Data Exploration and Preparation with BigQuery

A practical guide to cleaning, transforming, and analyzing data for business insights

Mike Kahn

BIRMINGHAM—MUMBAI

Data Exploration and Preparation with BigQuery

Group Product Manager: Kaustubh Manglurkar
Publishing Product Manager: Arindam Majumder
Content Development Editor: Shreya Moharir
Technical Editor: Sweety Pagaria
Copy Editor: Safis Editing
Project Coordinator: Shambhavi Mishra
Proofreader: Safis Editing
Indexer: Tejal Soni
Production Designer: Aparna Bhagat
Marketing Coordinator: Nivedita Singh

First published: November 2023

Production reference: 1251123

Published by Packt Publishing Ltd.
Grosvenor House
11 St Paul's Square
Birmingham
B3 1RB, UK

ISBN 978-1-80512-526-6

www.packtpub.com

To my wife, Jordana, for her endless support, love, and dedication to our family. Your encouragement, patience, and love has sustained me through the challenges and triumphs of writing this book. To my sons, Parker and Harrison, your curiosity and energy motivates me daily. To my parents, for always supporting me in my passions.

This book is dedicated to my family, whose love and encouragement make every achievement more meaningful and every challenge more surmountable.

– Mike Kahn

Contributors

About the author

Mike Kahn is a data and infrastructure enthusiast and currently leads a Customer Engineering team at Google Cloud. Prior to Google, Mike spent five years in solution architecture roles and worked in operations and leadership roles in the data center industry. His over 15 years of experience have given him a deep knowledge of data and infrastructure engineering, operations, strategy, and leadership. Mike holds multiple Google Cloud certifications and is a lifelong learner.

He is based in Boca Raton, Florida, in the US and holds a Bachelor of Science degree in **Management Information Systems** (**MIS**) from University of Central Florida and a Master of Science degree in MIS from Florida International University.

I want to thank the people who have been close to me and supported me, especially my wife, Jordana, and my parents, Abby and Steven Kahn, and my in-laws, Donna and Udy Nahum.

To all my colleagues and the customers that I have worked with, thank you for your inspiration and partnership.

About the reviewers

Suddhasatwa Bhaumik is an experienced data professional with 16+ years of experience in the industry. His primary expertise lies in data engineering and machine learning, with background experience in software development, cloud computing, and cloud architecture. He is currently working as an AI engineer at Google in Google Cloud Consulting, helping customers build their data and ML systems on **Google Cloud Platform (GCP)**. He has previously worked at industry giants including Vodafone, Infosys, and Tech Mahindra in various IT roles.

Guy Shilo is a data expert with more than 20 years of experience working with data, from a DBA of relational databases to big data analytical platforms and data engineering such as Hadoop, Splunk, Kafka NiFi, and others, to cloud data platforms (especially Google Cloud). Guy is a technology and data enthusiast and loves investigating, learning, and mastering new tools and technologies. Today, Guy works as a data and analytics customer engineer at Google Cloud, specializing in all Google Cloud data products. In this role, he helps identify customers' needs and translates objectives into action through product and service strategy and implementation, optimization, and architecture efforts. In the past, Guy used to work with Israeli military intelligence and various telecom companies as a data consultant.

Julio Quinteros is a co-founder of Axmos Technologies, a Google Cloud Premier Partner located in Latam. Julio is a Google Cloud Authorized Trainer and works in learning, research, and training with a focus on machine learning and data. Julio is also a co-founder and active organizer of the Google Developers Group in Santiago, Chile.

Nick Orlove is a product manager for BigQuery. He works with customers, engineering, and other teams to launch new products and features.

Kiran Narang is a big data analytics consultant at Google. She provides solutions and guidance to enterprises on how Google Cloud's data analytics products can solve latest business challenges.

Table of Contents

Part 2: Data Exploration with BigQuery

3

4

5

6

Exploring Data with Notebooks   83

7

Further Exploring and Visualizing Data   91

Part 3: Data Preparation with BigQuery

8

An Overview of Data Preparation Tools   109

9

Cleansing and Transforming Data   117

10

Best Practices for Data Preparation, Optimization, and Cost Control   139

Part 4: Hands-On and Conclusion

11

Hands-On Exercise – Analyzing Advertising Data   161

Preface

In the ever-expanding universe of data, the ability to explore and prepare information for meaningful insights is paramount. Welcome to *Data Exploration and Preparation with BigQuery*. This book is a guided journey into the world of leveraging Google BigQuery, a powerful and scalable data warehouse, for unraveling the potential within your data. Whether you're an analyst embarking on a quest for patterns or a seasoned data engineer forging pathways to actionable intelligence, this book is developed to be your companion.

In these pages, we will cover the art and science of data exploration and preparation, the foundational steps that begin the practice of data analytics. From structuring complex datasets to optimizing queries and using best practices, each chapter will direct you through the landscape of data analysis and transformation.

The book extends beyond technical nuances and dives into the philosophy of data, recognizing that behind every query, there is a story waiting to be unveiled. This book provides details beyond official documentation, providing strategies and approaches from years of customer interactions to accelerate your journey with data in BigQuery.

Google BigQuery is a leader in *Gartner Magic Quadrant for Cloud Database Management Systems* (2022), which recognizes its exceptional capabilities and industry impact. BigQuery has earned its place by demonstrating excellence as a data warehouse with its innovative architecture designed for scalable and high-performance analytics. BigQuery empowers organizations to unlock the full potential of their data through swift and sophisticated querying and seamless integrations with other Google Cloud services.

There is an increasing demand for data analysts and data engineers, and these roles will leverage the strategies and approaches outlined in this book.

Who this book is for

This book is for data analysts who want to learn how to explore and prepare data using BigQuery. If you are a data analyst who is experienced in SQL, reporting, data modeling, and transformations, this book is for you.

Business users who want to understand how to use BigQuery to make better data-driven decisions will also benefit from this book. Program and project managers and other data professionals will also benefit from the book's easy-to-follow approach. This book is excellent for any individuals who are planning to use BigQuery as a data warehouse to provide insights to their business from large data sets.

What this book covers

Chapter 1, Introducing BigQuery and Its Components, teaches how BigQuery operates to use it more effectively. We will take an "under the hood" look at the technologies that deliver BigQuery, and understand data exploration and preparation goals.

Chapter 2, BigQuery Organization and Design, teaches how to build a secure and collaborative BigQuery environment. You will gain a strong understanding of all services that deliver the BigQuery service beyond the SQL query. You will also understand design patterns for deploying BigQuery resources.

Chapter 3, Exploring Data in BigQuery, reviews various ways to explore data in BigQuery and reviews the process and steps of data exploration. You will learn about the different methods to access data in BigQuery and best practices to get started.

Chapter 4, Loading and Transforming Data, explores the techniques and best practices for loading data into BigQuery, and reviews the tools and methodologies for transforming and processing data with BigQuery. This chapter includes *Hands-on exercise – data loading and transformation in BigQuery*.

Chapter 5, Querying BigQuery Data, familiarizes you with the structure of a query and gives you a strong foundation in crafting queries. More complex querying practices will be reviewed as well. This chapter will give you the skills to begin writing queries.

Chapter 6, Exploring Data with Notebooks, helps you understand the value of using notebooks for data exploration and better understand the notebook options in Google Cloud. This chapter includes *Hands-on exercise – analyzing Google Trends data in Workbench*.

Chapter 7, Further Exploring and Visualizing Data, helps you better understand data attributes, discover patterns, and communicate findings effectively. You will learn about common practices for exploring data and review techniques and tools to analyze and visualize your data. This chapter includes *Hands-on exercise – creating visualizations with Looker Studio*.

Chapter 8, An Overview of Data Preparation Tools, explores approaches and tools that can be used with BigQuery for data preparation tasks to improve data quality.

Chapter 9, Cleansing and Transforming Data, reviews cleaning and transforming data in greater detail for optimizing table data after loading and initial exploration. You will learn about the skills to handle situations that you will encounter as you refine query results and reporting accuracy.

Chapter 10, Best Practices for Data Preparation, Optimization, and Cost Control, introduces the cost control and optimization features of BigQuery. You will learn how to use BigQuery in a cost-effective way.

Chapter 11, Hands-On Exercise – Analyzing Advertising Data, presents a use case including sales, marketing, and advertising data. Follow along with the exercise to learn how to analyze and prepare advertising data and utilize the steps as a repeatable process with your real data.

Chapter 12, Hands-On Exercise – Analyzing Transportation Data, presents a use case with vehicle data. Follow along with the exercise to learn how to analyze and prepare transportation data; the steps presented can be replicated with real data.

Chapter 13, Hands-On Exercise – Analyzing Customer Support Data, presents a use case with customer support data. Two different customer support data sources will be used, as well as BigQuery ML sentiment analysis, to better understand customer service data.

Chapter 14, Summary and Future Directions, recaps the key points discussed throughout the book. We will look into the future and learn about emerging trends and transformative directions that will shape the landscape of data exploration, preparation, and analytics with BigQuery.

To get the most out of this book

To get the most out of this book, you will want to have an active account with Google Cloud. The *Technical requirements* sections of each chapter provide specific directions and setup instructions.

Software/hardware covered in the book	Operating system requirements
Google Cloud	
GoogleSQL, SQL	Windows, macOS, or ChromeOS
Dataprep by Trifacta	

If you are using the digital version of this book, we advise you to type the code yourself or access the code from the book's GitHub repository (a link is available in the next section). Doing so will help you avoid any potential errors related to the copying and pasting of code.

The book can be read from front to back or as individual chapters on desired topics. For example, if you want to get right to loading data, start with *Chapter 4, Loading and Transforming Data*.

Download the example code files

You can download the example code files for this book from GitHub at `https://github.com/PacktPublishing/Data-Exploration-and-Preparation-with-BigQuery`. If there's an update to the code, it will be updated in the GitHub repository.

We also have other code bundles from our rich catalog of books and videos available at `https://github.com/PacktPublishing/`. Check them out!

Conventions used

There are a number of text conventions used throughout this book.

`Code in text`: Indicates code words in text, database table names, folder names, filenames, file extensions, pathnames, dummy URLs, user input, and Twitter handles. Here is an example: "The following SQL query will modify the `time` column name to `date` in our `jewelry_ads_data` table."

A block of code is set as follows:

```
CREATE TABLE `ch11.jewelry_sales_data2` (date DATE, order_id INT,
product_id INT, quantity INT, category_id INT, category_name STRING,
brand_id INT, price FLOAT64, gender STRING, metal STRING, stone
STRING)
```

Any command-line input or output is written as follows:

```
cd Data-Exploration-and-Preparation-with-BigQuery/ch4/
```

Bold: Indicates a new term, an important word, or words that you see onscreen. For instance, words in menus or dialog boxes appear in **bold**. Here is an example: "Click **BROWSE** to select a file from your GCS buckets. Find the file in your newly created bucket and click **SELECT**."

> **Tips or important notes**
> Appear like this.

Get in touch

Feedback from our readers is always welcome.

General feedback: If you have questions about any aspect of this book, email us at customercare@packtpub.com and mention the book title in the subject of your message.

Errata: Although we have taken every care to ensure the accuracy of our content, mistakes do happen. If you have found a mistake in this book, we would be grateful if you would report this to us. Please visit www.packtpub.com/support/errata and fill in the form.

Piracy: If you come across any illegal copies of our works in any form on the internet, we would be grateful if you would provide us with the location address or website name. Please contact us at copyright@packt.com with a link to the material.

If you are interested in becoming an author: If there is a topic that you have expertise in and you are interested in either writing or contributing to a book, please visit authors.packtpub.com.

Share Your Thoughts

Once you've read *Data Exploration and Preparation with BigQuery*, we'd love to hear your thoughts! Scan the QR code below to go straight to the Amazon review page for this book and share your feedback.

https://packt.link/r/1-805-12526-5

Your review is important to us and the tech community and will help us make sure we're delivering excellent quality content.

Download a free PDF copy of this book

Thanks for purchasing this book!

Do you like to read on the go but are unable to carry your print books everywhere? Is your eBook purchase not compatible with the device of your choice?

Don't worry, now with every Packt book you get a DRM-free PDF version of that book at no cost.

Read anywhere, any place, on any device. Search, copy, and paste code from your favorite technical books directly into your application.

The perks don't stop there, you can get exclusive access to discounts, newsletters, and great free content in your inbox daily

Follow these simple steps to get the benefits:

1. Scan the QR code or visit the link below

https://packt.link/free-ebook/9781805125266

2. Submit your proof of purchase
3. That's it! We'll send your free PDF and other benefits to your email directly

Part 1: Introduction to BigQuery

In the first part of this book, you will learn the mechanics behind BigQuery and how it operates. These chapters will cover BigQuery resource organization and design best practices. You will also understand the goals of data exploration and preparation after completing these chapters.

This part has the following chapters:

- *Chapter 1, Introducing BigQuery and Its Components*
- *Chapter 2, BigQuery Organization and Design*

1

Introducing BigQuery and Its Components

BigQuery is a fully managed serverless data warehouse that helps users and enterprises manage and analyze data with SQL. It includes features for data sharing, machine learning, geospatial analysis, and business intelligence.

In this chapter, you will be introduced to BigQuery and how the service operates. By gaining an understanding of how this service is delivered and how it functions, you will be able to use BigQuery more effectively.

This chapter will introduce and describe the first two, most critical steps of data analysis: data exploration and data preparation. By the end of this chapter, you will have a solid foundational understanding of BigQuery and how to begin preparing data to make it more useful and insightful.

In this chapter, we're going to cover the following main topics:

- What is BigQuery?
- How does BigQuery work?
- BigQuery administration and access
- BigQuery best practices and cost management
- Extending your data

Technical requirements

To get the most out of this chapter and the book, you will want to set up access to the **Google Cloud console** (`https://console.cloud.google.com/`). At the time of writing this publication, there is a free trial that will allow you to explore and build resources. Many services are also eligible for the Free tier (`https://cloud.google.com/free`), including BigQuery, which includes 1 TB of querying per month and 10 GB of storage each month. All you will need to get started is a

Google account (most people know this as their Gmail account). If you wish to use the Cloud console with your work email, you may be prompted to contact your organization administrator.

If you wish to explore BigQuery at no cost to determine whether BigQuery fits your needs, you can also utilize the **BigQuery sandbox** (`https://cloud.google.com/bigquery/docs/sandbox`). The sandbox lets you experience BigQuery and the Google Cloud console without enabling billing for your project. To access the BigQuery sandbox, follow these steps:

1. Visit `https://console.cloud.google.com/` and visit the BigQuery page. You can also open BigQuery directly by accessing `https://console.cloud.google.com/bigquery`.

2. Authenticate with your Google account or create one. Here is where you can utilize your existing personal Gmail account or attempt to use your organization or work credentials.

3. Follow the prompts to create a new Google Cloud project. Bypass setting up billing.

4. After you create a Cloud project, the Google Cloud console displays the sandbox banner.

Let's get started!

What is BigQuery?

BigQuery is Google Cloud's enterprise data warehouse, designed to help users ingest, store, visualize, and analyze data. BigQuery enables users to unlock insights across petabyte-sized datasets and enables business agility. In this chapter, we will explore BigQuery to give you a complete understanding of how the service operates so you can best utilize BigQuery to prepare and explore your data.

BigQuery's managed serverless infrastructure unlocks users from managing resources and allows for greater focus on data. BigQuery is a serverless enterprise data warehouse with analytic tools and machine learning services, with multi-cloud capabilities. BigQuery stores data in a columnar format that is optimized for analytics queries on structured and semi-structured data.

There are several ways to get data into BigQuery. You can ingest data into BigQuery by uploading it in one-time or scheduled batch loads or by streaming data to enable real-time insights. You can use queries to generate new data and append or overwrite the results to a table. Alternatively, you can use a third-party application or service to load data from external sources.

BigQuery supports a standard **Structured Query Language (SQL)** dialect that is **American National Standard Institute (ANSI)** compliant, which makes it easy for SQL practitioners and data analysts to use this service with a low learning curve and quick time to value. According to the documentation, BigQuery can be accessed via the Google Cloud console and through the BigQuery command-line tool. Developers and data scientists can use notebooks and client libraries as well as BigQuery's REST API and **Remote Procedure Call (RPC)** API to transform and manage data. **Open Database Connectivity (ODBC)** and **Java Database Connectivity (JDBC)** driver access allows interaction with existing applications and third-party tools.

BigQuery addresses the needs of data professionals including data analysts, data engineers, data scientists, and data developers. It allows these individuals to store and analyze large amounts of data to make the most out of datasets and enable data-driven decision-making and rich insights across data sources. Enterprises can easily turn complex data landscapes into compelling stories through analysis, reporting, and machine learning.

Understanding how BigQuery works

BigQuery is known for being a serverless, highly scalable, cost-effective cloud data warehouse. The power of this cloud-native service lies in the decoupled storage and compute resources. Unlike other data warehouse software or services, BigQuery service architecture has independent storage and compute infrastructure layers. This allows each layer to scale independently on demand. This decoupled architecture offers high flexibility and cost control for data analytics and data science workloads.

Underneath the user interface, BigQuery is powered by several Google technologies that have been in use since well before the 2011 general availability launch of this service. In this section, we will go over the primary technologies behind BigQuery – *Dremel*, *Colossus*, *Borg*, and *Jupiter*, so you can better understand how BigQuery is different from other enterprise data warehouse services.

Dremel, the execution engine

Dremel is the service that turns SQL queries into execution trees. BigQuery slots, which are compute reservations used by BigQuery to execute SQL queries, are the leaves of the tree and they read data from storage. The branches of the execution tree are called "mixers" and they perform aggregation.

The following diagram shows user data stored in Colossus distributed storage. The leaves are BigQuery on-demand or reserved slots for compute. The mixers perform different levels of aggregation, and in between the mixers is "shuffle," which moves data from one place to another on the Jupiter network. The mixers and slots are run by Borg.

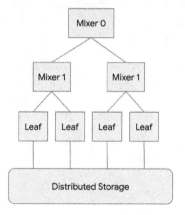

Figure 1.1 – BigQuery execution tree example

Dremel is a query system for the analysis of nested data that combines multi-level execution trees and BigQuery's columnar data layout. Dremel has tremendous power and can run aggregation queries over a trillion row tables in seconds. BigQuery offers query visualization through a query execution graph, which allows you to view performance insights for queries. The value delivered by Dremel in BigQuery is that it enables users the ability to run extremely complex queries over multiple large tables, better analyze query effectiveness, and optimize cost management. We will go over queries in detail in *Chapter 5, Querying BigQuery Data*. To learn more about Dremel, read the 2010 paper published by Googlers, linked at the end of this chapter [5].

Colossus distributed storage

BigQuery uses the columnar storage format, also known as Capacitor, to store data in Colossus, which is optimized for reading large amounts of structured data. Colossus also handles replication, recovery, and distribution management, so there is no single point of failure. The distributed storage system that BigQuery uses allows users to scale to hundreds of petabytes of data stored without the challenge of adding attached compute resources in most data warehouses. Herein lies one of BigQuery's differentiating features, decoupled storage, and the reduction of the burden of managing the infrastructure required for your cloud data warehouse.

The Borg compute platform

Borg is the service that paved the way for Kubernetes at Google. To give you hundreds of thousands of CPU cores or slots to process your task, BigQuery leverages Borg, Google's cluster management system. Borg is the platform that runs the slots and mixers and allocates compute resources for BigQuery jobs. Borg clusters run up to tens of thousands of machines.

Jupiter network infrastructure

Google has been a leader in developing distributed computing and data processing infrastructure since the early 2000s. From the early days of the company, it was known that great computing infrastructure requires great data center networking technology [1].

In order to support the billion user properties, such as YouTube and Gmail, that have been successful over the past two decades, Google developed Jupiter fabrics, networks that can deliver more than 1 petabit/second of total bisection bandwidth. To put this into perspective, such capacity would be enough for 100,000 servers to exchange information at 10 Gb/s each [1].

BigQuery uses Jupiter to move data extremely quickly between storage systems. Jupiter makes it appear that compute and storage systems are on the same physical machine, yet they are physically separated across machines in zones within a region.

Now that you have learned more about BigQuery and how the service is delivered, let's go over some foundational elements such as administration and access. The next section will help you understand how to access and use data in BigQuery. Get ready to gain an understanding of the different access features as well as the organization and team setup features available beyond a user account.

BigQuery administration and access

In this section, we will discuss how to administer and secure resources in BigQuery. We will describe access methods for users and services to access data. By the end of the section, you will have a basic understanding of the different approaches to securely allocate resources in BigQuery and how to enable access to users.

Tools for administration

BigQuery has several access methods for administration tasks. Most users and roles can do the same function, with multiple tools enabling point-and-click as well as automated task flows.

The Google Cloud console is the main user interface for the centralized management of data and compute resources. Users access the Google Cloud console to run SQL queries and create and manage BigQuery resources. In the BigQuery navigation menu, you can access options for analysis, migration, and administration.

When you access the SQL workspace in the BigQuery section of the Cloud console, you will be presented with an explorer tree view that will show all the projects, connections, datasets, tables, and shared queries available to your user account. Within the SQL workspace, you can open tables in different tabs and views. You can also collapse menus and star or favorite your datasets and tables for quicker access.

The **bq command-line tool** lets you perform administrative tasks using bq console commands. The bq command-line tool is a Python-based tool for BigQuery. You can create resources, manage resources, and run queries from the bq command-line tool. You can also run the bq command-line tool in a script or from a service account.

Understanding identity and access management

In Google Cloud, Cloud Identity is built-in **identity as a service (IDaaS)** that works across the Cloud console and with Google Workspace. If your organization already uses Workspace, you may already have access to the Cloud console.

> **Fun fact**
>
> The identity management service used at Google is called Gaia internally, which is an acronym for Google Accounts and ID Administration. Gaia is the same identity management system used across many commonly used Google products.

To manage individual accounts, you can set up users and groups in Cloud Identity to assign roles and permissions in the Cloud console. A user in Google Cloud is an individual user account. This may be an individual email address associated with a Google domain (for example, `user@gmail.com`) or an email address for another domain that has already been configured by a Cloud Identity or Google Workspace domain administrator (`https://developers.google.cn/issue-tracker/concepts/access-control`).

A group is a Google group that contains individual users, all of which need to share the same level of permissions. Many organizations will create groups for finance teams, data engineering teams, infrastructure teams, and network teams, to name a few. This allows organizations the ability to assign permissions to a group and those privileges cascade across multiple users that perform similar job functions.

Organizations with existing identity providers such as Active Directory can federate with Cloud Identity. This makes it easier to integrate and maintain governance with your primary identity provider. You can continue to use your existing **identity provider** (**IdP**) to handle tasks such as provisioning and managing users and groups, managing **single sign-on** (**SSO**), and configuring **multi-factor authentication** (**MFA**). Federating an existing IDP with Cloud Identity can simplify access and user management with Google Cloud.

Identity and access management (**IAM**) helps you secure data and compute resources with an access model that is used across Google Cloud. IAM lets you grant granular access to resources, prevents access to other resources, and helps you adopt the principle of least privilege [2]. When designing access management, the security principle of least privilege ensures that no one should have more permissions than they need to do their job. Learn more about IAM roles and permissions in the docs: `https://cloud.google.com/iam/docs/`.

A resource is an entity or container in reference to Google Cloud permissions. You will use resource hierarchy for access control, meaning you can set IAM policies at different levels of the Google Cloud console services resource hierarchy. Resources inherit the policies of the parent resource, so you will want to give users roles and permissions at the most granular levels (e.g., provide dataset-level permissions instead of project-level permissions). IAM permissions determine the operations that are allowed on a resource. Permissions cannot be assigned directly to users; users are assigned permissions through policies or roles. Roles are collections of permissions and can be assigned to Google identities and use a policy to enforce binding to Google Cloud resource levels:

- Organization
- Folder

- Project
- Service (e.g, datasets, tables, and views)

BigQuery allows you to go even more granular, assigning roles to resources within datasets, such as tables and views, without providing full access to the dataset's resources. Authorized views are another option for granting specific users access to query results without giving them access to underlying table data. You can create a dataset just for authorized views and assign access to that dataset or the view. We will go over resource hierarchy, roles, design, and real-life scenarios and examples in *Chapter 2, BigQuery Organization and Design*.

Now that you have learned about administration, access, and resources, let's discuss best practices and cost management. This will begin to introduce best practices for using BigQuery so you can start off using this service in the most economical and efficient manner.

BigQuery best practices and cost management

In this section, we will go over general best practices for using BigQuery. We will also touch on cost management and the different approaches to optimizing your spending on BigQuery. By the end of this section, you will have a good understanding of how to efficiently use BigQuery to control costs and optimize storage and queries.

Best practices

There are many best practices for using BigQuery. The following are a few best practices that are foundational for using this service efficiently. Take note and implement these approaches to get the most performance and benefit out of BigQuery:

- **Use the right data type for your data**: BigQuery supports many data types, each with its own storage cost. Keep in mind that a large string column takes up more space than an integer column. When designing your table schema, make sure to choose the right data type for your data.

- **Query only the columns you need**: Avoid using SELECT * as this is the most expensive way to query data as BigQuery does a full scan of every column in the table. If you are looking to explore data, use the **Preview** tab to sample data [3]. In *Chapter 3, Exploring Data in BigQuery*, we will go over different tools and features to preview and explore data. We will go into detail and present best practices for queries in *Chapter 5, Querying BigQuery Data*.

- **Filter (WHERE clause) your query as early and as often as possible**: This will help you improve performance and reduce costs. Operations on BOOL, INT, FLOAT, and DATE are typically faster than operations on STRING columns. Whenever possible, use a column that uses one of these data types in the WHERE clause.

- **Set up cost controls**: You can set up the expiration time at the dataset level, table level, and partition level. Consider expiration for temporary tables you will not need in the long term.

- **Use clustering to optimize table and querying performance**: Clustering groups similar data together based on its values. This reduces the amount of data that needs to be scanned for each query. Use the partitioning/cluster recommender for guidance to either cluster or partition a table and obtain the estimated monthly savings by applying the recommendation.

- **Partition data by date**: Partitioning tables by date lets you query relevant subsets of data, which improves performance and reduces cost. When you query a partitioned table using the _PARTITIONTIME pseudo column to filter for a date or range of dates, the query processes data only in the partitions that are specified by the date or date range [4]:

```
SELECT …
FROM `sales`
WHERE _PARTITIONTIME
BETWEEN TIMESTAMP("20230420")
        AND TIMESTAMP("20230431")
```

The following diagram shows how the partitioned table would look as a result of the preceding query:

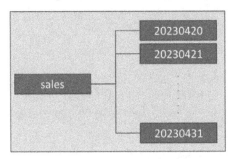

Figure 1.2 – Visual representation of a BigQuery data partitioned table

Note the sales table is partitioned by timestamp. The query is filtered by a timestamp range to only process data on those partitions.

Understanding and controlling costs

Start by choosing the right pricing model. BigQuery offers two pricing models: on-demand analysis and capacity pricing (BigQuery Editions). On-demand is the most flexible, but it can be more expensive if you don't optimize your queries. Capacity pricing, now known as BigQuery Editions, is less flexible but can be more cost-effective if you know (or have a trustworthy estimation of) how much you will be using BigQuery. Storage pricing is separate and is the cost to store data that you load into BigQuery.

On-demand compute analysis is the default billing, or per TB, where you pay for the data scanned by your queries. According to the BigQuery documentation on controlling costs (`https://cloud.google.com/bigquery/docs/controlling-costs`), you are charged according to the total data processed in the columns you select for your query, and the total data per column is calculated based on the types of data in the column. This is why it is very important to use the right data types for your data and optimize your queries.

You can set cost control mechanisms that enable you to cap your query costs. This would be useful for a department or project budget. Administrators and project owners can set the following:

- User-level and project-level cost controls
- The maximum bytes billed by a query

You can set a custom quota or modify existing custom quotas on the **Quotas** page of the Google Cloud console. To change quotas, you must have the `serviceusage.quotas.update` permission. This permission is already included in the following predefined IAM roles:

- Project Owner and Editor basic roles
- Quota Administrator (`servicemanagement.quotaAdmin`) Service Management role

Beyond setting a user- and project-level custom quota, you can set a limit on the number of bytes billed for a query using the **Maximum bytes billed** setting. When this is set, the number of bytes that a query will read is estimated before the query execution. If the number of estimated bytes is beyond the set limit, the query will fail without incurring a charge. Note that this is a per-query quota, yet can be used as a fail-safe if you are worried a query may have a high cost.

BigQuery offers a capacity-based analysis model for customers who may be already familiar with BigQuery and prefer a predictable cost for queries. This is known as **BigQuery Editions**. Capacity in BigQuery is measured in slots, which represent virtual CPUs used by your queries. In most cases, if you provision more slots, you can run more concurrent queries and complex aggregation queries will run faster. Slots are allocated in pools called reservations, and reservations let you allocate slots in ways that make sense for your use case. Slots or reservations allow you to separate workloads, for example, you may create a reservation for production workloads and another for development workloads. By doing this, your development jobs will not interfere with resources that are required by your production workloads.

BigQuery slots are available in three editions: Standard, Enterprise, and Enterprise Plus. They can be purchased without a usage commitment and are also available for one- or three-year periods with discounts. Slots are per region capacity and can be shared across an organization in Google Cloud.

As outlined in *Optimize Storage in BigQuery* at `https://cloud.google.com/bigquery/docs/best-practices-storage`, storage in BigQuery is broken into two categories: "*Active storage, which includes any table or partition that has been modified in the past 90 days, and long-term storage, which would be any table or partition that has not been modified for 90 consecutive days. The price of storage for that table automatically drops by about 50% of the initial cost and there is no impact on performance, availability, or durability between active and long-term storage."*

This is intentionally not an exhaustive list of best practices for BigQuery, but instead, a primer and introduction. For more best practices, check the BigQuery documentation: `https://cloud.google.com/bigquery/docs/best-practices-costs`.

Extending your data

In the world of data analytics and decision-making, having access to comprehensive and enriched datasets is crucial. The ability to extend data by incorporating external sources, using machine learning, and augmenting it with additional context can unlock new insights and empower organizations to make more informed decisions. In this chapter, we are exploring the techniques and strategies for extending data in BigQuery. This section equips data analysts and engineers with the tools and knowledge to extend their datasets and extract deeper value from their data.

BigQuery ML

BigQuery ML or **BQML** is a machine learning service that can be used to build and deploy machine learning models in BigQuery using SQL queries. BigQuery ML allows data analysts with limited programming expertise the ability to build models using their existing SQL expertise. This capability in BigQuery allows teams and organizations with limited data science resources the ability to use machine learning to better leverage their data and extract insights, predictions, and actionable intelligence directly within the BigQuery console. BigQuery ML offers a simplified process for machine learning tasks. Users can define and train models using SQL statements, eliminating the need to learn additional programming languages or frameworks. This SQL-based approach lowers the barrier to entry for data analysts and allows them to leverage their existing SQL skills to build and deploy models.

BigQuery ML supports the following use cases and models:

- Forecasting with linear regression models. Predict the sales of an item on a given day.
- Classification with binary and multiclass logistic regression. Determine whether a customer will make a purchase.
- Data segmentation with K-means clustering. Identify customer or user segments.
- Creating product recommendation systems using matrix factorization.
- Time series forecasts. Create forecasts able to handle seasonality and holidays.
- Identify the relationship between variables with regression models.
- Machine learning on tabular data using Vertex AI AutoML Tables.

BigQuery ML democratizes the use of machine learning by empowering data analysts to build and run models using existing tools. Predictive analytics can unlock greater insights, improve business agility, and guide business decision-making.

External datasets

BigQuery users can add public and private datasets to their projects to enrich proprietary data and add datasets to explore and determine whether a dataset may be relevant to the goals of the business.

Google pays for the storage of many public datasets through the Google Cloud Public Datasets program (`https://cloud.google.com/public-datasets`). These are public datasets that BigQuery hosts for users to access and integrate into existing queries and applications. You pay only for the queries that you perform on the data. At the time of writing this publication, the largest amount of datasets in the Public Datasets program were in science and research, healthcare, economics, and financial services.

Beyond the Google-offered datasets available in Cloud Marketplace, Google offers a Dataset Search product: `https://datasetsearch.research.google.com/`. Here, you can search topics and find data sources from other data providers around the world.

You may find that free data sources are most useful for experimentation; however, local data sources such as the **California Open Data Portal** (`https://data.ca.gov/`) could be highly useful to organizations that would benefit from integrating and studying government transportation, demographic, or transportation data.

Typically, when training ML models, specialized datasets deliver the highest value. More companies are working on data monetization strategies to externalize their data. Soon there will be more accessible paid data sources for integration and model development.

External connections

BigQuery allows you to query data that is stored in other services in Google Cloud, such as Cloud Storage, Cloud SQL, or Cloud Spanner, or in external sources such as AWS or Azure. These connections use the BigQuery Connection API.

Most data analysts are familiar with federated queries. Federated queries establish a connection to the database before sending the query. These connections handle credentials for the query. BigQuery supports federated queries with Cloud Spanner and Cloud SQL.

Remote functions let you use Cloud Functions or Cloud Run to implement functions in many programming languages. A BigQuery connection lets you connect to Cloud Functions to execute code. This opens BigQuery up to more Google Cloud services and allows non-Google API calls through SQL statements. This could be used to call Google Maps or the Translation API to translate data in a BigQuery table.

In this section, you have learned about a few ways to extend data in BigQuery and its features that help you do more with your data. This chapter will now conclude and we'll move on to BigQuery organization and design, and then to exploring data in BigQuery.

Summary

In this chapter, we described BigQuery and gained an understanding of the Google services that deliver the petabyte-scale trillion-row analytic serverless data warehouse. We discussed tools for the administration of BigQuery resources and went over IAM, including how to secure access, down to the table level.

We discussed cost and how to control costs via pricing models and query and table best practices. In the latter part of this chapter, we described how to extend data in BigQuery with BigQuery ML (BQML), public datasets, and external connections. By learning how BigQuery works, data analysts will be ready to gain skills to use this powerful data warehouse to reduce time to insights and derive more business value from large-scale datasets.

In the next chapter, we will go further into BigQuery organization and design. You will master BigQuery resource hierarchy and schema design practices.

References

The following are the links to the sources and documentation that we referred to in this chapter:

1. *A look inside Google's Data Center Networks*: `https://cloudplatform.googleblog.com/2015/06/A-Look-Inside-Googles-Data-Center-Networks.html`

2. *Roles and permissions*: `https://cloud.google.com/iam/docs/roles-overview`

3. *Estimate and control costs*: `https://cloud.google.com/bigquery/docs/best-practices-costs`

4. *Query partitioned tables*: `https://cloud.google.com/bigquery/docs/querying-partitioned-tables`

5. *Dremel: Interactive Analysis of Web-Scale Datasets*: `https://static.googleusercontent.com/media/research.google.com/en//pubs/archive/36632.pdf` or `https://research.google/pubs/pub36632/`

2
BigQuery Organization and Design

BigQuery is a serverless, highly scalable, and cost-effective cloud data warehouse that enables businesses to analyze all their data very quickly. It is a great choice for businesses that need to store and analyze large amounts of data as it can handle petabytes or even exabytes of data.

One of the most important aspects of using BigQuery is designing and organizing your data in a way that makes it easy to query and analyze. In this chapter, we will discuss some of the best practices and approaches for designing and organizing your BigQuery data for small to large complex organizational structures. We will also discuss resources and their relationships and provide details on design patterns around datasets, tables, and schemas to teach you how to best use this service.

By the end of the chapter, you will be able to effectively build a BigQuery environment for your business to securely structure and share data across teams and organizations with various use cases. You will gain a strong understanding of all of the elements that help deliver the BigQuery service experience beyond the SQL query and understand the value of using features for different scenarios. This chapter will present several unique design patterns for you to model and replicate for common deployments of BigQuery resources.

Specifically, we will cover the following main topics:

- Understanding BigQuery's resource hierarchy:

  - Organizations, folders, and projects

  - BigQuery-specific resources

  - BigQuery storage

- Exploring architecture patterns

Technical requirements

As mentioned in *Chapter 1*, to get the most out of this chapter, you will want to have access to the Google Cloud console (`https://console.cloud.google.com/`) to explore and build resources in BigQuery. You can also begin exploring the GitHub repository `https://github.com/PacktPublishing/Data-Exploration-and-Preparation-with-BigQuery` for this book to browse and download diagrams and code snippets.

In this chapter, we utilize a dataset made accessible through the Google Cloud Public Datasets Program. These datasets are hosted and maintained by Google, ensuring their availability to the public. You only incur charges for the specific queries you execute on the data, as Google covers the storage costs.

Add the Google Trends dataset to your Google Cloud project for hands-on examples. You can find the Google Trends dataset at `https://cloud.google.com/datasets`, and clicking **View Dataset** will bring the dataset into your SQL workspace in BigQuery. You can favorite the dataset to find it more easily. You can expand the dataset, click a table, and click **Preview** in the middle pane. You have just begun exploring a dataset in BigQuery. We will continue this exploration in this chapter to better understand resources and design patterns.

Understanding BigQuery's resource hierarchy

In this section, we will discuss the different types of resources that are available in BigQuery. We will also discuss how to manage these resources and how to optimize your BigQuery usage. Understanding BigQuery resources is not only foundational but it is critical to data warehouse setup, operations, and ultimately best utilizing BigQuery.

The following table describes the different types of BigQuery resources:

Resource Type	Description
Organization	An organization is a top-level container for all of your BigQuery resources
Folder	A folder is a container for projects
Project	A project is a container for datasets and other resources
Table	A table is a collection of rows and columns of data
View	A view is a virtual table that is based on one or more tables
Materialized View	A materialized view is a pre-computed view that is stored in BigQuery

Table 2.1 – BigQuery and Google Cloud resources

The resource hierarchy in BigQuery provides a logical organization method for managing resources and identity and access control. Folders can be used to group projects for products or regional locations. Projects can be used to separate different teams or business functions, while datasets can be used to separate different types of data within a project. Tables can be used to separate data within a dataset. Note the boundaries and nesting capabilities enabling team segmentation and administration capabilities:

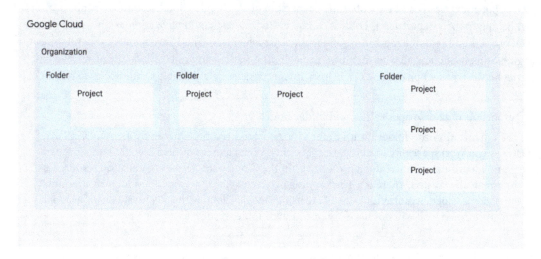

Figure 2.1 – Google Cloud's organization, folder, and project hierarchy

Furthermore, the resource hierarchy in BigQuery allows for fine-grained access control, where users can be granted different levels of access to projects, datasets, and tables. For example, a user can be granted read-only access to a dataset and not be allowed to modify the tables within it. This level of control provides a secure and structured environment for sensitive, private organizational and user data.

Organizations, folders, and projects

The Google Cloud *organization* resource is the root node in the resource hierarchy. It enables administrators to manage and control resources across multiple Google Cloud projects. An organizational resource serves as the top-level entity in a hierarchical structure that provides a centralized view of all of the resources in a Google Cloud account. An organization can contain multiple folders, projects, and policies.

The Google Cloud organization node can be thought of as an access boundary for specific groups that may need to serve a narrow function across your cloud resources. For example, it is common to assign the **Billing Account Viewer** role at the organizational level (`roles/billing.viewer`) to finance teams as it provides access to spending information across projects.

Folders are used to group related projects and resources within an organization. This resource is optional and provides an additional grouping and isolation boundary between projects and resources. Folders are typically used to model different departments or teams within a company. For example, if your organization had multiple international locations and you wanted to give those groups their own space to create and manage projects and cloud resources, you may consider giving them a folder. Folder resources can include other sub-folders to represent different teams or possibly applications.

In an individual (non-organization) enabled Google Cloud account, the primary layer of IAM and administration is the project. Folder resources allow for another layer of administration, for example, each department head can be granted full ownership of all Google Cloud resources within projects that belong to their department. Folders can be nested, so you could have a folder for international team projects and resource separation, and within that folder, you could have folders for development, staging, and production, all with their own projects. This folder and project hierarchy provides a strict barrier between project phases and can help maintain consistency and enable secure access to resources.

> **Important note on organization and folder nodes**
>
> The organization and folder nodes in the Google Cloud resource hierarchy are only available to Google Workspace or Cloud Identity accounts. When a user within a Google Workspace or Cloud Identity account creates a project within the Cloud console, an organization resource is automatically created. There is a 1:1 mapping between Workspace or Cloud Identity accounts and Google Cloud organizations. If you are using Google Cloud with a personal Google account (email address), you will not have organization or folder resources.

A Google Cloud *project* is a collection of resources that you will use to develop and run applications and set up and build your data warehouse. A project is associated with a billing account, activates Google Cloud APIs, and manages authentication and monitoring for those APIs. You can have one or more projects, and when you create a project, you will be prompted to select or create a billing account.

The project would be the main container for organizing resources that users (Google Workspace users, Cloud Identity users, or individual users using the console with their personal Google account) will activate and deactivate according to their needs, in comparison to the more complex to manage scenario where all resources coexist and are organized in a shared/global container, which would be the organization node. All project resources include a project name (or a display name) that will help you recognize them and an immutable project ID and project number that will work as an identifier for executing things on them. In order to access most resources within Google Cloud (via API, CLI, or even SQL), you must provide project resource information with every request. Being the minimal way to identify a project, most of the time, this will be precisely the project ID. When working with resources in the web Cloud console, the project selected persists across sessions and is bundled with any actions performed. When writing a SQL statement in BigQuery, you will use the project ID to identify your dataset and table in the FROM clause. It looks like this:

```
project-id.dataset.table
```

We will begin by using the Google Trends BigQuery public dataset as an example:

```
FROM `bigquery-public-data.google_trends.top_terms`
```

The preceding query parameter is referencing the `bigquery-public-data` project, which is globally accessible to anyone. The dataset is called `google_trends` and the table is called `top_terms`.

To conclude this section, review the following best practices and tips for managing Google Cloud organizations, folders, and projects:

- **Use a Google Cloud organization instead of individual projects**: This will make it easier to manage users, billing, and access control.

- **Create folders to organize your projects**: This will help you keep track of resources and make it easier to manage permissions.

- **Create projects for each application or service**: This will help you isolate resources and make it easier to manage costs.

- **Use a consistent naming convention for projects and resources**: This will make it easier to find and manage resources.

- **Use billing accounts, budgets, and resource quotas to track and control costs**: Each project can be associated with a billing account and each project can have budgets or quotas for usage. This will help you control costs and prevent users from accidentally using too many resources.

- **Use Cloud Identity and Access Management (IAM) to control access to resources**: IAM can be used to control who has access to resources and what they can do with them. This will help you to secure your environment and comply with security and regulatory requirements.

- **Grant users the least amount of access they need**: This will help you to protect resources by narrowing the potential risk – attack surface – in case of unauthorized access.

- **Use labels to tag your resources**: A label is a key-value pair that helps you organize and find resources. Common uses of labels are team or cost center labels (for example, `team:analytics` and `team:data_science`), environment or stage labels (for example, `environment:staging` and `environment:prod`), or component labels (for example, `component:process` and `component:source_data`).

- **Use the organization policy service**: The organization policy service gives you centralized control to configure restrictions on how resources can be used. This is one of the many reasons why organizations with multiple users are encouraged to adopt Cloud Identity or Workspace to access Google Cloud. This service lets you define guardrails for teams to stay within compliance boundaries, reducing risk, and helps project owners and teams move quickly. A common use case is restricting public IP addresses on compute instances or limiting resource sharing based on domains.

Google Cloud's resource hierarchy is a hierarchical structure that organizes Google Cloud resources into logical groups. This section outlined how the resource hierarchy can provide improved organization and management of resources and increase security and compliance by controlling who has access to resources. Let's now discuss more specific enterprise data warehouse resources in BigQuery.

BigQuery-specific resources

In addition to the general Google Cloud resources previously described, BigQuery has specific service resources that you will use to manage and analyze data. These resources include datasets, tables, views, jobs, routines, and storage. In this section, we will describe each resource and provide best practices for using each.

A *dataset* in BigQuery is a container for tables, views, and user-defined functions. It is a logical grouping of data that can be accessed and analyzed together. Datasets are created within a project and can be shared among different users or projects. Each dataset has a unique name and is stored in a specific location, regional or multi-regional. Table expiration can also be set at the dataset level. Users will want to use BigQuery datasets to store tables, for example, in a migration scenario. Datasets can be used to control access to data and prevent unauthorized users from accessing sensitive data.

Tables in BigQuery are like tables in a traditional database. BigQuery standard tables contain structured data and are stored in BigQuery storage in columnar format. They store data in rows and columns and can be queried using SQL. Each table is defined by a schema that describes the column names, data types, and encryption. Tables are created in a dataset and can be partitioned or clustered to improve query performance.

External data sources in BigQuery are tabular data that is stored outside of the BigQuery storage service. For example, you may have data stored in another Google Cloud database, files in Cloud Storage, or on another cloud platform. You can access external data in two different ways in BigQuery, by using external tables or federated queries. External tables store their metadata and schema in BigQuery storage, but their data is an external source. You manage external tables the same way that you manage a standard BigQuery table. A common external table could be multiple CSVs in a Cloud Storage bucket. Federated queries let you send a query to Cloud Spanner or Cloud SQL to get a result back as a temporary table. These queries use the BigQuery Connection API to connect to Spanner or Cloud SQL.

Views in BigQuery are virtual tables that can be used to simplify complex queries or create custom reports. A view is defined using a SQL query and can be created in a dataset. Views can be used to combine data from multiple tables or to filter data based on specific criteria. Authorized views are a particular type of view that permits users to run a query without having read access to the underlying tables.

Materialized views are precomputed views that cache the results of a view query for improved performance and efficiency. They are easy to set up and can greatly improve query performance. You will want to consider materialized views for common and repeated queries, as well as the following use cases:

- Data pre-aggregation, most useful for `SUM()` and `COUNT()` functions and so on.

- Data pre-filtering – if the column is not clustered, it will require a full table scan. For example, `WHERE status = 'EXPIRED'`.

- Pre-join tables allow you to keep the data normalized and still have good performance.

- Data re-clustering is used when there are different query patterns that would benefit from multiple clustering columns.

A *job* in BigQuery is an action that performs a specific task, such as querying a table, loading data into a table, or copying or exporting data. Jobs are created and managed using the BigQuery API, the web UI, or the command-line tool.

Further building upon *Figure 2.1*, the following diagram shows the relationship between datasets, tables, and views within a single project.

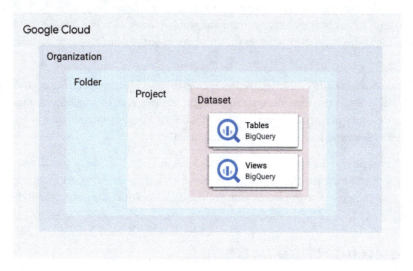

Figure 2.2 – BigQuery resources within a project

Overall, BigQuery offers a wide range of resources and tools that make it easy to store, manage, and analyze large and complex datasets. In *Chapter 4, Loading and Transforming Data*, we will further explore external connections and sources. By possessing knowledge about and beginning to properly leverage these resources, you can build powerful data pipelines, machine learning models, and business intelligence applications that deliver insights and value to your organization. Continue to the next section to learn more about specific patterns that use the resources we just discussed.

BigQuery storage

One of the key benefits of using BigQuery is its scalable and cost-effective storage capabilities. BigQuery offers two types of storage: active and long-term storage.

Active storage is used for tables that are frequently queried and updated. Active storage is any table or partition that has been updated in the past 90 days and has the standard per GB cost. *Long-term storage*, on the other hand, is used for data that is accessed less frequently. Tables and partitions that haven't been updated in 90 days have a reduced storage cost – about 50% less than active storage fees.

Compressed storage is a new storage model with BigQuery Editions pricing that is priced on the physical storage space taken up by data after compression. Whereas active and long-term storage are based on logical size, compressed storage lets you pay for data storage after it has been compressed.

BigQuery uses a columnar storage format called **Capacitor** that provides several benefits over traditional row-based storage formats. Capacitor stores data in a compressed columnar format that allows for efficient storage and retrieval of large volumes of data. It also allows for more efficient query processing by reducing the amount of data that needs to be read from disk.

BigQuery also provides several features to help users manage their data storage effectively. Partitioning allows users to split tables into smaller, more manageable pieces, making it easier to query large datasets. Clustering allows users to group data within a table based on similar values, further improving query performance.

BigQuery provides scalable and cost-effective storage capabilities for large volumes of structured and semi-structured data. By leveraging columnar storage and features such as partitioning and clustering, users can optimize query performance and manage their data storage more efficiently. In *Chapter 5, Querying BigQuery Data*, we will go over optimizing queries in detail.

Now that you have learned about resources in Google Cloud and BigQuery, let's discuss different design patterns that you may use as you build resources for your needs. The next section will present multiple scenarios and give you an idea of some of the common operating structures that you can configure in BigQuery.

Exploring architecture patterns

This section presents three architecture patterns for organizing BigQuery resources. The following three patterns should cover most of the common usage patterns for teams and organizations using BigQuery. It is important to understand these architecture patterns to determine what setup in BigQuery will work best for your usage. Each pattern has its advantages and most organizations combine elements of multiple patterns. We will lead with the recommended design and outline alternative approaches, including the considerations for each one:

- **Centralized enterprise data warehouse**: The BI and data team owns all department or business unit data. Departments have their own projects with views and dashboards for utilizing the organization's enterprise data warehouse.

- **Decentralized enterprise data warehouse**: Each department owns its raw data. The organization creates a central data warehouse project for analysis.

- **Cross-org data exchange**: Authorized views grant access from a private dataset to another Google Cloud organization. This scenario could be followed for a supplier and vendor relationship and could facilitate **Business-to-Business (B2B)** data sharing.

The centralized enterprise data warehouse

In the centralized enterprise data warehouse, departments have their own projects, with authorized views on top of the centralized **Enterprise Data Warehouse** (**EDW**). BI and data teams will have centralized access to manage raw and processed data, create specific views, and manage data on behalf of departments. The EDW project is essentially a data lake for the organization. Departments will be able to create their own visualizations and reporting or BI and data teams will be able to create them on their behalf. This arrangement will have a large amount of tables and views in a single project holding the EDW. In this recommended approach, data access control is easier to manage, and **Personally Identifiable Information** (**PII**) and sensitive data are protected in a single location.

The following is a centralized enterprise data warehouse example diagram. Note that the departments have virtual tables or views so the data team can manage raw data and create custom reports.

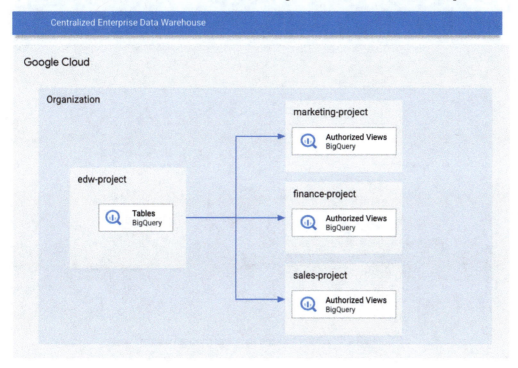

Figure 2.3 – The centralized enterprise data warehouse

The centralized data warehouse model provides the following features:

- Strategic business decision support
- Enterprise-wide data integration policies and security policies
- Higher cost and more time to implement

The decentralized data warehouse

In the decentralized enterprise data warehouse, departments own their raw and processed data. The central EDW project is essentially a project with authorized views and aggregations built on top of individual data marts. A data mart can be thought of as a subset of a data warehouse and is typically focused on a single department or source. This structure can make it simpler to manage data access at the department level with projects for each department. The BI and data teams have a single project for running analytics jobs. Analysts can query and read data from the data warehouse project. The data warehouse project can also be an access layer for reporting and visualization tools.

The following diagram of a decentralized data warehouse pattern shows how departments manage their own data in a more business-unit-administered data ecosystem.

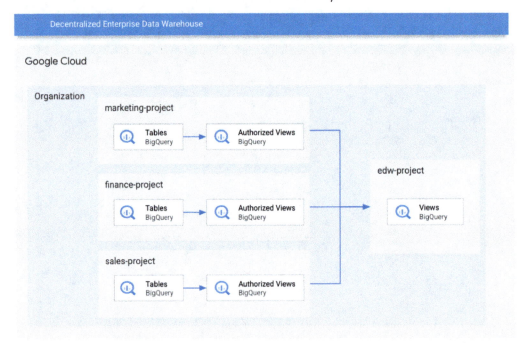

Figure 2.4 – The decentralized data warehouse pattern

The decentralized data warehouse model provides the following features:

- More tactical business decision support versus the previous centralized EDW
- Data integration is managed at the individual business levels
- Lower cost and less time to implement

The cross-org data exchange

In the cross-org data exchange design pattern, BigQuery views are used to share data with another organization or domain. This pattern could be used in organizations that are looking to set up data exchange with their suppliers, vendors, or business partners running on Google Cloud. By leveraging cross-org data sharing, companies using BigQuery have an opportunity to deliver or obtain data from partners, enabling rapid real-time decision making.

For example, if your company is a manufacturer and one of your product retail or construction distributors is also using BigQuery, you would have the opportunity to facilitate data sharing. The manufacturer could obtain product feedback data or inventory and stock levels, and quickly adjust their fulfillment and product demands. This would allow the manufacturer to act quickly to improve their sales and relationships with important partners with the power of data exchange on BigQuery. The Google Cloud features that enable this design pattern are VPC service controls ingress and egress policies and BigQuery authorized views.

The following diagram shows the cross-org data exchange design. It uses a project with authorized views from private datasets to share specific, determined data outside of the organization. **VPC service controls (VPC-SC)** create a service perimeter (dotted line) and control ingress and egress into projects.

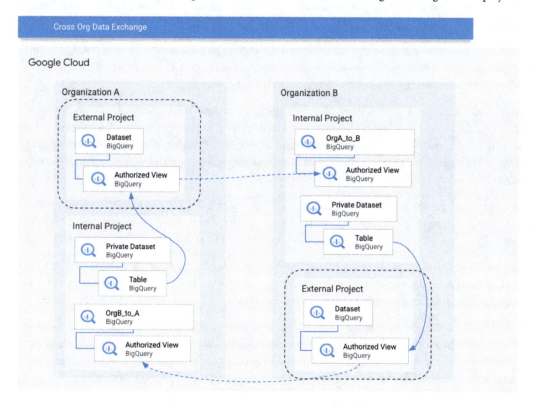

Figure 2.5 – The cross-org data exchange

Another approach to data sharing is Analytics Hub in Google Cloud. This service is a data exchange that allows you to securely share data across organizations with added subscription management and governance over the cross-org data exchange approach. Analytics Hub is a gateway-type service between data publishers and data subscribers that should be evaluated if the goal is to share data broadly for data monetization purposes. This service is a more managed approach to the cross-org data exchange that should be evaluated when seeking to share data for profit purposes externally to your organization.

In this section, we outlined three approaches for designing enterprise data warehouses in Google BigQuery. Each design has its advantages and organizations should determine whether the top-down, centralized or the bottom-up, decentralized approach makes the most sense for how their teams operate and their capabilities. Now let's discuss schema design in the next section, to continue good practices for BigQuery setup at the table level.

Schema design

One important aspect of working with BigQuery is designing an effective schema for your data as you build tables. The schema is the way in which you structure your data within BigQuery, including the types of data you store, how you organize it, and how you define relationships between different pieces of data.

A schema defines the structure of a database or a data table. In BigQuery, a schema consists of one or more columns, where each column can have a specific data type. When designing a schema in BigQuery, there are several important considerations to keep in mind.

First, consider the *types of queries* you plan to run against your data. Your schema should be optimized for the types of queries you will be running most frequently. For example, if you plan to run a lot of aggregations, you may want to pre-aggregate some of your data to reduce the query processing time. On the other hand, if you plan to do a lot of filtering on specific columns, you may want to create separate tables for each filter.

Second, consider the *size and complexity* of your data. BigQuery is designed to handle massive datasets, but the size and complexity of your data can still impact query performance. You may want to consider denormalizing your data or breaking it up into smaller tables to reduce the query processing time.

Third, consider the *accessibility* of your data. BigQuery provides several access control mechanisms, including project-level, dataset-level, and table-level permissions. You should design your schema to ensure that data is accessible only to those who need it and that sensitive data is properly secured.

Finally, consider the *ease of maintenance and scalability* of your schema. As your data grows and evolves, your schema should be able to accommodate changes without requiring significant changes to your query logic or data pipelines. You should also design your schema to be easy to maintain and update, with clear naming conventions and well-documented data types and relationships.

Table design

When designing a BigQuery table, it is important to consider several factors, such as the data types being used, the relationships between tables, and the intended use cases for the data. One important consideration is the use of *nested and repeated fields*. These can be used to group related data and reduce the number of tables required to represent a data model.

By partitioning tables based on a specific column or field, data can be organized into smaller, more manageable sections. Clustering, which involves sorting data within partitions, can further improve query performance by reducing the amount of data that needs to be scanned.

It is important to consider the use of denormalization and nested and repeated fields when designing tables in BigQuery. Traditional databases are typically normalized, or data is divided into multiple tables. Normalized table design increases the number of joins in your queries. Joins are the process of combining rows from two or more tables based on a common column. In most cases, denormalized or combined tables are preferred in BigQuery because they improve the performance of queries, and schemas are simplified.

When you denormalize your data, you are storing redundant data in one table. This can help to improve the performance of your queries because BigQuery does not have to join tables together to find the data that you need. Nested fields allow you to store related data together and repeated fields allow you to store multiple values for a single column. Nested and repeated fields can help you store more data in a single row, which can improve the performance of your queries.

In the following diagram, you can see the difference between normalized tables and what normalized tables could look like if denormalized with repeated and nested fields.

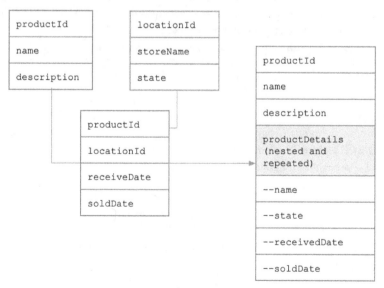

Figure 2.6 – Shifting from normalized to denormalized tables with nested and repeated columns

> **Don't optimize prematurely**
>
> Postpone optimizations such as denormalization or query refactoring. First, try out your existing schemas and queries, and if they are fast or inexpensive enough, leave them alone! The beauty of BigQuery is the ability to handle large amounts of data in different forms. Don't let optimization hold up the querying and exploring of your tables. You can always optimize later if you notice challenges writing queries or with query performance.

Here are best practices for schema and table design in BigQuery:

- Denormalization is not a requirement but can speed up queries by reducing the need for joins.
- Take advantage of nested and repeated fields in denormalized tables when you have situations with related data.
- Design for performance – when designing your schema, you must consider how the data will be used.
- Keep it simple. The more complex your schema, the more difficult it will be to manage and maintain.
- Choose the right data types. The data type of each column should be appropriate for the data that will be stored in the column. For example, if the column will store numbers, you should use a numeric data type, not a string.
- Migrate the current table schema as is to BigQuery and optimize as necessary.

BigQuery table and schema design is an important part of building an operationally efficient BigQuery data warehouse. If a table has redundant or unnecessary data, this can result in larger storage costs and slower query performance. If tables have many columns but only a few columns are used in queries, this may lead to slower query performance and unnecessary costs. By following the tips in this section, you can design a schema that will help you to store, query, and analyze your data efficiently.

Summary

Designing and organizing your BigQuery data is an important part of using BigQuery effectively. In this chapter, we outlined Google Cloud's resource hierarchy and BigQuery resources and provided best practices for each feature. This chapter's diagrams were built upon as the chapter progressed, providing a visual approach to understanding BigQuery resources, design, and organization.

In conclusion, designing and organizing a BigQuery environment requires a good understanding of resources and consideration of several key factors, including pattern and schema design. By following the best practices in this chapter, you can create a data warehouse that is easy to query and analyze, cost-effective, and performant. In the next chapter, we will shift to exploring data. Read on to learn about the various tools and approaches to continue to build your data analysis skillset.

Part 2:
Data Exploration
with BigQuery

In this part of the book, we will move on from theory and concepts and review tactical approaches to exploring, loading, and querying data in BigQuery. Various best practices and solutions will be covered that will help you get started on analyzing and exploring your data.

This part has the following chapters:

- *Chapter 3, Exploring Data in BigQuery*
- *Chapter 4, Loading and Transforming Data*
- *Chapter 5, Querying BigQuery Data*
- *Chapter 6, Exploring Data with Notebooks*
- *Chapter 7, Further Exploring and Visualizing Data*

3

Exploring Data in BigQuery

In this chapter, we will review various ways to explore your data in BigQuery and introduce the practice of data exploration. We will review examining tables and data in the BigQuery web UI, the BigQuery bq command-line interface, and exploring data with visualization tools. After learning about the different methods to access your data in BigQuery, this chapter will outline the best practices and approaches to get started.

Completing this chapter will establish a strong foundation for the topics covered in the remainder of this book. We are going to compare common data exploration techniques and begin writing SQL queries to interact with data in BigQuery. After reading this chapter, you will be prepared to start your journey of data exploration and preparation. You will be equipped to begin integrating your data in BigQuery to accelerate your data analysis capabilities and build a strong data analytics practice for yourself or your organization.

We are going to cover the following topics:

- What is data exploration?
- Exploring data in BigQuery
- Additional approaches and best practices

Technical requirements

As mentioned in previous chapters, to get the most out of this chapter, you will want to have access to the Google Cloud console (`https://console.cloud.google.com/`). You can begin exploring the GitHub repository (`https://github.com/PacktPublishing/Data-Exploration-and-Preparation-with-BigQuery`) for this book to browse and download diagrams and code snippets. If you have not already, you will also want to view and add the Google Trends dataset to your Google Cloud project for hands-on examples. Visit the Google Trends dataset at `https://console.cloud.google.com/marketplace/product/bigquery-public-datasets/google-search-trends` and click **View Dataset**. This will bring the dataset into your SQL workspace in BigQuery. You may star (add to favorites) the dataset to find it more easily.

Expand the dataset, click a table, and click **Preview** in the middle pane. You have just begun exploring a dataset in BigQuery. Continue in this chapter to better understand resources and design patterns.

What is data exploration?

Data exploration is the process of examining, analyzing, and visualizing data in order to discover patterns, relationships, and insights. It involves the use of various query and data visualization techniques to understand the underlying structure of the data, identify trends, and gain a deeper understanding of the data. Data exploration is essential for making informed decisions about your data.

Data exploration is typically one of the first steps in data analysis and is used to get a sense of what the data contains, to identify potential problems or errors in the data, and to form hypotheses about the relationships between columns and tables. By exploring data, analysts can better understand the characteristics of the data, such as its distribution, variance, and range, and identify any outliers or anomalies that may need to be addressed. This process can also help identify opportunities for further analysis or data collection.

Data exploration can help you to do the following:

- Understand the structure of the data
- Identify outliers and missing values
- Identify relationships between variables
- Discover patterns in the data
- Generate hypotheses about the data
- Communicate findings to others

It is important to keep in mind that data exploration is an iterative process. As you explore your data, you may identify new questions that you want to answer. You may also need to go back and clean the data or transform it in new ways. The goal of data exploration is to gain a better understanding of the data so you can make informed decisions about how to use it.

As a data analyst, you are not necessarily limited to just using SQL in the BigQuery console. There are other services and features in Google Cloud and data preparation tools that we will introduce later on in *Chapter 8, An Overview of Data Preparation Tools*.

You may be wondering: what do you have to do before you begin exploring data? You have to find a question, something unknown, or perhaps something interesting that you want to learn from a dataset. You could look for something simple such as the most sold products or revenue from product groups. Often, one of the greatest challenges in data exploration is coming up with the right questions. A dataset can be a blank slate and you'll need to figure out where to start. If you are new to data exploration, here are a few tips to get you started:

- **Understand the context**: Before diving into data exploration, take the time to understand the context and objectives of the analysis. Clearly define the questions you want to answer or the problems you want to solve. This will guide your exploration and help you focus on relevant aspects of the data.

- **Get familiar with the data**: Start by getting familiar with the dataset's structure, including the columns, datatypes, and relationships between tables. Understand the meaning of each variable and any data limitations or quality issues. This will help you make informed decisions during exploration and avoid misinterpretations.

- **Start with a small dataset**: When you are first starting out exploring data, it is a good idea to start with a small dataset if possible. This will make it easier to learn how to use the BigQuery tools and techniques as well as optimize cost.

- **Use the built-in functions and operators**: BigQuery offers a variety of built-in functions and operators that can be used to manipulate and analyze data. These functions can save you a lot of time and effort.

- **Visualize the data**: Visualizations are powerful tools for data exploration. Use charts, histograms, scatter plots, and other visual techniques to gain insights into patterns, relationships, and distributions within the data. Visualizations can reveal trends, anomalies, and potential correlations that might not be apparent from raw tabular data.

- **Stay curious and learn continuously**: Data exploration is an ongoing learning process. Stay curious, explore different techniques, and learn new tools and methodologies. Keep up with the latest trends in data analysis and stay informed about advancements in data exploration techniques. Continuous learning will enhance your skills and expand your capabilities as a data analyst.

Now that you understand what data exploration is, let's dive into its fundamentals in the next section.

Fundamentals

The goal of data exploration is to identify patterns and trends in the data that can be used to answer questions, make predictions, or develop new insights. Data exploration can be done using a variety of techniques, such as the following:

- Descriptive statistics can provide a summary of the data, enabling analysts to understand the variability and distribution of variables. Think mean, median, mode, and standard deviation here.

- Data sampling involves selecting a representative subset of data from a larger dataset. This technique allows for faster exploration at times.

- Creating charts, graphs, and other visualizations can help identify patterns and trends in the data. Visualizations provide an intuitive means for exploring and communicating findings.

- Machine learning models can be used to identify patterns in data that are not easily detected by humans. Regression analysis explores relationships between variables, allowing for prediction or inference on data patterns. Time series analysis provides insights into patterns and helps with forecasting future values.

Data exploration is an iterative process. As you explore the data, you will likely identify new questions that need to be answered. This will lead to further exploration and analysis that will in turn lead to new insights.

The key principles of data exploration are as follows:

- Start with a clear understanding of the question. What do you want to learn from the data?

- Use a variety of tools and techniques. There is no single right way to explore data. The best approach will vary depending on the data and question.

- Be patient. It takes time to get to know the data and to identify patterns and trends.

Let's further expand our knowledge of data exploration by learning about the data life cycle in the following section.

Data life cycle

The data life cycle is the process that describes the stages that data goes through from its creation to its eventual deletion at the end of its useful life. By understanding the data life cycle, you can better plan your activities around data exploration and preparation:

- **Data creation** is the stage where data is first created. Data can be created in a variety of ways such as through sensors, interactions, or logging.

- **Data collection** is the process of gathering data from a variety of sources.

- **Data preparation** is the stage where data is cleaned, transformed, and organized so that it is ready for analysis.

- **Data analysis** is the stage where data is analyzed to identify patterns and trends.

- **Data visualization** is the stage where data is presented in a way that makes it easy to understand for consumers.

- **Data sharing** is the process of making data available for others to use.

- **Data archiving** is the process of storing data for future use. This can include backing up data to cloud storage or switching to long-term storage at a reduced cost.

Common challenges and solutions

There are several common challenges that can be encountered when exploring data. Some of these challenges involve data volume, data quality, and data variety. Data may be incomplete, inaccurate, or inconsistent. Data could be scattered across tables and require complex joins to derive any value. Poor data quality can make it difficult to identify patterns and trends in data.

In a general sense, data volume can be very large, making it difficult to store, process, and analyze. Fortunately, with BigQuery and optimized SQL queries, you can analyze large datasets with ease. Data variety can also make exploring and preparing data challenging. Data can come in a variety of formats and types, structured and unstructured, making it difficult to prepare for analysis.

There are many solutions that can be used to address challenges with exploring and preparing data. Many of these solutions we will outline in the chapters of this book.

Data visualization can help overcome some of the common challenges with data exploration. Data visualization is the process of presenting data in a way that is easy to understand. This can include creating charts and graphs. By looking at data beyond the query tabular results, naturally, you will be able to slice and dice columns and identify trends and useful details.

> **Explore BigQuery results within a sheet**
>
> BigQuery users can quickly explore query results within a Google Sheet for sharing. To take advantage of this option from within the SQL workspace in BigQuery's Cloud console, execute a query. After the query has been completed, within the query results you will see a drop-down menu with an option to **Explore Data**. Choose **Explore with Sheets** and your data will be connected. From here, you can create connected charts, pivot tables, and functions that work on the entire dataset. This functionality makes it easy to collaborate with partners or other interested parties in a familiar spreadsheet interface. Connected sheets also provide a more updated single source of truth for analysis without relying on continual `.csv` exports.

As you can see, exploring data is a vital step in the data analysis process, enabling analysts to gain insights, discover patterns, and make informed decisions. So far, we have defined data exploration and explained the value that it delivers. The next section will pivot from theory to practice, introducing more advanced topics in data analysis so you can begin hands-on work in BigQuery.

Introduction to exploring data in BigQuery

BigQuery offers a variety of features that make it easy to explore data. The approaches and tools described in this section can be used in parallel and by preference. You can use each of these tools in any order you would like, and it is encouraged to have knowledge and experience with each, so you have the flexibility to choose what works best for you. The BigQuery web UI is the best way to get started with exploring data. It is a web-based interface that allows you to import, modify, and query your data. The BigQuery page in the Cloud console is fully featured and most data analytics teams will spend a lot of time there. In this section, we will continue to use the Google Trends public dataset to introduce practices around data exploration.

Exploring data in the BigQuery SQL workspace

The SQL workspace (refer to *Figure 3.1*) is the main view where you can open multiple tabs, view datasets, and begin your data exploration journey. You will use the SQL workspace in the BigQuery web UI to create visualizations and reports from your data, save your queries and view query history, import and export data, understand query performance, and much more. The SQL workspace is the primary area for data analysis that you will use when interacting with BigQuery.

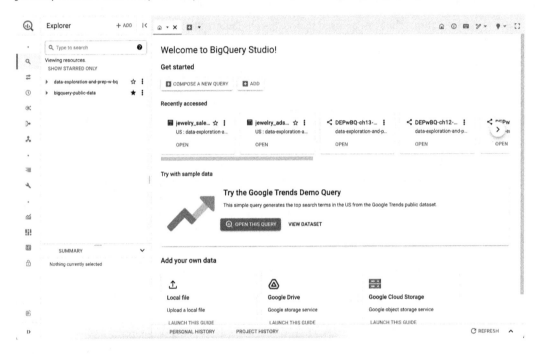

Figure 3.1 – The SQL workspace in BigQuery analysis

Before writing queries, it is important to gain an understanding of your table's properties. It is important to know and understand the metadata, or data about your data, before proceeding to run queries and gain insights.

Exploring schema and table structure

To begin exploring data in BigQuery, you will want to understand table schema and properties. Imagine we have just loaded our company's massive sales dataset into BigQuery. It has many tables and fields, so how do we decide which columns and tables we should query? How do we work to gain an understanding of the tables before actually writing a query and beginning to formulate questions to ask the data? There are a few ways to do this. First, we will explore table schema and table metadata to gain a better understanding of our tables.

Using the *Google Trends* public dataset as mentioned in the *Technical requirements* section of this chapter, we will explore the schema data for the Google Trends tables within the Cloud console. If you have not done so already, visit the datasets homepage at `https://cloud.google.com/datasets`, click **Explore all datasets**, search for the `Trends` dataset, then click **View dataset**. This will open BigQuery and allow you to browse the data in your Cloud console.

Start by clicking on the `top_terms` table inside the `google_trends` dataset within the SQL Explorer view in BigQuery. See *Figure 3.2* for this view in the Cloud console:

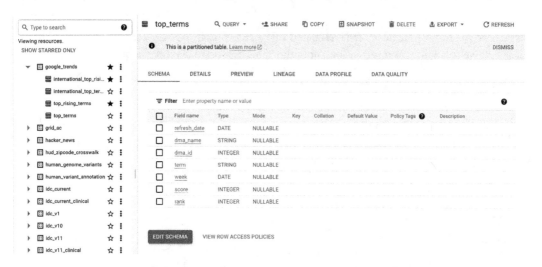

Figure 3.2 – Table schema details for the Google Trends public dataset in BigQuery

In the preceding screenshot, you can see the datatype for each column in this table (**DATE, INTEGER,** and **STRING**). By understanding the table's datatypes, you can better understand how to write queries. For example, knowing the refresh date is a `DATE` datatype enables you to take advantage of **BigQuery GoogleSQL date functions** (`https://cloud.google.com/bigquery/docs/reference/standard-sql/date_functions`). Knowing the correct datatype for each field allows you to better explore your table's data. Looking at this dataset, you may want to filter by `refresh_date`, which is a `DATE` datatype. See the following example:

```
WHERE refresh_date >= DATE_SUB(CURRENT_DATE(), INTERVAL 1 WEEK)
```

The preceding statement on the `refresh_date` column uses two date functions in GoogleSQL: `DATE_SUB` and `CURRENT_DATE`.

DATE_SUB subtracts the specified interval (1 week) from the CURRENT_DATE, which returns the current date as a DATE datatype value. The WHERE statement is filtering data, telling the BigQuery SQL engine to only provide rows selected that have a refresh date greater than or equal to dates in the last week. This type of table query filtering with date functions is only possible as the datatype on this field is set as DATE on the schema. If the datatype was STRING or plain text, this filtering would not be possible and the query would not execute.

> **Schema validation and the right datatypes**
> You will want to validate and correct table datatypes during schema creation or after you load data into BigQuery. Correct datatypes will allow you to better interact with your data. Schema validation is critical to best leveraging your data in BigQuery.

Next up, we will browse the table's **DETAILS** and **PREVIEW** tabs in SQL Explorer in BigQuery. These areas will give us additional information about our table before we explore via queries.

Let's explore the **DETAILS** tab to continue learning about this table's structure:

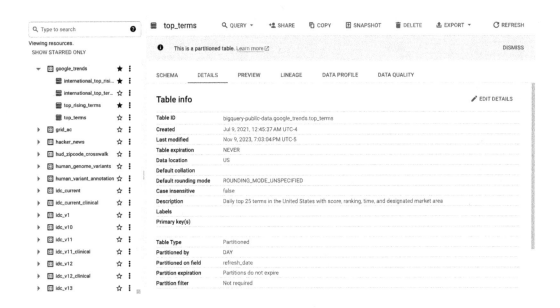

Figure 3.3 – Table details for the Google Trends public dataset in BigQuery

Displayed in *Figure 3.3*, the table details let you view basic table info such as creation and modification timestamps, expiration date, data location, table type, and partition information. This `top_terms` table is partitioned by `DAY`, which is the default partition type and a good choice when data is spread out over a wide range of dates or when the table is continuously updated over time.

Next, we will look at the **PREVIEW** tab, which allows you to explore rows of data in your table without a query:

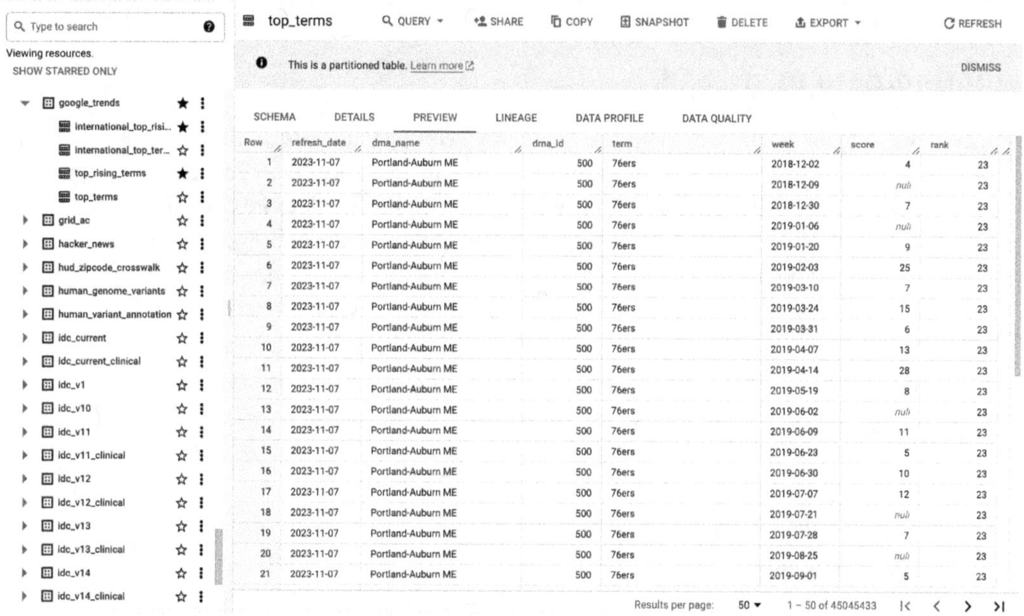

Figure 3.4 – Table preview for the Google Trends public dataset in BigQuery

When first exploring a dataset, the **PREVIEW** tab is useful to give you a basic understanding of the table structure and patterns around the data. The first observation is that this table is large. Checking the preview tells us that the total number of results is nearly 44 million rows, as displayed at the bottom of *Figure 3.4*. Another observation as you scroll through the preview rows is that the `dma_name` column has many rows with different weeks and that they are incremented by 7 days in the `week` column. This tells you that if you want data by a specific `dma_name`, you have information for the search terms at the start of the week.

Going through further pages of rows in this table, you can see that there are null values in the `score` column. This is a useful piece of information to know about the table as you begin to formulate queries. This means the table does not have a popularity score for the term in the `dma_name` for every `refresh_date`.

Just by browsing the table preview, we have learned that the table is large, there are null values in the score column, and there are multiple date columns (we also could have identified that by observing the schema earlier). We have now completed the first step in exploring data in BigQuery: understanding table schema and properties. You may want to continue to page through the table rows in the table preview to better understand the table before writing a query, or you may have already reached a good baseline understanding of the data. When you have a good basic understanding of how the table looks and feels, then you should be ready to begin formulating questions to ask the table in the form of a SQL query.

Exploring data using SQL

BigQuery's SQL engine is very powerful and can handle complex queries. In the previous sections, we manually went through table properties and schema and browsed a table row preview. Now, we will begin using queries and **Structured Query Language** (**SQL**) to ask more complex questions of our data. SQL is an important skill to have as a data analyst and it is one of the fastest ways to interact with large datasets of data inside BigQuery.

To explore data with SQL in the BigQuery web UI, follow these steps:

1. Go to the BigQuery SQL workspace in the Cloud console.

2. Select a table.

3. Select the query drop down menu and choose a new or split tab.

4. In the Query Editor, type your SQL query.

5. Click the **Run** button.

The results of your query will be displayed in the results pane.

Query example 1

Let's build a SQL query from top to bottom and show the results of that query. Follow along in the console and feel free to modify the query and see the results.

The SELECT clause is used to select columns from a table. For example, the following query selects the refresh_date, term, and rank rows from the top_trends table:

```
SELECT refresh_date, term, rank
```

The FROM clause tells SQL what table to select rows from. The format in BigQuery is `project. dataset.table` and uses a backtick or ` around the location:

```
SELECT refresh_date, term, rank
FROM `bigquery-public-data.google_trends.top_terms`
```

The WHERE clause is used to filter rows from a table. AND is a between operator to combine filtering requests. For example, the following query selects all rows from the customers table where the rank is 1 and the refresh_date is within the week. You may change the interval number or substitute the date_part values for DAY, WEEK, MONTH, QUARTER, and YEAR:

```
SELECT refresh_date, term, rank
FROM `bigquery-public-data.google_trends.top_terms`
WHERE rank = 1
AND refresh_date >= DATE_SUB(CURRENT_DATE(),
    INTERVAL 1 WEEK)
```

The GROUP BY clause is used to group rows from a table by a common value. For example, the following query groups rows from the top_terms table:

```
SELECT refresh_date, term, rank FROM `bigquery-public-data.google_
trends.top_terms`
WHERE rank = 1
AND refresh_date >= DATE_SUB(CURRENT_DATE(),
    INTERVAL 1 WEEK)
GROUP BY refresh_date, term, rank
```

The ORDER BY clause is used to sort the results from the query. Using the DESC argument will sort from latest to oldest. Conversely, ASC will sort from oldest to latest. Here is the completed query:

```
SELECT refresh_date, term, rank FROM `bigquery-public-data.google_
trends.top_terms`
WHERE rank = 1
AND refresh_date >= DATE_SUB(CURRENT_DATE(),
    INTERVAL 1 WEEK)
GROUP BY refresh_date, term, rank
ORDER BY refresh_date DESC
```

In *Figure 3.5*, we have the results from running this query on the Google Trends top terms table. You can see the top terms for the past week, sorted from latest to oldest:

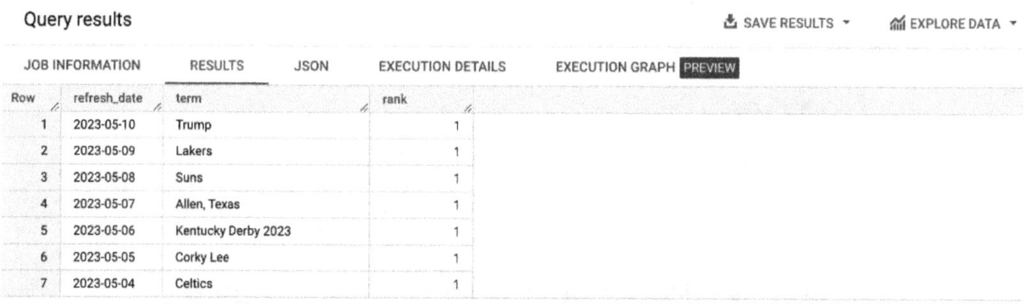

Row	refresh_date	term	rank
1	2023-05-10	Trump	1
2	2023-05-09	Lakers	1
3	2023-05-08	Suns	1
4	2023-05-07	Allen, Texas	1
5	2023-05-06	Kentucky Derby 2023	1
6	2023-05-05	Corky Lee	1
7	2023-05-04	Celtics	1

Figure 3.5 – Results from querying the Google Trends top_terms dataset

Query example 2

Let's try another query example. The question I want to ask the Google Trends top terms dataset is: *How many DMAs (designated market areas) in the table are in the state of Florida?* Let's write a SQL query that will do this.

We will start by selecting columns that will give us this information. Since we already have a good understanding of the Google Trends dataset from working with it earlier in this chapter, we know there is a column called dma_name. If we use a SQL COUNT function, we should be able to get this data quickly. We'll also want to only look for distinct values to make sure we are only returning unique matches. We are using as to give the result of the function a more descriptive name (DMA_COUNT) in the results. The SQL COUNT function is an aggregate function. More information can be found in the docs at **BigQuery GoogleSQL Aggregate functions** (https://cloud.google.com/bigquery/docs/reference/standard-sql/aggregate_functions).

```
SELECT COUNT(DISTINCT(dma_name)) as DMA_COUNT
```

Next, in the FROM clause, we are just referencing the same dataset that we have continued to work with:

```
FROM `bigquery-public-data.google_trends.top_terms`
```

So far, we have selected the column we need (dma_name) and specified the table location we want to read from. Now, we need to filter by FL to just give us dma_name columns in the state of Florida. We will use the REGEXP_CONTAINS function here, specify the column, and specify the string. This is a SQL function that can only be performed on STRING columns (see **BigQuery GoogleSQL string functions** at https://cloud.google.com/bigquery/docs/reference/standard-sql/string_functions):

```
WHERE (REGEXP_CONTAINS(dma_name, r"FL"))
```

Here is our completed query to count the number of dma_name columns that include the state of FL:

```
SELECT COUNT(DISTINCT(dma_name))
FROM `bigquery-public-data.google_trends.top_terms`
WHERE (REGEXP_CONTAINS(dma_name, r"FL"))
```

We get the following result:

Figure 3.6 – Results from querying the Google Trends top_terms dataset
and counting the distinct dma_name rows that contain FL

The preceding query asked the dataset how many dma_name columns contained FL, or how many unique dma_name columns in the dataset are in Florida. This could be useful to understand how Florida compares to other states in the Google Trends dataset.

In the previous examples, we ran two queries, one to return filtered data from the 43 million rows in our dataset, and an aggregate query to count the number of unique entries for the state of Florida in the dataset. You can begin to see how understanding how your table is structured and running basic SQL queries allows you to be more prepared to explore data with advanced approaches. This section was intended to be an introduction to exploring data with SQL. We will go over SQL queries in BigQuery in more detail in *Chapter 5, Querying BigQuery Data*.

> **Exploring BigQuery docs to understand the available functions**
>
> When you begin writing SQL queries to explore data in BigQuery, you will want to know the available functions that you can perform on different fields or datatypes. As you begin to ask questions of your data, you will want to match your questions with available functions. There will be a process of testing the functions, looking for examples, and writing them in your own queries. Remember, SQL is a language used in programming and for managing data, so if it takes a while to get a SQL query and function to run, that is completely normal. For more information, you can refer to https://cloud.google.com/bigquery/docs/reference/standard-sql/functions-and-operators.

Exploring data using the bq command-line interface

In addition to the BigQuery web UI, you can also use the bq **command-line interface (CLI)** to explore data in BigQuery. The bq CLI is a powerful tool that allows you to interact with BigQuery using commands and scripts. To invoke the bq CLI, you will need the **gcloud CLI** (https://cloud.google.com/cli) installed. This can be installed on most Linux, Windows, and macOS operating systems. Alternatively, you can use the bq CLI that is preinstalled on Cloud Shell in the Cloud console.

Locate the **Activate Cloud Shell** button in the Cloud console to bring up a terminal window at the bottom of the Cloud console:

Figure 3.7 – Activating Cloud Shell from the console

Cloud Shell is a browser-based terminal that comes preloaded with the gcloud command-line tool and 5 GB of storage. It comes with a code editor (see *Figure 3.8*)and is a powerful tool for development and deployment practices. Use Cloud Shell to interact with Google Cloud resources, scripts, and other integrations.

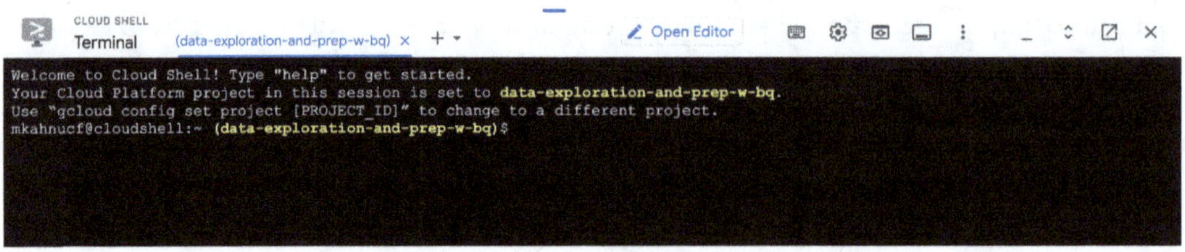

Figure 3.8 – Cloud Shell activated in the Cloud console

Here are some common bq commands that you can use to explore data:

- `bq ls`: This is used to list datasets and tables
- `bq query`: This is used to run SQL queries
- `bq load`: This is used to load data into BigQuery
- `bq export`: This is used to export data from BigQuery

There are several reasons why someone might choose to use the bq CLI to explore data in BigQuery:

- **Automating tasks**: The bq CLI allows you to automate repetitive tasks, such as running SQL queries, exporting data, or loading data into BigQuery. By using scripts and the CLI, you can perform these tasks more efficiently and save time.
- **Command line flexibility**: Some users may prefer the flexibility and control of the CLI over the **graphical user interface** (**GUI**) of the BigQuery web interface. With the bq CLI, you can quickly navigate through datasets and tables, execute SQL queries, and perform data operations without using a mouse or navigating through menus.
- **Integration with other tools**: The bq CLI integrates with other command-line tools and scripts, allowing you to incorporate BigQuery data into your workflows and data pipelines. For example, you can use the bq CLI to extract data from BigQuery and load it into other systems or combine BigQuery data with data from other sources.

Overall, the bq CLI provides a powerful and flexible way to explore and work with data in BigQuery. It can help users streamline workflows, automate tasks, and control costs, making it a valuable tool for data professionals and developers alike.

Now, let's discuss another more visual way to explore data, with visualization tools.

Exploring data with visualization tools

Data visualization is a critical aspect of data exploration and analysis. It allows you to present data in a graphical format, making it easier to understand and identify patterns or trends. In addition to the BigQuery web interface and the bq CLI, there are several visualization tools that you can use to explore and analyze data in BigQuery. These tools can help you to communicate your findings to others via reports and charts.

Looker Studio is a web-based data visualization tool that integrates with several Google products, including BigQuery. It allows you to create interactive reports and dashboards using a drag-and-drop interface. With Looker Studio, you can connect to BigQuery, create charts, graphs, and tables, and share your visualizations with others. Looker Studio also provides several pre-built templates and connectors to popular data sources, making it easy to get started with your visualizations.

> **Fun fact**
> Looker Studio was previously known as Data Studio and was a part of the **Google Marketing Platform** (**GMP**), closely coupled with Google Analytics and Google Ads services. Today, Looker Studio is a part of Google Cloud.

Tableau is a popular data visualization tool that allows you to connect to a wide range of data sources, including BigQuery. With Tableau, you can create interactive visualizations and dashboards using a drag-and-drop interface. It provides a wide range of chart types and visualization options, including geographic mapping, trend analysis, and data blending. Tableau also supports advanced analytics and machine learning capabilities, allowing you to perform predictive analysis and data modeling.

Looker is a cloud-based business intelligence platform that provides data modeling, exploration, and visualization capabilities. It allows you to connect to various data sources, including BigQuery, and provides a SQL-based interface for querying and analyzing data. Looker also provides several pre-built templates and visualization options, allowing you to quickly create reports and dashboards. Additionally, Looker provides a wide range of customization options, making it easy to tailor your visualizations to your specific needs. Looker is a platform that includes LookML and other robust tools for transforming your presentation layer for reporting across your organization.

Power BI is a business analytics tool developed by Microsoft that supports connectivity with BigQuery. It offers a user friendly interface and a wide range of visualization options to create insightful reports and interactive dashboards. Power BI allows users to connect to BigQuery datasets, transform and shape the data, and create compelling visualizations with powerful filtering and drill-down capabilities. Many organizations that run Microsoft 365 (formerly known as Office) and use BigQuery will choose to use PowerBI as their visualization tool of choice.

The tools outlined in this section provide a range of options for visualizing data stored in BigQuery, enabling users to explore, analyze, and communicate insights effectively. They empower organizations to make data-driven decisions and derive value from their BigQuery datasets. It's important to choose a visualization tool that aligns with your organization's specific needs, skill level, capabilities, and budget.

Now that we have described tools to help data exploration, next up, we will go through advanced approaches and best practices to continue to build your knowledge in data exploration.

Enhancing data exploration in BigQuery

In the previous sections, we outlined a few approaches for beginning to understand your data and beginning data exploration in BigQuery. Now we will outline some additional approaches and touch on best practices.

Advanced approaches

Jupyter Notebooks are popular for data exploration and analysis. They are tools commonly used by data scientists. However, notebooks are becoming more common in interacting with ML models and large datasets. You can leverage BigQuery's integration with Jupyter Notebooks to write SQL queries and perform data exploration in a collaborative and interactive environment. By using libraries such as `google-cloud-bigquery`, you can execute queries, fetch results, and visualize data within the notebook itself.

BigQuery Studio provides an analytics workspace of notebooks within the BigQuery console. BigQuery Studio helps integrate tools into a single experience that can reduce the need to utilize other tools, making teams more efficient. BigQuery Studio includes assistive code development in the SQL editor and within notebooks using Duet AI (generative AI).

BigQuery integrates with Google Cloud's AI and machine learning tools such as Google Cloud AutoML and BigQuery ML. These tools allow you to perform advanced data exploration by leveraging machine learning algorithms. For example, you can use BigQuery ML to build and deploy machine learning models directly within BigQuery, enabling you to uncover patterns and make predictions from your data.

Best practices

When dealing with large datasets in BigQuery, it can be time-consuming and costly to explore the entire dataset. In such cases, you can use sampling techniques to select a representative subset of the data for exploration. As described in this chapter, take the time to understand the data's structure, meaning, and limitations. Familiarize yourself with the variables, datatypes, and any data quality issues that may impact your analysis. This understanding will ensure accurate interpretation of the results.

Visualizations are powerful tools for exploring data. Utilize charts, graphs, and interactive visualizations to identify patterns, trends, and correlations within the data. Visual representations make complex data more accessible and facilitate clearer insights.

Remember, data exploration is an iterative process. Continuously refine your analysis, ask new questions, and explore different angles to gain deeper insights. The exploration process should be flexible, so adapt to new findings and adjust the approach accordingly.

These best practices are guidelines for the process of exploring and analyzing data. The choice of approach you take depends on the nature of the data, the questions you want to answer, the complexity of analysis required, and your preferred tools and techniques. Combining multiple approaches can often yield richer insights and facilitate a comprehensive exploration of your BigQuery datasets.

Summary

In summary, this chapter on data exploration in BigQuery served as a guide for data analysts, offering insights into the various approaches, tools, and best practices available for effective exploration and analysis within BigQuery. It equipped you with the necessary knowledge and skills to navigate and derive valuable insights from your datasets in BigQuery. In the upcoming chapters, we will move past introductory concepts into repeatable technical practices you can use in your data analysis practice.

4

Loading and Transforming Data

In the previous chapters, we introduced BigQuery and some of its foundational features. We introduced best practices and described the design and organization of resources, enabling you to understand the service. We also began defining different approaches for exploring data in BigQuery and went over the iterative process of exploration as a data analyst. Now that much of the foundational concepts have been covered, in this chapter, we will shift to the concepts and practices around loading and transforming data in BigQuery.

Loading and transforming data are critical steps in the data analysis process. These steps allow organizations to store data efficiently to begin leveraging data for insights and decision-making. In this chapter, we will explore the various techniques and best practices for loading data into BigQuery, including batch loading, streaming data, and data connections from external sources. Additionally, we will delve into the tools and methodologies available for transforming and preprocessing data with BigQuery. The last section of this chapter will present a scenario and a guided hands-on exercise to follow, covering some of the discussed concepts.

We will begin to move from foundational to more technical and tactical approaches in this chapter, helping you understand different data loading and transformation scenarios. By understanding the intricacies of loading and transforming data in BigQuery, data analysts and engineers can streamline this process and ultimately maximize the value of data assets.

Specifically, we are going to discuss the following main topics:

- Data loading
- Data transformation
- Evaluating the **extract, transform, load** (ETL) and **extract, load, transform** (ELT) approaches
- Hands-on exercise – data loading and transformation in BigQuery

Upon completion of this chapter, you will have a strong understanding of the different ways to load data into BigQuery. The hands-on exercise at the end of this chapter will reinforce the concepts in this chapter and help you build your proficiency using BigQuery.

Technical requirements

To get the most out of this chapter, you will want to have access to the Google Cloud console (`https://console.cloud.google.com/`).

Visit and clone this book's GitHub repository to begin downloading technical artifacts for the hands-on example: `https://github.com/PacktPublishing/Data-Exploration-and-Preparation-with-BigQuery`

Exploring data loading techniques

There are various ways to ingest data into BigQuery. Data loading can be broken up into a few approaches: batch, streaming, and scheduled. Data load jobs can be executed via the console, the bq command-line interface, the API, other Google Cloud service integrations, and scheduled jobs. In this section, we will discuss each approach to help you understand the best data loading technique to get started and establish a data loading strategy for one-time or regular ingestion and analysis.

Batch loading data

Batch loading or bounded data is a process of loading data into BigQuery in a single operation. This can be done from a variety of sources, including files located in Google Cloud Storage or Google Drive, and local files. Acceptable file types include CSV, JSON, Apache Avro, ORC, and Apache Parquet formats. Batch loading is typically driven through the console UI, automated via API, or via scheduled jobs.

When loading data from a source, you must first have a dataset where the table will be located. The dataset is a logical container for your table data. This is also where you select the region for your data to reside. After creating a dataset, you will create a table in BigQuery to store your data.

> **Choosing the location of your data**
>
> It's important to consider the location of your data when creating a dataset and, ultimately, your tables. The dataset location determines the region where your data will be stored. If you plan to transfer data from a Cloud Storage bucket on a regular basis, optimize your architecture by having both the storage bucket and the BigQuery dataset location in the same region. Location proximity is a common best practice to optimize the performance of your cloud services.

Empty tables can be created without loading data. You may use this table creation flexibility for situations where data is coming in the future via a pipeline or automated data loading scenario. In these cases, you will want to specify a schema to minimize issues when data arrives. For most batch scenarios, the source file will define the schema and BigQuery will autodetect it for you. There may be some adjustments to the schema you will want to make to validate whether all column data types are accurate. As we previously highlighted, the most accurate data type for each table column will allow you to write better queries and use SQL functions in your queries. Refer back to *Chapter 3, Exploring Data in BigQuery* for recommendations on exploring schemas and best practices around data types.

We will also spend some time on SQL functions that rely on correct schema data types in *Chapter 5, Querying BigQuery Data*.

Once your dataset is created, you can use the BigQuery API or the BigQuery console to load your data into tables. The BigQuery API provides a variety of methods for loading data, including the `LOAD DATA` statement, the `LOAD DATA LOCAL` statement, and the `LOAD DATA FROM STORAGE` statement. The BigQuery console provides a graphical interface for loading data and to use the console, you must first create a load job. A load job specifies the source data, the destination table, and the loading options. This is the workflow that you see when you select the **CREATE TABLE** option in your dataset in the BigQuery SQL Explorer:

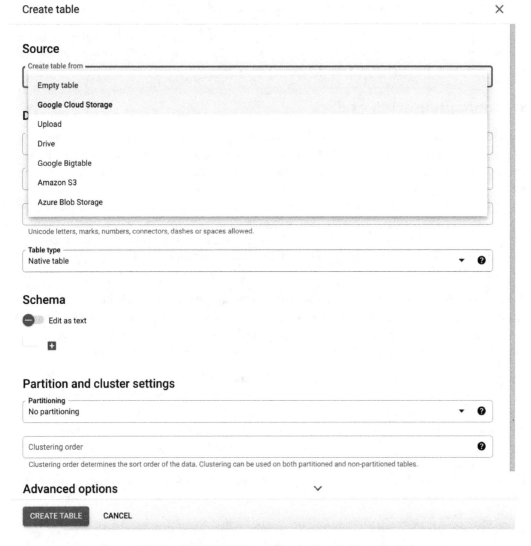

Figure 4.1 – The CREATE TABLE workflow in Google Cloud BigQuery

Creating a table within your dataset and using the source as a CSV upload or a CSV in Google Cloud Storage is the quickest way to get started loading data in BigQuery. At the end of this chapter, we will walk through an example that will show you how to do this.

There are several benefits to batch loading data into BigQuery:

- It is a simple and efficient way to load large amounts of data
- There is no charge for loading batch data
- It can be scheduled to run on a regular basis, which makes it ideal for loading data that is updated frequently
- It can be used to load data from a variety of sources, including both local and cloud-based sources

Batch loading is the approach you will likely begin with when getting started with BigQuery. In the next two sections, we will cover streaming ingestion and scheduled jobs in BigQuery to acclimate you with other options for loading data into tables.

Streaming ingestion of data

Streaming data, also known as unbounded data, to BigQuery allows you to ingest and analyze real-time data in a scalable and efficient manner. When it comes to streaming data in BigQuery, there are several options available that we will discuss in this section. You must know your data source characteristics before considering a streaming ingestion method. You may have devices that are collecting sensor data you wish to analyze. You may have application, service, or event data from systems running on Google Cloud or another cloud. These are two basic example scenarios where you will want to consider bringing a steaming data source into BigQuery. Some of these streaming options we will discuss also have capabilities for batch processing. This flexibility allows you to adopt a single ingestion method for various data sources.

One of the primary methods for streaming is to use the **Storage Write API**, which allows for real-time ingestion of data into BigQuery with exactly-once delivery guarantees. Records become available for query as they are written to the table. The Storage Write API combines the functionality of streaming and batch loading into a single API and is the recommended way to stream data into BigQuery.

Another option for streaming is to leverage **Cloud Dataflow**, a fully managed, highly capable service for stream and batch data processing. With Dataflow, you can design and deploy data pipelines that can ingest, transform, and load streaming data into BigQuery. Dataflow allows for control over your streaming data pipeline with session windowing and watermarks. Windowing divides unbounded or streaming data into windows for processing, and watermarks indicate when Dataflow expects all data to have arrived for that window. These features allow you to better control large amounts of incoming data and how they are delivered to BigQuery. Google provides open source Dataflow templates that make it easy to get started. More details are available at `https://cloud.google.com/dataflow/docs/guides/templates/provided-templates`.

The classic BigQuery streaming pipeline is PubSub -> Dataflow -> BigQuery. Integrating services such as Apache Kafka or Google Cloud PubSub into your application will set up intermediate message queues to stream data into BigQuery. These services enable the decoupling of data sources and provide scalable, reliable, and fault-tolerant data ingestion capabilities.

> **Streaming isn't always necessary**
>
> Oftentimes, data analysts will look at a business data scenario and determine that they must have the data streamed and delivered in real time. Many times, a regular scheduled batch job can be efficient and provide equivalent value. We often see real-time data opportunities and our eyes light up in excitement for the possibilities. While there may be reporting and analytic value, you will want to spend time understanding your business case and data consumers' needs before choosing a streaming architecture. Streaming data ingestion pipelines will require more management, maintenance, and monitoring. The cost and overhead may not be worth the value in your data warehouse.

The availability of multiple streaming options for data in BigQuery empowers you to choose the most suitable method based on your specific requirements and existing data infrastructure. Next up, we will discuss the scheduled loading of data and the **BigQuery Data Transfer Service** (**BQDTS**) and other scheduled loading services that give you an option between manual batch and streaming to schedule data ingestion into BigQuery.

Scheduled loading of data

There are various ways to schedule the loading of data in BigQuery. You may be familiar with the cron command-line utility on Unix operating systems. This is a simple service that schedules and orchestrates the execution of any command-line service. There are a few cron-like job schedulers that include service integrations you can take advantage of to schedule and automate loading jobs from sources. Start by knowing your data source. If there is a service that has existing integration, consider using it to simplify your data loads. In this section, we will discuss the BQDTS, **Cloud Composer**, and other approaches to schedule data loads.

The BQDTS is a managed service that simplifies the process of ingesting data from various sources into BigQuery. It enables you to schedule and automate the transfer of data from common data sources such as Google Marketing Platform, Google Ads, YouTube, and more, directly into BigQuery for analysis.

The BQDTS eliminates the need for manual data extraction, transformation, and loading (ETL) processes by providing pre-built connectors and configurations for different data sources. It ensures data is transferred securely and efficiently, maintaining data integrity throughout the process. You can set up scheduled transfers to regularly pull data from the data sources into BigQuery. This allows for the automatic and timely refresh of data for analysis.

By utilizing the BQDTS, organizations can streamline the process of bringing data from different sources into BigQuery, enabling faster and more efficient data analysis. It simplifies data integration tasks, reduces manual effort, and ensures the availability of up-to-date data for business insights and decision-making. The BQDTS can be accessed via the Google Cloud console, the bq command-line tool, and the BQDTS API.

Cloud Composer, a managed workflow orchestration service on Google Cloud, can also be used for scheduling data loading jobs in BigQuery. With Composer, you can create and manage workflows using **directed acyclic graphs (DAGs)**. By defining tasks within the DAGs that interact with BigQuery, you can orchestrate the data loading process. Composer allows you to set schedules or triggers for the DAGs, ensuring regular and timely execution of data loading jobs. Consider Cloud Composer if you have existing experience with Apache Airflow or plan to schedule other tasks in Google Cloud.

The best way to schedule the loading of data into BigQuery will depend on your specific needs and requirements. If you need to load data from a variety of sources, the BQDTS may be a good option. If you need more flexibility to plan other scheduled events in Google Cloud, Cloud Composer may be an option to consider. Before selecting an approach, start exploring integration capabilities and know your data source well.

Next up, we will review cases where you do not need to load data and you will instead use BigQuery functionality to integrate with other services to access data stored outside of BigQuery.

Situations where you do not need to load data

Loading shared, public, and external data sources and services into BigQuery storage is not necessary thanks to the powerful BigQuery analysis layer. In BigQuery, an external data source is a data source that you query from the BigQuery query engine, even though the data is not stored in BigQuery storage. There are several types of external data sources that do not require loading data, so let's go over them in this section.

With the concept of external tables, table metadata and schema information are stored in BigQuery but the data resides in an external location. You manage external tables the same way you would a regular BigQuery table, as they are contained within a dataset. You can query these tables and join them with other tables. External tables can take advantage of table access controls and row- or column-level security. Available data sources for external tables include Cloud Bigtable, Cloud Storage, and Google Drive.

Federated queries are when BigQuery sends a query to an external database and the results are returned as a temporary table. These queries are read-only and do not have access controls. Available data sources for federated queries include Cloud Spanner and Cloud SQL. See the following diagram for a visual example of external table and federated queries:

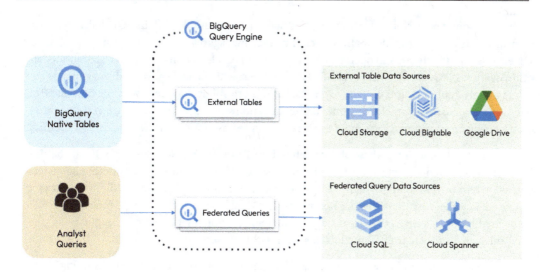

Figure 4.2 – BigQuery table and analysts interacting with external and federated data sources

Lastly, BigQuery Omni enables you to query and analyze data stored across multiple cloud platforms. With BigQuery Omni, you can leverage the power of BigQuery to seamlessly access and analyze data in different cloud environments, such as AWS and Azure, without the need for data movement or duplication. Remember in *Chapter 1, Introducing BigQuery and its Components*, in the section *Understanding how BigQuery works*, we mentioned that "*the power of this cloud-native service lies in the decoupled storage and compute*." BigQuery Omni follows that design principle by decoupling compute and storage so that compute can run on Google Cloud while data remains on the cloud where it is stored. This allows you to analyze data without having to move it, which presents opportunities for unifying environments and saving costs.

So far in this chapter, we have covered the various methods for loading data into BigQuery, including batch loading, streaming, scheduled loading, and external and federated tables, and some of the characteristics of each approach. Next up, we will discuss data transformation and preparing your data to be analyzed. Data transformation is important to understand because as a data analyst, you have options to transform data during data load, in a pipeline into your cloud data warehouse, or once it has landed in BigQuery. In the next two sections, we will explore these concepts in detail.

Data transformation with BigQuery

Data transformation is a critical step in the data analytics process, where raw data is processed, cleaned, and restructured to better derive insights and support decision-making. This section explores the various features and techniques available in BigQuery for transforming data, enabling you to shape and prepare data for analysis.

BigQuery supports powerful SQL capabilities for data transformation. With its SQL dialect, you can perform a wide range of transformations including filtering, aggregating, joining, and sorting data. SQL expressions, functions, and operators allow for complex calculations and manipulations of data within queries. BigQuery also supports window functions, which enable advanced analytics such as running totals, rankings, and moving averages. Read more about BigQuery window functions, or analytic functions, in the official documentation on window function calls at `https://cloud.google.com/bigquery/docs/reference/standard-sql/window-function-calls`.

BigQuery allows the creation and use of **user-defined functions** (**UDFs**) to extend its SQL capabilities. UDFs enable you to define custom functions in JavaScript, SQL, or other programming languages such as Python or Java to apply them to transform data within queries. This flexibility allows for complex data transformations that are not directly achievable with standard SQL functions. UDFs can be used for tasks such as data cleansing, string manipulation, mathematical computations, and more, enhancing the data transformation capabilities of BigQuery.

Stored procedures are another way to automate data loading and transformation tasks in BigQuery using SQL. They are similar to functions but can also contain multiple statements, which makes them ideal for tasks that require a series of steps to be performed. Stored procedures allow you to build and save data loading and transformation logic and provide a reusable approach to data transformation. You should consider using stored procedures if you need to call a function within your queries or automated queries on a regular basis. BigQuery also features remote functions that let you use GoogleSQL functionality with code and integrations with serverless development tools such as Cloud Run and Cloud Functions. This allows you to build and deploy functions and call them in your queries. Imagine the possibilities here with me for a moment. One example could be calling the DLP API (`https://cloud.google.com/dlp/docs/reference/rest`) to remove **personally identifiable information** (**PII**) data from tables and write the sanitized, non-PII data to another table for data consumers. Another example may be to call the Cloud Translation API to translate support case data in a BigQuery table from one language to another for processing.

BigQuery's **data manipulation language** (**DML**) capabilities enable you to perform data transformations using SQL statements beyond traditional query operations. DML operations such as `INSERT`, `UPDATE`, `DELETE`, and `MERGE` can be utilized to modify and transform data within BigQuery tables. This provides the ability to perform in-place transformations and updates on the data, making it suitable for tasks such as data cleansing, data enrichment, and data quality improvements.

One common use for DML is to clean up data. For example, you can use DML to remove duplicate rows or rows that contain incorrect data. To remove duplicate rows with DML, you can use the following DML statement:

```
DELETE FROM table WHERE id IN (
    SELECT id FROM table GROUP BY id HAVING COUNT(*) > 1);
```

This statement will delete all rows in the table where the `id` column has more than one value.

To remove rows that contain incorrect data, you can use a WHERE clause to filter out the rows that you want to remove. For example, the following DML statement will delete all rows where the age column contains a value that is less than 18:

```
DELETE FROM table WHERE age < 18;
```

Another common use for DML is to integrate data from different sources. For example, you can use DML to join two tables together. To join two tables together, you can use the following DML statement:

```
SELECT * FROM table1 INNER JOIN table2
ON table1.id = table2.id;
```

At times with streaming data or multiple data sources, you may want to perform regular transformations. Using scheduled queries with DML in BigQuery provides a powerful way to automate data transformations on a regular basis. Scheduled queries allow you to define DML statements such as INSERT, UPDATE, and DELETE and schedule them to run at specific intervals. This enables you to perform data transformations without the need for manual intervention or external tools. If you want to periodically insert new data, update existing records, or delete obsolete information, scheduled queries and DML in BigQuery provide a convenient approach to automate and maintain data transformations over time. By leveraging the scheduling capabilities, you can ensure that your data is always up to date and reflects the desired transformations without the need for manual work.

As previously mentioned in the *Streaming ingestion of data* section, BigQuery seamlessly integrates with Cloud Dataflow, a fully managed stream and batch processing service. Dataflow allows you to design and deploy complex data pipelines for data transformation before loading it into BigQuery. In addition to its integration capabilities with BigQuery and other services, Dataflow offers powerful transformation capabilities, including data cleansing, normalization, enrichment, and complex data manipulations using its programming model based on Apache Beam. Dataflow is a common service used by large enterprises for their data processing pipelines in BigQuery. By leveraging Dataflow with BigQuery, you can handle large-scale data transformations efficiently, enabling real-time and near-real-time analytics workflows.

We will discuss more strategies for data transformation in *Chapter 9, Cleansing and Transforming Data*. The transformation strategies we will present in this upcoming chapter will be centered around cleaning table data.

As you can see, data transformation is a crucial step in your data analytics practice. BigQuery offers a range of powerful features and techniques to facilitate efficient data transformation. With SQL transformations, UDFs, DML operations, Dataflow integration, and scheduled queries, BigQuery empowers you to shape and prepare data for analysis. By leveraging these capabilities, organizations can improve data quality and drive informed decision-making from their data stored in BigQuery.

We will now pivot to the next natural step, the end-to-end processes for going from data source to destination. It is important to understand the value behind ETL and ELT before you adopt any of the previously mentioned approaches to save you time and make your data analysis efforts more efficient.

Evaluating ETL and ELT approaches for data integration

ETL and ELT are two main approaches to integrating, loading, and preparing data in BigQuery. When building a data analytics practice, to provide ongoing data value, you will want to decide on one of these approaches.

In ETL, data is extracted from a data source, transformed, and then loaded into a data warehouse or other target system. The transformation step is often complex and time-consuming, as it involves cleaning, validating, and standardizing the data. There are SaaS tools that automate and manage ETL pipelines, and there are many options today to create your own ETL pipelines by joining multiple services before the data arrives in BigQuery.

The other primary data integration approach is ELT. ELT is when data is extracted from a data source and loaded directly into a target system. Any transformation steps are then performed in the target system. This approach is often faster than ETL as the transformations can be performed in parallel with the loading step. The data is loaded as-is from the source system to BigQuery and then transformed using SQL, or with other approaches we previously discussed within BigQuery. See the following diagram for a visual representation of ETL and ELT to better understand the difference in each approach:

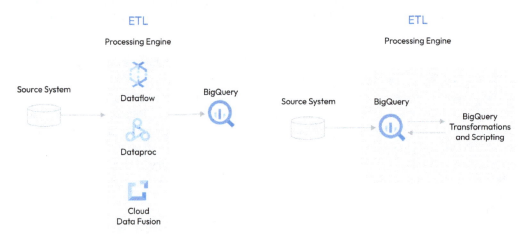

Figure 4.3 – The ETL and ELT processes

Many organizations are shifting to ELT processes in BigQuery due to the growing capabilities and ease of transformation with SQL and the options for creating secondary tables and views, with ease. In ELT, data is loaded into raw and staging tables before transformation and publishing into reporting "production" type accessible tables. The choice of whether to use ETL or ELT depends on a number of factors, including the size and complexity of the data, the performance requirements, and the budget.

For smaller teams and organizations starting their data warehousing practice in BigQuery, ELT will be the preferred, simpler approach. This way, you just write SQL queries, transform data, and move data around between tables. With ELT, you do not have to worry about managing a separate transformation service and can avoid the complexities of an ETL pipeline.

The best approach for you will depend on your specific needs. If you have a large dataset and need to process it quickly, ELT may be a good option. If you need to perform complex data transformations or comply with strict data security regulations, ETL may be a better choice. If your team has existing Apache Beam pipelines (Dataflow) and may be integrating multiple data sources, you will want to explore ETL. These approaches can be used in parallel and organizations typically will blend approaches, grounding their decisions on the level of effort for data engineering teams and the data value to end users.

The concepts we discussed in the previous sections of this chapter will come to life in the next section, where there will be an opportunity for hands-on loading and transforming data in BigQuery. Follow along to add a hands-on experience dimension to your knowledge quest on understanding the loading and transforming capabilities of BigQuery.

Hands-on exercise – data loading and transformation in BigQuery

To assist with your learning of the concepts in this chapter, we will take you through a hands-on example, including loading data from a local file and preparing some basic transformations on the table data. This hands-on exercise will prepare you for loading your own data in the future and give you experience of doing some basic processing of that data. We will follow a scenario that utilizes a traffic collision dataset. This example and the scenario will build in the future chapters. Follow along by reading the scenario and following it step by step in your Google Cloud console. It may be useful to do a little role-playing here, as follows!

Understanding the scenario

Consider yourself as the Head of Data Analytics for the company described in this scenario. Your company is building a service to reduce users' cellphone usage while driving. The company's data team is just beginning to bring in datasets to help the marketing and product departments better promote the service and refine the product development. As a first attempt to identify data sources that may provide useful insights, the data team decides to start with collision data from Los Angeles. It will attempt to find patterns around certain driver demographics. This will attempt to validate some of the marketing team's plans such as focusing on younger drivers, and some of the engineering team's features that are being developed.

This example can take anywhere from 10-30 minutes, depending on your experience.

Loading data from a local file

For this example, we will use the Cloud Shell terminal and the bq command-line tool to load data.

We will be using the Los Angeles Traffic Collision Data (`https://data.lacity.org/Public-Safety/Traffic-Collision-Data-from-2010-to-Present/d5tf-ez2w`) provided by the Los Angeles Open Data catalog (`https://data.lacity.org/`). Let's load this data into BigQuery to see whether this dataset has any useful insights for our scenario. The raw data is available at the preceding link. For convenience, we also have it available at ch4/`archive.zip` in the GitHub repository for this book: `https://github.com/PacktPublishing/Data-Exploration-and-Preparation-with-BigQuery/tree/main/ch4`. The bq command-line tool provides a terminal approach to interact with BigQuery and your Google Cloud resources. Everything you do with the bq tool, you can also do with the REST API or in the Cloud console:

1. Open Cloud Shell in your browser by visiting `https://console.cloud.google.com/cloudshell`.

2. Authorize Cloud Shell and make sure you are in the correct project. Also, select the default region zone for your resources:

    ```
    gcloud init
    ```

3. After your project has been selected, clone the GitHub repository for this book:

    ```
    git clone https://github.com/PacktPublishing/Data-Exploration-
    and-Preparation-with-BigQuery
    ```

4. Navigate to the folder containing the traffic collision dataset:

    ```
    cd Data-Exploration-and-Preparation-with-BigQuery/ch4/
    ```

5. Unzip the `archive.zip` file:

    ```
    unzip archive.zip
    ```

6. Preview the data in the file that was just extracted. Use the spacebar to preview the data and use Q to quit:

    ```
    zless traffic-collision-data-from-2010-to-present.csv
    ```

7. Now, create a dataset and table for our data:

    ```
    bq mk collisions
    bq mk -table collisions.data
    ```

8. Load data into the table:

    ```
    bq load --source_format=CSV --autodetect collisions.data
    traffic-collision-data-from-2010-to-present.csv
    ```

9. Examine the schema and table metadata:

```
bq show collisions.data
```

We have now successfully loaded a local dataset into BigQuery in just a few steps. Next up, we will perform some light transformations to prepare our data in different ways.

Preparing and transforming data

There are several ways to prepare and transform data in BigQuery. You can use Cloud Dataprep, which provides a graphical interface for cleaning and transforming data. We will discuss Cloud Dataprep in *Chapter 9, Cleansing and Transforming Data*. You can use SQL to perform data transformations, or you can use a third-party tool to prepare and transform it before loading it into BigQuery. In this example, we will use SQL to perform data transformations. This follows the previously mentioned ELT approach.

We will now move from the bq command-line tool to using the BigQuery SQL Explorer, the query editor on the Cloud console BigQuery page.

Example 1

For the first example of preparing and transforming data, we will use a SQL query to write results to a new table. The table we loaded previously may contain many columns that we do not need. In this case, it is possible to create a smaller, more specific table from the original table using the CREATE TABLE statement. The following example uses the CREATE TABLE statement to create the demographic_1 table from the collisions.data table that we loaded previously:

1. Open the BigQuery page in the Google Cloud console by visiting https://console. cloud.google.com/bigquery.

2. If you are unable to find the newly created dataset and table, enter collisions in the search box.

3. In the SQL workspace query editor, enter the following query:

```
CREATE TABLE collisions.demographic_1 AS (
    SELECT date_reported, date_occurred,
        time_occurred,     area_name, crime_code,
        crime_code_description,     victim_age,
        victim_sex, victim_descent, premise_code,
        premise_description, address, cross_street,
        location,    zip_codes
    FROM `<your project name>.collisions.data`
    WHERE Victim_Age > 16
    AND Victim_Age <= 18
);
```

Make sure to replace <your project name> with your actual project name. If you are not sure of your project name, you can find this in the **Cloud Overview** dashboard in the Cloud console.

As a result, you should see a message that says **This statement created a new table named demographic_1**.

This query has created a new table in our collisions dataset for individuals between the ages of 16 and 18 in a new table called demographic_1. This new table has 3,091 rows where the original table had 502,858 rows, so our dataset has been reduced significantly. By preparing smaller tables, it can be easier to keep data secure and control who has access to each table. This is important to understand as a data analyst as you will often need to prepare data for different teams and individuals.

Example 2

In the second example, we will transform the data by calculating the total number of collisions for both victim_age and area_name columns.

In the SQL workspace query editor, enter the following query:

```
SELECT victim_age, area_name, COUNT(*) as total_accidents FROM ` <your
project name>.collisions.data`
WHERE victim_age is not NULL
GROUP BY victim_age, area_name
ORDER BY victim_age asc
```

Here, we are filtering out columns with a null value in victim_age and creating a new column for the total number of accidents per victim_age and area_name. This query allows us to view the total amount of collisions per age and area name, another way to potentially transform the original dataset to provide specific answers in the data.

In this section, we have presented an example of loading and transforming data on a transportation dataset containing collision data. We have loaded data from a GitHub repository and performed some preprocessing and data transformation, creating a smaller specific table and creating a query that uses the COUNT() aggregation function and the GROUP BY clause to organize data.

This example shows a few ways to transform a large dataset after loading the dataset into BigQuery. In the presented scenario in the beginning of this section, we wanted to analyze a collision dataset to better understand patterns in data sources for a service that our company is building to reduce users' cellphone usage while driving. With just a few lines of SQL, we have managed to begin unlocking insights and answering questions that may help better inform the teams working on a product. We can now provide some statistics and basic reporting to teams by loading and transforming data in BigQuery.

Summary

This chapter has provided a comprehensive overview of loading and transforming data in BigQuery, demonstrating the power and flexibility of this powerful data warehouse and analytics solution. We have explored various methods for ingesting data into BigQuery, including batch loading, streaming, and the use of data transfer services. Additionally, we have delved into the data transformation capabilities of BigQuery, highlighting its SQL-based querying language and advanced functions for data manipulation and enhancement. This chapter provided perspectives on using ETL approaches as well as ELT. Finally, the hands-on example helped wrap knowledge on these concepts and provided you an opportunity to experience loading and transforming data in BigQuery on your own.

In conclusion, BigQuery offers a comprehensive set of tools and features for loading and transforming data at scale. Whether it's handling massive volumes of data, conducting real-time analysis, or executing complex data transformations, BigQuery provides a flexible and powerful environment that empowers organizations to unlock the full potential of their data assets. As a data analyst, you have the responsibility of choosing the right tool and approach for the job, determining how you can gain the greatest return from your time and investment in cloud-based data services.

In the next chapter, we will go further into queries, covering the approaches, best practices, and tools associated with writing powerful SQL queries in BigQuery. You will gain a strong understanding of the value of using the BigQuery analysis engine to query your data and learn about some of the unique query features available.

5

Querying BigQuery Data

In data analytics and business intelligence, the ability to query large amounts of data quickly and effectively is a fundamental skill. In this chapter, we will begin a journey into the world of querying BigQuery data. We will explore best practices and advanced features that enable you to extract meaningful information from datasets efficiently. If you are a data analyst, data scientist, or business leader seeking to leverage data for strategic decision-making, understanding how to query BigQuery data is a critical skill to possess.

This chapter will begin by familiarizing you with the structure of a BigQuery query. This will give you a strong foundation in crafting queries and the basics. Continuing, we will layer on features and cover more complex querying practices, such as aggregations, joins, and functions, and conclude with saving, optimizing, and troubleshooting queries.

By the end of this chapter, you will possess the understanding and skills necessary to query BigQuery data effectively. Whether you are working with small or massive datasets, you will be equipped to build queries that derive valuable insights, enabling you to drive data-based decision-making in your organization.

In this chapter, we are going to cover the following main topics:

- Understanding query structure
- Understanding data types
- Using expressions and aggregations
- Joining tables
- Using functions
- Advanced querying techniques
- Saving, sharing, and scheduling queries
- Optimizing queries
- Troubleshooting queries

Technical requirements

As mentioned in earlier chapters, to get the most out of this chapter, you will want to have access to the Google Cloud console (`https://console.cloud.google.com/`) to explore and build resources in BigQuery. You can also begin exploring this book's GitHub repository (`https://github.com/PacktPublishing/Data-Exploration-and-Preparation-with-BigQuery`) so that you can browse and download diagrams and code snippets.

In this chapter, we will revisit the Google Trends dataset we explored in *Chapter 2*. If you have not already, you will want to view and add the Google Trends dataset to your Google Cloud project. Visit the Google Trends dataset at `https://console.cloud.google.com/marketplace/product/bigquery-public-datasets/google-search-trends` and click **View Dataset**; this will bring the dataset into your SQL workspace in BigQuery. You may mark the dataset as a favorite to find it easier. You can expand the dataset, click a table, and click **Preview** in the middle pane, at which point you have just begun exploring a dataset in BigQuery. We will continue this exploration in this chapter to better understand how to query BigQuery data.

Understanding query structure

A BigQuery query is an SQL statement that is used to select, filter, and transform data stored in BigQuery tables. To effectively query data in BigQuery, it is essential to understand the structure of a query and the purpose of each element. A BigQuery query follows a specific syntax and consists of various clauses that work together to retrieve the desired information from your datasets. Let's break down the sections of a SQL query in BigQuery in detail.

Action command – the SELECT clause

The commands that are used in the `SELECT` area of your query tell the analysis engine what needs to be done. `SELECT` extracts data from a table.

The `SELECT` clause chooses the columns you want to retrieve in the result. It determines what data you want from a table and defines calculations or transformations. You can specify columns to be returned by name or use the wildcard operator (`*`) to select all columns (note that it is not advised to use this wildcard when you're determining columns to be retrieved due to costs; this will be described later in this chapter). You can also add `DISTINCT` after `SELECT` to return unique values.

Here's an example:

```
SELECT col1, col2, DISTINCT(col3) AS unique_filtered
FROM `project_id.dataset.table`
GROUP BY unique_filtered
```

Location command – the FROM clause

The location command specifies which dataset tables contain the columns we want to show in our results.

The FROM clause specifies the table or tables you want to retrieve data from. In BigQuery, you need to provide the dataset and table names in the `project.dataset.table` format. The project. dataset.table is encapsulated in backtick characters (`). This clause allows you to query a single table, multiple tables via a wildcard table (https://cloud.google.com/bigquery/docs/querying-wildcard-tables), or combine data from different tables with a JOIN clause using a common field.

Here's an example:

```
SELECT *
FROM `project_id.dataset.table1` as table1
JOIN `project_id.dataset.table2` as table2
  ON table1.id = table2.id
```

Filtering command – the WHERE clause

Next in our query structure are commands that tell the BigQuery analysis engine what data to filter for in our tables via SQL. Filtering is optional yet allows you to be more granular with specificity in your query results.

The WHERE clause is optional and used for filtering. WHERE can be followed by a comparator operator such as =, >, and < or BETWEEN, IN, and LIKE. You can specify multiple conditions using operators such as AND, OR, and NOT. This helps you narrow down the dataset and retrieve only the rows that meet your criteria. You can learn more about operators in the BigQuery documentation: https://cloud.google.com/bigquery/docs/reference/standard-sql/operators.

Here's an example:

```
SELECT *
FROM `project_id.dataset.table`
WHERE category = 'Electronics'
  AND price > 1000;
```

Selection handling commands – the GROUP BY, HAVING, ORDER BY, and LIMIT clauses

Once we have the fields we want to return from our data, we can specify how we want them to be handled.

The **GROUP BY** clause is used to group rows based on common values. It needs to be used by aggregate functions such as COUNT, SUM, and AVG. GROUP BY enables you to perform calculations and analysis on subsets of data. When using GROUP BY, you must group the results by one or more columns in the SELECT clause. We will cover expressions and aggregations later in this chapter. Here's an example:

```
SELECT category, SUM(quantity) AS total_quantity
FROM `project_id.dataset.table`
GROUP BY category
```

The **HAVING** clause is used with the GROUP BY clause to filter the grouped rows based on a condition. It is similar to the WHERE clause, which filters data on specific rows and provides another level of filtering results. You can use HAVING and WHERE together; the WHERE clause would filter the individual rows, group those rows, and perform aggregation calculations, after which the HAVING clause would filter the groups. Here's an example:

```
SELECT category, SUM(quantity) AS total_quantity
FROM `project_id.dataset.table`
GROUP BY category
HAVING total_quantity > 1000
```

The **ORDER BY** clause is used to sort results in a specific way based on specific columns. You can sort by listing rows with columns with no data first (NULLS FIRST) or last (NULLS LAST) or in ascending (ASC) or descending (DESC) order. If you do not specify the ORDER BY clause, sorting is done in ascending order. You can specify multiple columns for sorting and can also use different sorting orders for each column. Here's an example:

```
SELECT *
FROM `project_id.dataset.table`
ORDER BY column1 ASC, column2 DESC, column3 NULLS LAST
```

The **LIMIT** clause restricts the number of rows returned by the query. It should be used when you only need a subset of the results. *Note that this clause only affects data displayed, not data queried.* So, do not use LIMIT as a strategy to reduce the amount of processing in a large query. LIMIT can be useful when dealing with large datasets. The LIMIT clause is often used in combination with sorting to retrieve the top or bottom (head or tail) rows in a query. Here's an example:

```
SELECT *
FROM `project_id.dataset.table`
LIMIT 10
```

> **Note**
> If your goal is to explore the very first or last rows of a table, remember that you can use the **Preview** tab in the BigQuery web console.

As you can see, understanding the structure of a BigQuery query is critical for crafting accurate and efficient queries. These are the basic building blocks of your BigQuery queries. Combining these clauses enables you to create complex queries that can be used to analyze your data. By mastering the query structure, you will be equipped to extract meaningful information from your BigQuery datasets. For additional information, check out the BigQuery documentation reference on *Query Syntax* at `https://cloud.google.com/bigquery/docs/reference/standard-sql/query-syntax`.

In this section, we looked at query structure and explained and provided examples for each clause in a query. While a basic concept in SQL and data analysis, it has been included here as a building block for understanding how to best leverage BigQuery. Next, we'll dive into data types and how to best leverage data types in schemas and tables, thereby enabling query best practices.

Understanding data types

When querying data in BigQuery, it is essential to have a solid understanding of the various data types and their characteristics. Data types determine how values are stored, interpreted, and processed in BigQuery. By correctly identifying and handling data types, you can ensure accurate and efficient querying. Let's explore some key considerations when working with data types in BigQuery.

BigQuery supports a wide range of data types, including integers, floats, strings, Booleans, dates, times, and more. It is more important to use the appropriate data type for each column in your tables to ensure compatibility with the data being stored. We covered the importance of setting the right data types in a table's setup and schema in *Chapter 3, Exploring Data in BigQuery.*. When querying data, ensure the data types of the columns being compared or joined are comparable. Incompatible data types may result in unexpected behavior or errors with the query. You may need to perform data type conversions such as CAST when you are joining two columns with different datatypes.

> **Using CAST when joining two tables**
>
> When the columns you want to join have different data types, you may encounter an error during the JOIN operation. To resolve this, you can use the CAST function to convert one or both columns into a compatible data type. Using the CAST function can make joins easier and data more readable. The CAST function uses the `cast(column_name AS new_data_type)` format.

For example, you can use the CAST function to perform a join between the `products` and `inventory` tables:

```
SELECT *
FROM products
JOIN inventory
ON products.product_id = CAST(inventory.product_code AS INT64)
```

In this example, we are joining the `products` table with the `inventory` table on the `product_id` and `product_code` columns. Since `product_id` is stored as an integer and `product_code` is stored as a string in the inventory table, we can use the `CAST` function to convert `product_code` into an integer for the join condition.

Numeric data types such as `INT64`, `FLOAT64`, and `NUMERIC` have different precision and scale characteristics:

- `INT64` represents whole numbers without decimal places.

- `FLOAT64` represents floating-point numbers with decimal points.

- `NUMERIC` or `DECIMAL` is a decimal data type with arbitrary precision and scale. It is suitable for calculations that require exact decimal accuracy, such as financial calculations.

You will want to make sure you have columns set with the right numeric data type to ensure accuracy with reporting.

In BigQuery, **strings** are represented using the `STRING` data type, which stores variable-length character sequences. Strings can be encoded using different character sets, such as UTF-8. BigQuery supports case-sensitive and case-insensitive string comparisons based on collation. By default, string comparisons are case-insensitive.

BigQuery provides various data types to handle date and time values, such as `DATE`, `DATETIME`, and `TIME`. When querying date and time data, be sure that you are using the appropriate data type for your requirements – for example, use `DATE` when working with dates only, `DATETIME` when both date and time are needed, and `TIME` when dealing with time values independent of any specific date. Be mindful of time zone considerations when working with date and time data. BigQuery stores timestamps in UTC by default, but you can adjust the time zone for queries using the appropriate data type, such as `TIMESTAMP` and `TIMEZONE`.

BigQuery also supports complex data types such as **arrays** and **structs**, allowing you to store and query nested or repeated values within a single field. An array is an ordered list containing zero or more values of the same data type. When working with arrays, be aware of the indexing and querying syntax to access specific array elements or perform operations on an array as a whole. Structs enable the creation of nested and hierarchical structures within a table. Here are some examples of structs and array applications in tables:

- **Nested data**: When data has a hierarchical relationship, such as employee records with nested department information, you can use structs to represent these relationships.

- **Event data**: In event-driven data such as user activity logs, you can use arrays to store a series of events over time, such as page views, clicks, or actions. This makes it easier to analyze user behavior and perform time series analysis.

- **Time series data**: Arrays are useful for storing historical records, sensor readings, or financial data, where each element in the array corresponds to a specific time point.

- **Log data**: When storing logs, structs and arrays help organize the various attributes associated with each log entry. In a server log, a struct may contain details such as IP address, timestamp, and request type. An array can hold additional information such as error codes or response time.

To access `struct` fields, you must use dot notation. For example, if you have a struct named `employee` with `name` and `email` fields, you can query them like this:

```
SELECT employee.name, employee.email
FROM table
```

To access elements within an array, you must use the `OFFSET` keyword. For example, if you have an array named `users`, you can query the second item like this:

```
SELECT users[OFFSET(1)]
FROM table
```

Understanding data types is important for performing accurate queries and ensuring that data is interpreted correctly during analysis. By choosing the appropriate data type, considering precision requirements, and handling data conversions when necessary, you can avoid data inconsistencies and achieve reliable results when querying BigQuery data. The next important area to understand when querying BigQuery is how to use expressions and aggregations to make your query results highly useful.

Using expressions and aggregations

In BigQuery, expressions and aggregations play a crucial role in performing calculations and summarizing data during querying. They allow you to transform and manipulate data to derive meaningful insights from your datasets. Let's explore how expressions and aggregations are used in BigQuery.

Expressions

In BigQuery, **expressions** are used to perform calculations, create derived columns, and apply transformations to table data. You can use various operators, functions, and literals within expressions to manipulate values. Let's look at some key aspects of using expressions in BigQuery.

BigQuery supports a wide range of operators, including arithmetic operators (+, -, *, /), comparison operators (=, <, >), logical operators (AND, OR, NOT), and string concatenation operators (| |). These operators allow you to perform mathematical operations, compare values, and combine conditions.

BigQuery provides an extension library of built-in functions to manipulate data. These functions allow you to perform string manipulations, mathematical calculations, date and time operations, type conversion, and more. You can also create custom functions using SQL **user-defined functions (UDFs)** to meet specific requirements.

Conditional expressions such as IF, CASE, and COALESCE allow you to control the flow of the query and apply different logic based on specific conditions. They help in implementing conditional transformations or handling NULL values effectively.

Aggregations

In BigQuery, **aggregations** are used to summarize and aggregate data across rows or groups of rows. They allow you to calculate metrics, perform statistical analysis, and generate summary reports. BigQuery provides a wide range of built-in aggregation functions such as SUM, COUNT, AVG, MAX, MIN, and more. These functions allow you to perform calculations on groups of rows and generate summary statistics. Here's an example:

```
SELECT AVG(age)
from customers
```

The following query uses an aggregation to find the maximum order amount for each customer:

```
SELECT customer_id, MAX(order_amount)
FROM orders
GROUP BY customer_id
```

Expressions can help manipulate and transform individual values, while aggregations allow you to summarize and analyze data across multiple rows or groups. Understanding and utilizing these capabilities allows you to derive valuable information from your BigQuery datasets. Now, let's go over the JOIN operation in BigQuery, which allows you to combine data from multiple tables or views.

Joining tables

BigQuery supports a variety of join types that can be used to combine data from two or more tables. The most common join types are inner joins, outer joins, and self joins.

Inner joins

An inner join returns rows that match the JOIN condition from both tables. It only returns the rows where the joining condition is met on both tables. The JOIN condition is a Boolean expression that compares values in the two tables. For example, the following query joins the customers table and the orders table on the customer_id column:

```
SELECT customer_id, name, order_id, order_date
FROM customers
INNER JOIN orders
ON customers.customer_id = orders.customer_id
```

This query will return all rows from the customers table that have a matching row in the orders table. Inner joins are useful when you want to focus on the intersection of data between tables.

Outer joins

An outer join returns all rows from the left table, even if there is no matching row in the right table. The rows from the right table that do not match any rows on the left table are returned with null values for the columns from the left table. There are two types of outer joins – left outer joins and right outer joins.

A *left outer join* returns all rows from the left table and the matching rows from the right table. The rows from the right table that do not match any rows in the left table are returned with null values for the columns from the left table. For example, the following query joins the customers table and the orders table on the customer_id column and returns all rows from the customers table even if there is no matching row on the orders table:

```
SELECT customer_id, name, order_id, order_date
FROM customers
LEFT OUTER JOIN orders
ON customers.customer_id = orders.customer_id
```

Left joins are commonly used when you want to include all rows from the left table, regardless of matches on the right table.

A *right outer join* returns all rows from the right table, and matching rows from the left table. The rows from the left table that do not match any rows in the right table are returned with null values for the columns from the right table. For example, the following query joins the customers table and the orders table on the customer_id column and returns all rows from the orders table, even though there is no matching row in the customers table:

```
SELECT customer_id, name, order_id, order_date
FROM orders
RIGHT OUTER JOIN customers
ON customers.customer_id = orders.customer_id
```

Right joins are useful when you want to include all rows from the right table, regardless of matches in the left table.

A *full outer join*, or *full join*, returns all rows from both tables, regardless of whether there is a match between the tables. For rows where there is no match, null values are returned for the columns from the other side. For example, the following query performs a full outer join on the customers and orders tables using the customer_id column:

```
SELECT customer_id, name, order_id, order_date
FROM customers
FULL OUTER JOIN orders
ON customers.customer_id = orders.customer_id
```

Full outer joins are beneficial when you want to include all rows from both tables, regardless of matches.

When joining tables in BigQuery, it is important to ensure that the columns that are used for joining have the same data type and format. By leveraging join capabilities in BigQuery, you can combine and analyze data from multiple tables, gain deeper insights, and unlock the full potential of your data for reporting, business intelligence, and data-driven decision-making.

Using functions

When working with BigQuery, one of the most powerful features is your ability to leverage various functions to manipulate and analyze your data. Functions allow you to perform calculations, transformations, aggregations, and more with your SQL queries. This section explores the different types of functions available and shows how they can be used to enhance your data querying capabilities.

BigQuery supports a variety of functions that can be used to manipulate and analyze data. These functions can be used to perform a variety of tasks:

- Data transformation functions can be used to transform data from one format into another. For example, you could use a function to convert a CSV file into a JSON file.

- Machine learning functions can be used to train and deploy machine learning models. For example, you could use a function to train a model to predict customer churn.

- Functions can be used to perform analytics on large datasets. For example, you could use a function to calculate the average order value for a customer segment.

BigQuery provides a wide range of built-in functions that are available for performing common operations. These functions include mathematical calculations (SUM, AVG, MAX, MIN), string manipulations (CONCAT, SUBSTR, LENGTH), date and time operations (DATE, TIMESTAMP, EXTRACT), and more. By using these functions in your queries, you can efficiently manipulate and transform your data.

When you need to summarize or aggregate data, BigQuery's aggregate functions come in handy. These functions allow you to calculate metrics across groups of rows, such as computing the total count, average, sum, or maximum values within a set of records. By using aggregate functions in combination with the GROUP BY clause, you can generate insightful summaries regarding your data.

This section went over just a few of the many functions that are available in BigQuery. For a complete list of functions, please refer to the BigQuery documentation at https://cloud.google.com/bigquery/docs/reference/standard-sql/functions-and-operators. By using functions in your BigQuery queries, you can perform complex calculations and manipulate data in a variety of ways. This can help you get more insights from your data and make better decisions.

Advanced querying techniques

BigQuery offers various advanced querying techniques that allow users to perform complex analyses and extract valuable insights from their datasets. These techniques leverage advanced SQL functionalities and BigQuery-specific features to handle challenging querying scenarios.

Subqueries

Subqueries allow you to nest one query inside another, enabling you to break down complex problems into smaller more manageable parts. You can use subqueries in various ways, such as performing calculations based on the results of a subquery, filtering data, or creating temporary tables for further analysis. In the following example, which was performed on the Google Trends dataset, an aggregate subquery calculates the average rank of a search term in the `top_terms` table in the `Charlotte NC` **designated market area** (**DMA**):

```
SELECT DISTINCT(term), rank, refresh_date,
   (SELECT AVG(rank) FROM `bigquery-public-data.google_trends.top_
terms` WHERE refresh_date = "2023-06-10"
AND dma_name = "Charlotte NC") AS avg_rank
FROM `bigquery-public-data.google_trends.top_terms`
WHERE refresh_date = "2023-06-10"
```

> **Note**
>
> The Google Trends dataset's `top_terms` table only keeps a few weeks of data. Before running this query, replace the `06` month in `refresh_date` with the current month.

We get the following results:

Query results

⬇ SAVE RESULTS ▾   📊 EXPLORE DATA ▾   ↕

< | JOB INFORMATION | RESULTS | JSON | EXECUTION DETAILS | EXECUTION GRAPH | >

Row	term ▾	rank ▾	refresh_date ▾	avg_rank ▾
1	NBA	1	2023-06-10	12.99999999999...
2	Champions League	2	2023-06-10	12.99999999999...
3	Mike Batayeh	3	2023-06-10	12.99999999999...
4	Walt Nauta	4	2023-06-10	12.99999999999...
5	Novak Djokovic	5	2023-06-10	12.99999999999...
6	Kelis Bill Murray	6	2023-06-10	12.99999999999...
7	Niall Horan	7	2023-06-10	12.99999999999...
8	Lexus	8	2023-06-10	12.99999999999...
9	Johnny Depp	9	2023-06-10	12.99999999999...
10	Egypt shark attack	10	2023-06-10	12.99999999999...
11	Boris Johnson	11	2023-06-10	12.99999999999...
12	Taurine	12	2023-06-10	12.99999999999...

Figure 5.1 – Results from a subquery that finds the average rank across top terms

Window functions

Window functions provide a powerful way to perform calculations over a specific subset or window of rows within a query result set. They allow you to calculate running totals, rankings, and moving averages, and perform other analytics operations. Window functions operate on a partition of rows and can be combined with ORDER BY to specify the order of rows within the partition.

Common table expressions

A **common table expression** (CTE) is a temporary table that can be used in a query. If you need to reference a subquery multiple times in your main query or have to reference a value multiple times, you can use the WITH clause to define it as a CTE. For example, the following query on the Google Trends dataset's top_terms table finds the terms with the highest peak search interest each year:

```
WITH yearly_peaks AS (
  SELECT
    term,
    EXTRACT(YEAR FROM week) AS year,
    rank,
    ROW_NUMBER() OVER (PARTITION BY EXTRACT(YEAR FROM    week) ORDER
BY rank DESC) AS peak_rank
  FROM `bigquery-public-data.google_trends.top_terms`
)
SELECT term, year, rank
FROM yearly_peaks
WHERE peak_rank = 1
ORDER BY year
```

We get the following results:

Query results

⬇ SAVE RESULTS ▼   📊 EXPLORE DATA ▼   ↕

| < | JOB INFORMATION | RESULTS | JSON | EXECUTION DETAILS | EXECUTION | > |

Row	term ▼	year ▼	rank ▼
1	LIV Golf	2018	25
2	Nicolas Cage	2019	25
3	Denver Nuggets	2020	25
4	Vanderpump Rules reunion	2021	25
5	Doc Rivers	2022	25
6	LIV Golf	2023	25

Figure 5.2 – Using the WITH clause with a subquery to find the peak rank for terms over multiple years

Array functions

Array functions enable users to work with arrays within their data. These functions support aggregations, transformations, and element comparisons. Array functions are especially valuable when dealing with nested or repeated data structures, where arrays represent relationships or collections of values. The following query returns the top 25 terms for the latest week available, creates an array for the rank and the week, and orders the results by the rank in the array (called `x`). This is a filtering array, allowing you to extract only the elements that meet certain criteria – in this case, the latest data (`MAX(refresh_date)`):

```
SELECT term, ARRAY_AGG(STRUCT(rank,week) ORDER BY week DESC LIMIT 1)
AS x
FROM `bigquery-public-data.google_trends.top_terms`
WHERE
    refresh_date = (SELECT MAX(refresh_date) FROM `bigquery-public-
data.google_trends.top_terms`)
GROUP BY term
ORDER BY (SELECT rank FROM UNNEST(x))
```

We get the following results:

Query results — SAVE RESULTS — EXPLORE DATA

JOB INFORMATION | RESULTS | JSON | EXECUTION DETAILS | EXECUTION GRAPH

Row	term	x.rank	x.week
1	NBA	1	2023-06-04
2	Champions League	2	2023-06-04
3	Mike Batayeh	3	2023-06-04
4	Walt Nauta	4	2023-06-04
5	Novak Djokovic	5	2023-06-04
6	Kelis Bill Murray	6	2023-06-04
7	Niall Horan	7	2023-06-04

Figure 5.3 – Results from a query that creates an array from the x.rank and x.week columns

So far, we've seen how BigQuery provides advanced querying techniques such as subqueries, common table expressions, window functions, and array functions. By harnessing these features, users can optimize performance, reduce costs, and perform sophisticated analytics on large datasets efficiently. Exploring and mastering these techniques can significantly enhance the data analysis capabilities of BigQuery users.

Saving, sharing, and scheduling queries

BigQuery also provides features for saving, sharing, and scheduling queries, allowing you to collaborate with others, reuse queries for future analysis, and schedule queries to run at a future time. Understanding how to save, share, and schedule queries will help improve your productivity in BigQuery.

To save a query in BigQuery, you first need to write the query in the BigQuery Query Editor. Once you have written the query, you can save it by clicking the **Save** button. When you save a query, you can choose to save it as a **Personal query**, **Project query**, or **Public query** types. A personal query can only be accessed and edited by you. A project query can be edited by other project users with appropriate permissions. Finally, a public query can be accessed by anyone outside of your project with your query-shared URL.

Sharing queries in BigQuery allows you to collaborate with others and distribute query results. There are a few ways to share query results; there could be a situation where you want to send the insights from your created query to others or business users so that they can explore the data. After running your query in the **Query results** window, you will have a dropdown for **Save results** and **Explore data**. **Save results** allows you to export to CSV, JSON, a new BigQuery table, Google Sheets, and copy to the clipboard (refer to *Figure 5.4*). Savings results is useful if you need to send someone a CSV or JSON file so that they can import it into another tool, save the results to a new BigQuery table for a sanitized or filtered view for someone to do further analysis or reporting, or to Google Sheets for a data user in another organization to perform reporting and analysis in a spreadsheet:

term	year	rank
Ted Lasso	2018	25
Preakness 2023	2019	25
Nicolas Cage	2020	25
DaniLeigh	2021	25
DaniLeigh	2022	25
Ted Lasso	2023	25

Figure 5.4 – BigQuery query results copied to the clipboard and shared in plain text

BigQuery gives you options to explore query data after a query has been executed. Within the BigQuery console, you can explore data in Sheets, Looker Studio, and with a Colab notebook. This rich extensibility allows you to take your queried data and explore it or share it with a few clicks. Sheets allows you to quickly export your data to a Google Sheet, and Looker Studio allows you to create various visualizations with your data to present your data in a visually pleasing way. In *Chapter 6, Exploring Data with Notebooks*, we will dive deeper into exploring and sharing data with Colab notebooks.

Scheduling queries in BigQuery allows you to automate the execution of your queries and can be used as a strategy for optimizing data processing tasks. This is beneficial in scenarios where you are dealing with periodic reporting, data maintenance, or other routine tasks. Scheduled queries help distribute the query workload over time, reducing the risk of resource contention and often resulting in more consistent query performance. For more on scheduling queries, review the official docs: `https://cloud.google.com/bigquery/docs/scheduling-queries`.

By leveraging BigQuery's saving, sharing, and scheduling capabilities, you can improve your collaboration with others and enable data sharing across your team or organization. Saving queries for reuse or collaboration, or saving and sharing results in different ways, enhances productivity and promotes different levels of data analysis with BigQuery.

Optimizing queries

Efficient query performance is important for maximizing the potential of BigQuery and ensuring quick and reliable data analysis. This section provides guidelines and best practices to optimize your queries in BigQuery, thereby improving execution speed, reducing costs, and enhancing productivity.

Before optimizing a query, it's important to have a good understanding of your data and query patterns. You need to have a good understanding of the size and distribution of your data before working to optimize. First, understand how tables are partitioned or clustered as it can impact query performance and how you write your query. Then, identify common query patterns and possible recurring tasks, look for opportunities to optimize patterns, or use BigQuery features such as caching and table partitioning to speed up execution. Let's review some query optimization techniques that can help you understand some main considerations when you're optimizing your queries.

Here are some query optimization techniques you can use:

- Minimize the columns returned in the `SELECT` clause. Only retrieve the necessary columns to reduce data transfer and processing overhead. If you need to select all of the columns in the table except for a couple, use the `EXCEPT` keyword. Here's an example:

    ```
    SELECT * EXCEPT (col1, col2)
    FROM `project_id.dataset.table`
    ```

- Utilize materialized views to precompute and store the results of complex queries. Materialized views can speed up subsequent queries that can utilize the precomputed data.

- Use a `LIMIT` clause with `ORDER BY`. When using `ORDER BY`, sorting is done at the end of the query's execution on a single resource slot. If you are ordering a very large set, it can overwhelm the slot processing the data. As mentioned previously, `LIMIT` does not reduce the amount of data that's scanned, just the results that are displayed.

- When comparing strings, use LIKE over REGEXP_CONTAINS. LIKE is a lighter way to search for values and may be quicker for wildcard matching. Save REGEXP_CONTAINS for more complex searching of columns. Let's look at some examples of using these options:

  - REGEX_CONTAINS filtering:

    ```
    where
      REGEXP_CONTAINS(col1, '.*test.*')
    ```

  - LIKE filtering:

    ```
    where
      col1 LIKE '%test%'
    ```

- If the I/O stage is slow in terms of queries, reduce your network overhead or make sure resources are in the same region. Revisit your storage format and consider partitioning or clustering tables. We will go over *query troubleshooting* in the next section.

- Place filtering conditions (WHERE) as early as possible in the query to limit the amount of data that's processed.

- Optimize join operations by considering table size, join type, and data distribution. Consider denormalization and combining tables to avoid multiple tables and joins when possible.

Please note that this is not an exhaustive list of optimization approaches and techniques for BigQuery queries. For additional information, please review the following documentation: https://cloud. google.com/bigquery/docs/best-practices-performance-overview.

BigQuery provides rich tools and features to assist in query optimization and troubleshooting. While you optimize your queries, you can review the execution details and query plan to understand how BigQuery executes your query. Data analysts should review the steps involved in the query execution, identify potential bottlenecks, and optimize accordingly. In the next section, you will learn how to further optimize and work with queries that may not be working properly.

Troubleshooting queries

Query troubleshooting is an important area to be knowledgeable about when working with BigQuery as it helps identify and resolve issues that may arise during query execution. This section will provide an overview of common query troubleshooting techniques and best practices to give you an understanding of approaches to take while writing queries to resolve any issues that may arise.

The first step in query troubleshooting is to analyze any error messages encountered during query execution. BigQuery will give you an explanation of the error and give you the line number where the error is occurring. At that point, it is up to you to review your query and determine if you may have missed a comma between columns in the select statement or mistyped the table name.

> **Comment sections of your query during troubleshooting**
>
> If your query is taking too long, returning zero results, or giving an error and not running at all, you have the opportunity to rewrite your query! Consider commenting out parts of your query using a "#" at the beginning of the line or highlighting the section of the query and pressing *Cmd + /* (Mac) or *Ctrl + /* (Windows). This will allow you to remove lines in your SQL query that may be causing execution issues.

BigQuery provides execution details and an execution graph for each query that outlines the steps involved in processing the query, the time, and the estimated resources required. Understanding the execution plan can help you identify potential bottlenecks and optimize your query. *Figure 5.5* shows an example of a query visualization. The longest step that's selected takes .49 seconds. This presents a potential opportunity to optimize this query. This is the query graph for the query in the *Advanced query techniques* section (*Figure 5.2*). Don't worry if you can't read the text in it – the idea is to show you what a query graph looks like:

Figure 5.5 – An overview of using the query results execution graph
to visualize the steps required to process a query

If your query is taking too long, you will want to explore the query visualization graph to determine where the bottleneck exists. You may determine that you have an aggregation that allows the query to execute but takes far too long to process. You may be processing too many unnecessary columns to obtain your data and find yourself returning to your query to adjust columns and re-run them.

BigQuery includes *monitoring* and *logging* features to help track query performance and further troubleshoot issues. You can use the BigQuery web UI, command-line tools, or APIs to monitor the progress of your queries, view query statistics, and identify any errors or warnings. BigQuery keeps a log of personal and project query history. You can go back through your query history and show job details or bring the query into the editor to run again.

Query troubleshooting in BigQuery involves analyzing error messages, reviewing the query execution details and graph, and monitoring query progress and durations. By following steps to troubleshoot your queries, you can overcome challenges, optimize query performance, and achieve accurate and efficient data analysis in BigQuery.

Summary

This chapter covered various aspects of querying data, enabling you to extract valuable insights efficiently. It emphasized the importance of understanding SQL query syntax and the structure of BigQuery queries. You were introduced to essential concepts such as SELECT statements, filtering data with WHERE clauses, aggregations with GROUP BY, and sorting results with ORDER BY.

This chapter also explored advanced querying techniques such as JOIN to combine data from multiple tables and subqueries to extract data subsets. The opportunity to save and share your queries improves data team productivity, and tools to optimize and troubleshoot queries allow you to be efficient with your analysis usage. With practical examples and best practices, you now have the skills to write complex queries and analyze data effectively in BigQuery.

In the next chapter, we will cover another approach to querying and exploring data in BigQuery: using notebooks. We will cover the various Google services that provide an interactive environment that allows data analysts to write, execute, and modify code in real time. Notebooks provide a reproducible, collaborative environment that includes code execution and visualization capabilities. They can enhance productivity and are another excellent tool for analysts to leverage alongside BigQuery.

Further reading

To learn more about the topics that were covered in this chapter, take a look at the following resources:

- *Query syntax*: `https://cloud.google.com/bigquery/docs/reference/standard-sql/query-syntax`

- *Data types*: `https://cloud.google.com/bigquery/docs/reference/standard-sql/data-types`

- *Aggregate functions*: `https://cloud.google.com/bigquery/docs/reference/standard-sql/aggregate_functions`

- *Functions, operators, and conditionals*: `https://cloud.google.com/bigquery/docs/reference/standard-sql/functions-and-operators`

- *Introduction to optimizing query performance*: `https://cloud.google.com/bigquery/docs/best-practices-performance-overview`

6

Exploring Data with Notebooks

In previous chapters, we have discussed the BigQuery fundamentals – design, loading and preparing data, and querying it. We will now discuss and demonstrate the use of notebooks to explore your data in BigQuery.

Workbench instances are the managed data analysis and data science notebooks provided in Google Cloud Vertex AI. Also known as Vertex AI user-managed notebooks, or notebooks, Workbench instances are a powerful tool to explore and prepare data. Notebooks allow you to run queries, visualize data, perform transformations, and execute all of your data analysis tasks in a single application. They make it easy to iterate on your analysis and quickly see the results of your progress and changes. Think of a notebook as an interactive space to create and process the various steps of data analysis in a single page, capturing history and creating visualizations, with the ability to share and easily collaborate with others.

In this chapter, we will start by introducing the concept of notebooks and discussing their benefits. Then, we will show you how to create a notebook and connect it to a BigQuery dataset. We will walk through a few examples of how to use notebooks to explore data. Finally, we will explore the notebook options in Google Cloud.

By the end of this chapter, you will be able to create a notebook and connect it to a BigQuery dataset, create notebooks to interactively analyze data, create visualizations of your data, and share your findings with others.

In this chapter, we are going to cover the following main topics:

- Understanding the value of using notebooks
- Using Workbench notebook instances in Vertex AI
- Using Colab notebooks

Technical requirements

At this point of the book, it is assumed that you have access to the Google Cloud console: `https://console.cloud.google.com`. If this is not the case, please check the *Technical requirements* section in *Chapter 1, Introducing BigQuery and Its Components*, for setup instructions. You can find code samples discussed in this chapter in the book's GitHub repo: `https://github.com/PacktPublishing/Data-Exploration-and-Preparation-with-BigQuery`. Furthermore, we will continue our exploration of the *Google Trends* dataset in this chapter. If you have not already, import this dataset into your Google Cloud project so that you can access it and get hands on. You can find the Google Trends dataset at `https://cloud.google.com/datasets`; click **View Dataset**, which will import the dataset into your SQL workspace in BigQuery.

Understanding the value of using notebooks

There are many benefits of using notebooks to explore data in BigQuery. Here are the most important:

- **Interactive analysis**: Notebooks allow you to interactively analyze data, which means that you can manipulate the results of your queries immediately. This makes it easy to explore different datasets and find patterns that you might not have otherwise seen. The interactivity of notebooks fosters a deeper understanding of the data, as analysts can experiment with different types of queries, visualizations, and transformations with ease. The ability to mix code cells with text explanations and visualizations within a notebook empowers analysts to tell a comprehensive data story, making it easier to work with others and communicate insights to stakeholders.

- **Visualizations**: Notebooks make it easy to create visualizations of your data. This can help you understand your data better and communicate your findings to others.

- **Collaboration**: Notebooks can be shared with others, which makes them a great way to collaborate on data analysis projects. Notebooks facilitate seamless collaboration among data analysts. Multiple team members can work on the same notebook simultaneously, sharing code, insights, and annotations. This collaborative environment promotes knowledge sharing, encourages collective problem-solving, and accelerates the exploration process. Notebooks can be easily shared, allowing reviewers access and the ability to provide feedback, ensuring transparency and accountability in the data exploration process. Also, given they are code and text, versioning them is a natural strategy for adoption as part of a collaborative workflow.

- **Documentation**: Notebooks serve as an excellent means of documenting the data exploration process. Every step, including queries, visualizations, and data transformations, can be captured and preserved within a notebook. This enables reproductivity, as anyone can rerun the notebook and obtain the same results. Notebooks facilitate transparent and auditable analysis, ensuring that the decision-making process is well documented and traceable.

Jupyter notebooks

Notebooks are based on **JupyterLab** (`https://jupyter.org`), which is a web application and development environment for notebooks, data, and code, with extensive language support to create and share computational documents. It allows you to configure and arrange workflows. Utilizing Jupyter notebooks can enhance the data exploration process. The benefits come from the interactivity and BigQuery's computational power, resulting in a powerful workflow option.

Jupyter notebooks provide an interactive Python-based environment, where data analysts and data scientists can execute queries, visualize results, and iterate on their analysis in real time.

Jupyter notebooks have an ecosystem of libraries and packages that help the data exploration experience. Analysts can leverage popular Python libraries such as Pandas, Matplotlib, and Seaborn to perform advanced data manipulation, statistical analysis, and visualizations seamlessly within the notebook environment. This ecosystem provides a wide array of tools and techniques to tackle complex data exploration tasks effectively.

Jupyter has a feature called magic commands that enhance the functionality and interactivity of Jupyter notebooks. These commands, prefixed by `%` for line magics and `%%` for cell magics, provide shortcuts to perform tasks, access system utilities, and interact with the notebook environment. Later in this chapter in the hands-on example, we will use the BigQuery `%%bigquery` magic command. The `%%bigquery` magic command lets you run SQL queries in regular syntax, making it easy to interact with data. Magic commands offer flexibility and efficiency when running and using notebook-integrated services.

In the next section, we will explore the Google Cloud service to run Jupyter notebooks and Vertex AI Workbench notebook instances.

Using Workbench notebook instances in Vertex AI

This section provides an overview of the notebooks available in Google Cloud and their significance in relation to data exploration and preparation in BigQuery. **Workbench notebooks** are a powerful component of the Vertex AI platform, enabling data analysts and data scientists to perform data exploration within a collaborative and unified environment. Workbench notebooks are a JupyterLab VM-based offering that can be configured for specific usage scenarios. Let's discuss this data exploration tool in more detail.

Workbench notebooks provide a unified interface, where data analysts and scientists can work seamlessly on projects. Multiple team members can collaborate on the same notebook, making it easy to share insights, exchange ideas, and work toward data goals. **Vertex AI Workbench** (`https://cloud.google.com/vertex-ai-workbench`) offers two types of notebook options, **managed notebooks** with built-in integrations, and **user-managed notebooks** that are highly customizable. As managed notebooks are the most common choice for data exploration, analysis, and modeling, the remainder of this chapter will focus on that option.

Creating a managed notebook

The process of creating a managed notebook in the Google Cloud console is relatively straightforward. Inside the **Vertex AI** section of the Google Cloud console, **Workbench** can be found under **Notebooks**. After selecting **New Notebook**, you can get started with a notebook with relatively little configuration. In the standard configuration for managed notebooks, you have the ability to configure the notebook name, region, and permission (single user or service account with multiple user access option). That's it! Just like that, you can create a managed notebook for data exploration. In the next section, we will review advanced options to configure your notebook environment further.

> **Note**
>
> If you plan to share a Workbench-managed notebook with other users, use the service account permission. By default, the Compute Engine service account is selected, but you can create and specify a new service account if you wish. Users that wish to access the notebook will need the `iam.serviceAccounts.actAs` IAM role. For more information on how to use the `serviceAccounts.actAs` role, visit `https://cloud.google.com/iam/docs/service-accounts-actas`.

In the notebook's advanced options, during the creation process, you can modify the environment, hardware, networking, and security for your notebook. In this advanced configuration for notebooks, you can specify the type of machine type, add a **graphics processing unit** (**GPU**), modify a network, place the notebook in your own VPC instead of being in the Google-managed network, or place it in a shared network for sharing across connected locations or sites, using private services access (`https://cloud.google.com/vpc/docs/private-services-access`).

Executions and schedules

Once set up, you can schedule notebook files to be executed. This can be a method of scheduling regular tasks to automate and improve your workflow with notebooks. With executions and schedules, users can automate and manage the execution of BigQuery queries directly from a notebook environment. Executions enable users to run SQL queries on their BigQuery datasets and receive real-time results within the notebook, offering an option to streamline the data analysis process. Users can schedule query executions to run at specified intervals, automating repetitive tasks and ensuring data refresh. This feature is particularly valuable for creating data pipelines and generating up-to-date reports. If you plan to utilize notebooks, executions and schedules are valuable features to improve your workflow.

Hands-on exercise – analyzing Google Trends data with Workbench

In this exercise, we will use a managed notebook in Vertex AI Workbench to analyze the Google Trends dataset we worked with previously. We will load the dataset into a Pandas DataFrame, perform data preprocessing, and visualize data as follows:

1. **Setting up the notebook**:

    I.   Launch the Vertex AI Workbench (`https://console.cloud.google.com/vertex-ai/workbench`) and create a new managed notebook instance.

    II. Browse the advanced settings. Adjust the instance configuration, such as machine type, CPU, memory, and storage options, or keep the options as default. As this is just a hands-on example, it is recommended to choose the smallest hardware configuration.

    III. Once the instance is provisioned, open the notebook in the Workbench interface by clicking **OPEN JUPYTERLAB**.

2. **Inspecting the data**:

    I.   As this is a managed notebook, it will come preloaded with most packages that you will need for data exploration. You will not need to load any packages at this point.

    II. Examine your table using the built-in `%bigquery_stats` command:

    ```
    %bigquery_stats bigquery-public-data.google_trends.top_terms
    ```

3. **Data exploration and preprocessing**:

    I.   Use the BigQuery `%%bigquery` *magic command* before your commands to run SQL queries and return results as a pandas DataFrame. Jupyter magics are notebook-specific shortcuts that let you run commands and accept variables with low code. In the following example, we will provide a variable name (`top_terms_FL`) as a parameter to `%%bigquery`.

For example, this query will find top terms for designated market areas in the state of Florida and save the results in the `top_terms_FL` DataFrame:

```
%%bigquery top_terms_FL
SELECT score, rank, MAX(refresh_date) as date, dma_name, term
  FROM `bigquery-public-data.google_trends.top_rising_terms`
WHERE refresh_date = DATE_SUB(CURRENT_DATE(), INTERVAL 1 DAY)
AND dma_name LIKE '%FL%'
AND score IS NOT NULL
GROUP BY score, rank, percent_gain, term, dma_name, week
ORDER BY score asc
```

> **A note on Pandas DataFrames**
>
> A Pandas DataFrame is a two-dimensional, tabular data structure in Python that organizes data into rows and columns, similar to a table in a spreadsheet. It is a primary data structure provided by the Pandas library and is widely used in data analysis and manipulation tasks. In Jupyter you can use DataFrames to assign query results to a variable and do further manipulation on that variable.

II.   Explore our data with the following commands:

```
top_terms_FL.tail(10)
top_terms_FL.head(10)
```

III.   Clean the data by dropping duplicates:

```
top_terms_FL.drop_duplicates()
```

4. **Deriving insights**: Analyze the numbers in the DataFrame, and identify interesting patterns or insights:

```
top_terms_FL.plot.hist()
```

This query produces the following result that shows a skew to the left:

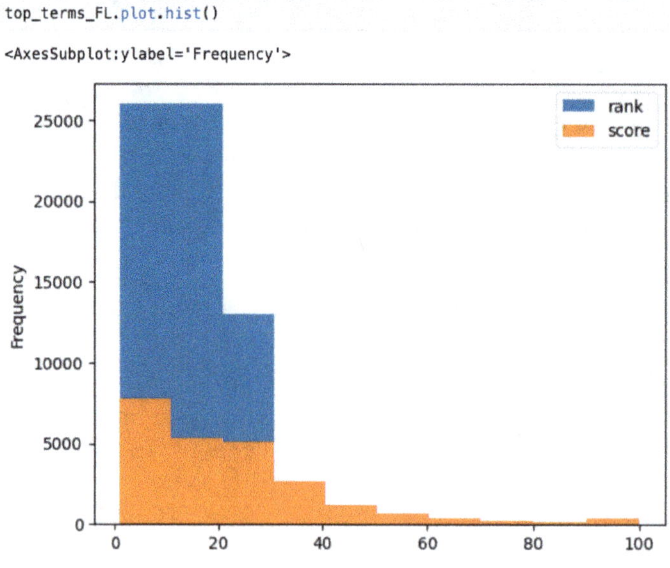

Figure 6.1 – Using a pandas histogram visualization

With just a few commands you can see that using a notebook is a highly interactive extensible method to explore your data in BigQuery. Notebooks complement BigQuery with Python environment capabilities and libraries, allowing you to use different tools for the exploration and preparation of your data.

Managed notebooks in Workbench Vertex AI provide data analysts with a fully managed, scalable, and secure environment to perform their data exploration and analysis tasks. With integration with Vertex AI services, flexible configurations, collaboration capabilities, and access to pre-installed libraries and tools, Workbench notebooks streamline the workflow and empower users to focus on their data analysis tasks. If you are an individual user and do not need to adhere to organizational compliance, you should consider Colab notebooks for a more serverless option to leverage JupyterLab.

What about the announced BigQuery notebooks?

At the time of writing, they are a closed preview, but by the time this book is published or you are reading this, they probably will be at the state of **General Availability (GA)**: `https://cloud.google.com/bigquery/docs/create-notebooks`.

Using Colab notebooks

Colab notebooks, powered by Google Colaboratory, are another powerful and convenient tool for data exploration and analysis. Colab notebooks provide a cloud-based environment that allows you to write and execute code, collaborate with others, and utilize powerful hardware resources, all without the need for any setup or installation.

Google Colab is a free online Jupyter Notebook environment that runs on Google's cloud infrastructure. It allows you to write and run Python code, as well as other languages such as R and Julia. Colab is a powerful tool for data analysis, machine learning, and education.

One of the key advantages of Colab notebooks is its collaboration features. You can share your notebooks with others, allowing them to view and edit your code and analysis in real time. This makes it easy to work on data exploration projects as a team, facilitating collaboration and knowledge sharing. Sharing Colab notebooks is similar to sharing a Google document; access to the notebook can be sent to anyone with an email address.

Colab notebooks seamlessly integrate with various Google services, such as Google Drive and Google Sheets. This allows you to access and manipulate data stored in these services directly from your notebook. You can read data from Google Sheets, save analysis results to Google Drive, or even perform collaborative editing with team members on the same Google sheet.

Comparing Workbench instances and Colab

Colab notebooks have a similar look and purpose to Workbench instances and are based on the same Jupyter platform. Colab notebooks are zero config and serverless, meaning you do not have to worry about building an instance to run your environment or managing that instance, such as starting or stopping the instance when not in use. Colab notebooks are geared toward organizations who want Google to manage everything – libraries, frameworks, security, and costs. They are geared more toward individual or educational usage.

Workbench instances are intended to be a laptop or workstation replacement. Data analysts who are transitioning from a local machine to the cloud typically want a lot of flexibility. Workbench instances provide that flexibility, with greater configurations and options for performance and setup. Power users who value greater system access will find notebook environment flexibility with Workbench instances in Vertex AI. Organizations that have very specific requirements for OSs, libraries, and extensions will also likely opt for Workbench instances. Hence, this book will utilize and reference Workbench instances for the remainder of the chapters.

Summary

This chapter went through the power and versatility of using Jupyter notebooks for data exploration. We went over the different notebook options available for usage in Google Cloud including Vertex AI Workbench instances and Colab notebooks. Each service has a specific target user and both are collaborative and have the same general purpose – extending your BigQuery data exploration with Python and JupyterLab. With practical examples and step-by-step instructions, the chapter equips you with the necessary knowledge to effectively explore and prepare data, using notebooks in conjunction with BigQuery.

In the next chapter, we will delve into exploring and visualizing data to enable you further, with even more options to explore data in BigQuery. Take a look at the links in the Further reading section for additional information related to this chapter.

Further reading

- *Data Wrangling with pandas Cheat Sheet*: `https://pandas.pydata.org/Pandas_Cheat_Sheet.pdf`

- *Vertex AI notebooks*: `https://cloud.google.com/vertex-ai-workbench`

Further Exploring and Visualizing Data

In the previous chapters, we learned about the basics of BigQuery and the practice of data exploration, how to load and transform data, how to query data in BigQuery, and how to use notebooks to explore your data. Now, we will dive further into the world of data exploration and visualization in BigQuery. Further exploring and visualizing data allows us to better understand data attributes and peculiarities, gain insights, discover patterns, and communicate our findings effectively. In this chapter, we'll discuss common practices for exploring data and review various techniques and tools available for BigQuery to analyze and visualize your data.

In this chapter, we are going to cover the following main topics:

- Understanding data distributions
- Uncovering relationships in data
- Exploring BigQuery data with Google Sheets
- Visualizing BigQuery data using Looker Studio
- Hands-on exercise – creating visualizations with Looker Studio
- Integrating other visualization tools with BigQuery

Technical requirements

In this chapter, we will be using the Los Angeles Traffic Collision data from the hands-on exercise in *Chapter 4, Loading and Transforming Data* (`https://data.lacity.org/Public-Safety/Traffic-Collision-Data-from-2010-to-Present/d5tf-ez2w`) provided by the Los Angeles' Open Data catalog (`https://data.lacity.org/`). For convenience, we also have it available as `ch4/archive.zip` in this book's GitHub repository: `https://github.com/PacktPublishing/Data-Exploration-and-Preparation-with-BigQuery/tree/main/ch4`. We will review how to analyze your BigQuery data in Looker Studio and Google

Sheets in this chapter. It is really easy to integrate BigQuery with Looker Studio and Google Sheets. You will want to select the table you used to load the collision data into BigQuery. Click your table in the BigQuery **Explorer** pane and, in the table query pane, click the **EXPORT** button, then **Explore with Looker Studio** or **Explore with Sheets**. We will walk you through this later in this chapter.

Understanding data distributions

The distribution of a dataset is how the data is spread out or clustered around certain values or ranges. By understanding the distribution of a dataset, we can gain insights into the characteristics and patterns of the data, which can be useful in making informed decisions and predictions. Understanding the distribution of data is important for identifying patterns, detecting outliers, and making informed decisions about how to explore data.

Data distributions can be examined through descriptive statistics, which provide summary measures that help us understand the central tendency, variability, and shape of the data. Measures such as mean, median, mode, range, and standard deviation provide a snapshot of the dataset's overall characteristics. BigQuery offers SQL functions that allow us to compute these descriptive statistics efficiently. Some of the most commonly used functions are as follows:

- COUNT(*): This function returns the total number of rows in a table or group
- SUM(column_name): This function returns the sum of all the values in a column
- AVG(column_name): This function returns the average of all the values in a column
- MIN(column_name): This function returns the minimum value in a column
- MAX(column_name): This function returns the maximum value in a column

For example, the following query would calculate the descriptive statistics for the victim_age column in the collision dataset we loaded and had hands-on experience within *Chapter 4, Loading and Transforming Data*:

```
SELECT
   COUNT(*) AS count,
   AVG(victim_age) AS avg,
   MIN(victim_age) AS min,
   MAX(victim_age) AS max
FROM `data-exploration-and-prep-w-bq.collisions.data`
```

The results of this query show that there's a total of 502k rows, an average victim age of 41, a minimum age of 10, and a maximum age of 99 in the dataset. This query gives us an idea of the data distribution for the victim_age column in our dataset. These results could lead to asking further questions about the dataset, such as what was a 10-year-old doing driving?

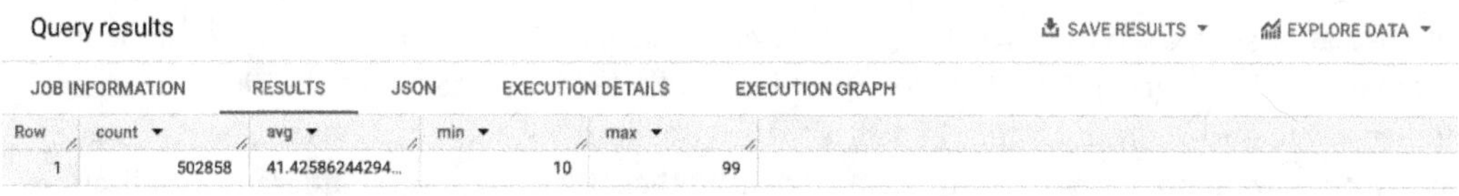

Row	count ▼	avg ▼	min ▼	max ▼
1	502858	41.42586244294...	10	99

Query results   SAVE RESULTS ▼   EXPLORE DATA ▼

JOB INFORMATION   RESULTS   JSON   EXECUTION DETAILS   EXECUTION GRAPH

Figure 7.1 – Using descriptive statistics aggregate functions in BigQuery

Understanding the distribution of categorical data is also important for exploration and analysis. You can use aggregate functions such as COUNT and COUNTIF to analyze categorical statistics and also bar charts in visualizations to identify categorical distributions. By examining the distribution of categorical data, we can uncover patterns, identify dominant categories, and explore relationships between variables. A histogram is a graphical representation of the data distribution of numerical values. It shows how many values fall within each range of values. We will go over bar charts and histograms later in this chapter in the *Visualizing data* section.

Why is it important to understand data distributions?

Understanding data distributions is important for several reasons. First, it can help you identify outliers in the data. Outliers are values that are far outside the normal range of values. They can be caused by errors in data entry or by unusual events. Note the very young and elderly individual records in our collisions dataset that we found previously. You will want to know about these occurrences in your dataset so that you can be more knowledgeable and report on them.

Second, understanding data distributions can help you choose the right statistical tests for your data. Different statistical tests are designed for different types of data distributions. If you choose the wrong statistical test, you may get inaccurate results.

Ultimately, understanding data distributions can help you make better decisions about your data. For example, if you know that your data is normally distributed, meaning no serious deviations in values, you can use the mean and standard deviation to make predictions about the data. Let's explore the value of uncovering relationships before we begin reviewing visualization approaches.

Uncovering relationships in data

In addition to understanding data distributions, exploring relationships between variables is important for gaining insights into how different factors interact and affect each other. By understanding how different variables are related to each other, you can gain insights into your data that would not be possible otherwise. You will be ready to write the queries that will unlock insights from your data.

There are several ways to uncover relationships in data. One common approach is to use correlation analysis. Correlation analysis measures the strength and direction of the relationship between two variables. A correlation coefficient of 1 indicates a positive relationship, a correlation coefficient of -1 indicates a perfect negative relationship, and a correlation coefficient of 0 indicates no relationship. For example, if you had a table of customer data that includes the customer's age, gender, and income, you could use correlation analysis to see if there is a relationship between the customer's age and income. If there is a positive correlation, then you would know that older customers have higher incomes. Another way to uncover relationships in data is to use visualizations. Visualizations can help you easily understand how different variables are related to each other. There are several different visualization techniques that you can use, such as scatter plots, bar charts, and line charts. We'll discuss these in the next section. For example, you could use a line chart to visualize the relationship between a customer's age and income. If you see a cluster of points that form a line, then you would know there is a linear relationship between the two variables:

customer_id	age	income
1	20	30000
2	25	40000
3	30	50000
4	35	60000
5	40	70000
6	45	80000

Table 7.1 – Example data showing a customer's age and income relationship

When these values are plotted on a graph, we get the following result:

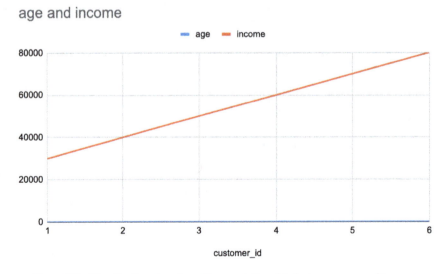

Figure 7.2 – Visualization showing a linear relationship between age and income

Here are some additional tips for uncovering relationships in data:

- **Use different techniques**. Don't rely on just one technique to uncover relationships in data. Use a variety of techniques, such as correlation analysis and visualization, to get a more complete picture of the relationships in your data.

- **Look for patterns**. When you are exploring your data, look for patterns that suggest relationships between different variables. For example, you might notice that a particular variable tends to increase or decrease as another variable increases or decreases.

- **Ask questions**. As you are exploring your data, ask yourself questions about the relationships between different variables. What are the possible explanations for these relationships? What are the implications of these relationships?

Uncovering relationships in data can be a challenging task at first, but it is an important step in the data analysis process. By doing variable relationship analysis, you can increase your chances of uncovering meaningful relationships in your data. Next, let's see how we can use visualization techniques for our purpose.

Exploring BigQuery data with Google Sheets

If you are a Google Workspace or Google account user, you may be familiar with Google Sheets, the spreadsheet tool that allows users to input and manage data in a workbook with rows and columns. Google Sheets gives users the ability to easily connect or input data, create tables, charts, and graphs, and perform statistical analysis. Sheets is integrated with BigQuery, offering another option to explore your BigQuery data. Exploring BigQuery data in sheets can be a quick and productive option, especially for sharing findings.

Connecting to Sheets from BigQuery using Explore with Sheets

You may consider exporting your data to Google Sheets for further exploration and relationship analysis from within BigQuery. Select your table in the BigQuery **Explorer** pane and, in the table query pane, click the **EXPORT** button, then **Explore with Sheets**:

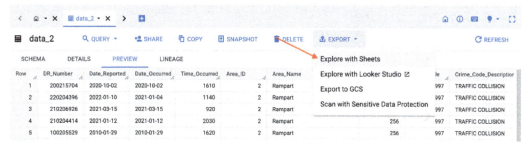

Figure 7.3 – Explore with Sheets

Once your table is connected to Google Sheets, you will be able to browse a limited row preview, create charts, pivot tables, extract rows, add a calculated column, and view column stats. Sheets provides you with the option to do many common data exploring and visualization tasks on your tables in BigQuery. You can insert formulas and additional sheets for analysis or visualizations through charts. You can also build other spreadsheets and bring your BigQuery table data into a workbook for additional insights and data enrichment purposes, making it easy to input and work alongside BigQuery data.

Connecting to BigQuery using Connected Sheets

Another way to explore your BigQuery data can originate from within Sheets. Connected Sheets combines the UI-friendly version of Google Sheets on top of the powerful and limitless engine of BigQuery. This approach uses the **Data Connector** feature within Google Sheets. To connect BigQuery within a Sheets workbook, visit the **Data** menu, then **Data connectors**, then **Connect to BigQuery**. Here, you can select your Google Cloud project, then select a dataset, then a table or view to connect to and begin exploring.

The previous data exploration approaches we outlined are mostly for data engineers and analysts. Connected Sheets enables anyone to analyze data at scale and make more data-driven decisions. Data analysis with Sheets can be done by most business users familiar with spreadsheet tools and provides the opportunity to analyze billions of rows of data in BigQuery with a simple connection. Connected Sheets can help accelerate time to insights across large groups.

Column statistics

After connecting your BigQuery table to Sheets, you can view column size, min and max values, distribution information, unique values, and null value information. This is an alternate query-less approach to finding this information via a SQL query. Sheets' BigQuery column statistics give you an easy and quick way to understand data distributions and relationships in your data – that is, important data attributes you will want to know as a data analyst:

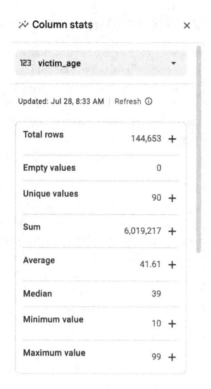

Figure 7.4 – Viewing BigQuery Column stats in Google Sheets

Collaboration with BigQuery data in Sheets

Google Sheets makes it easy to collaborate with others on your BigQuery data. When you connect to a BigQuery table or view in Sheets, you can share the spreadsheet with others so that they can view or edit it. This makes it easy to work together with your team on data analysis projects. Sheets includes real-time collaboration, which means that when one person makes a change to the spreadsheet, everyone else who is viewing the spreadsheet will see the change immediately. Sheets is highly secure as it follows your Google Workspace organization policies for sharing. It is flexible for individual Google account users, giving you the ability to share data with anyone with a Google account.

Google Sheets, when connected to tables and views in BigQuery, can be a familiar data analysis playground for you to explore and visualize your data. It is a great option for enabling business users to connect to and analyze data in BigQuery. This analysis option can also be useful for single small to medium-sized quick turnaround data analysis. For larger datasets, you may find it is easier and more effective to do your analysis using other visualization tools, such as Looker Studio. We'll discuss visualizing data in Looker Studio in the next section.

Visualizing BigQuery data using Looker Studio

Visualizing data is an essential step in your data exploration and analysis work. It allows you to gain insights, discover patterns, and communicate findings to stakeholders. We will use **Looker Studio** (`https://cloud.google.com/looker-studio`), formally known as **Data Studio**, in this section. Looker Studio enables an out-of-the-box native integration to BigQuery and makes it easy to visualize data quickly. It is free to use with any Google account and easy to share reports and enable collaboration if your organization uses Google Workspace.

Creating the right visualizations

Choosing the right visualization approach is important in communicating insights and patterns hidden within your BigQuery data. The appropriate visualization technique can bring clarity to complex datasets, highlight trends, and aid in decision-making. Before creating visualizations, it is essential to have a clear understanding of your data and the objectives you aim to achieve. Consider the type of data you are working with, be it numerical, categorical, or geospatial, and determine the key questions you want to answer or insights you want to convey. Understanding the data and objectives will guide you in selecting the most appropriate visualization techniques.

Different types of data call for different visualization approaches and techniques. Numerical data, such as sales figures or temperature readings, can be effectively represented using bar charts, line charts, scatter plots, or heat maps. Categorical data such as product categories or customer segments can be visualized using bar charts, pie charts, or stacked bar charts. Geospatial data can be represented using maps or scatter plots on a map. Match the visualization type to the data type to ensure clarity and meaningful representation.

> **Note**
>
> Having correct data types on your tables is critical to generating valuable visualizations. For example, there may be a situation where you are unable to generate a histogram or bar chart visualization because a numerical field has been loaded into a string or text data type. In these situations, you will need to revisit your table data and schema and adjust or reload data into the correct data type. Revisit *Chapter 5*, *Querying BigQuery Data*, for more on data types and *Chapter 4*, *Loading and Transforming Data*, for more on data loading. Also, see *Chapter 9*, *Cleansing and Transforming Data*, for more on data type conversions.

Creating the right visualization is often an iterative process. Start with initial visualizations, evaluate their effectiveness, and seek feedback from reviewers. Refine and iterate based on the feedback received and adjust it to improve clarity, visual appeal, and alignment with objectives. Consider different perspectives and iterate until the visualizations effectively convey the desired insights and support decision-making.

Hands-on exercise – creating visualizations with Looker Studio

Visualizations enable you to uncover patterns, identify trends, and make informed decisions. For the visualizations in this section, we will be using the Los Angeles Traffic Collision Data mentioned in the *Technical requirements* section. You will want to select the table you used to load the collision data into BigQuery. Select your table in the BigQuery **Explorer** pane and, in the table query pane, click the **EXPORT** button, then **Explore with Looker Studio**:

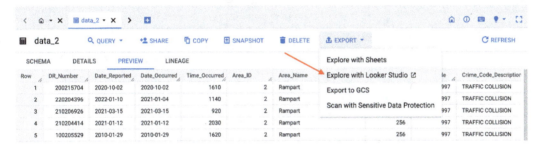

Figure 7.5 – Explore with Looker Studio

Let's explore some of the most common visualization techniques.

Commonly created charts

Bar charts are effective for visualizing categorical data and comparing different categories in groups. For example, with our collision dataset, we can create a bar chart that visualizes the ages of individuals who were in car collisions, with `victim_age` displayed on the *X* axis and `DR_number` (the unique ID) on the *Y* axis with the count metric applied. Here is how the chart setup looks in Looker Studio:

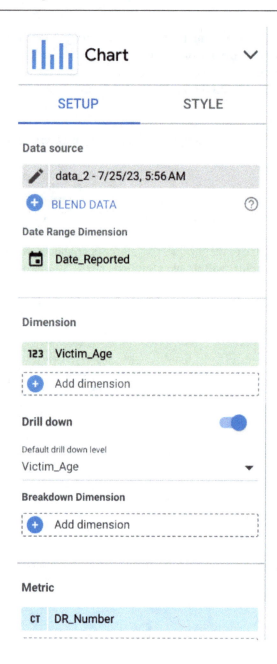

Figure 7.6 – Bar chart setup in Looker Studio

Looking at this chart quickly tells us that the largest distribution of values is at age 30, followed by age 25. The possible highest concentration of records in this dataset is at these two victim ages:

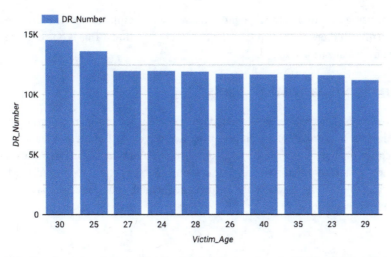

Figure 7.7 – Bar chart showing age distribution for the Los Angeles Traffic Collision Data dataset

Time series charts are useful for visualizing trends and patterns over time or continuous variables. In the Los Angeles Traffic Collision Data dataset, you can create a time series chart to show the fluctuation of traffic incidents over time. Create a line chart by visiting the **Insert** menu and choosing the **Time series chart** option. The chart shown in *Figure 7.9* was built with the following setup after we used our Los Angeles Traffic Collision Data dataset:

- **Date Range Dimension**: Date_Reported
- **Dimension**: Date_Reported
- **Metric**: Crime_Code (Count)

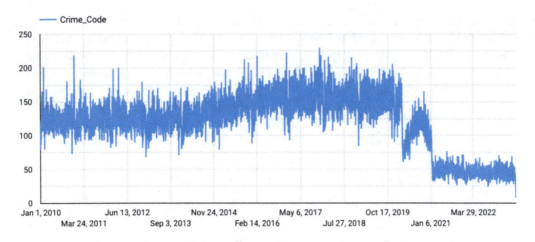

Figure 7.8 – Line chart showing a reduction in traffic incidents in the past few years

You may consider using a custom date range filter to narrow the results of the visualization. This will allow you to determine if there have been trends over different periods. This is one of the many ways you can refine your visualization data.

Calculations in visualization tools

In *Chapter 5*, *Querying BigQuery Data*, we discussed using expressions and aggregations in your queries before visualizing data. If your dataset is not pre-processed or you determine you want to do further processing outside of BigQuery, you can do your aggregations and calculations in most visualization tools. It is common to start to visualize data while creating charts as you can determine whether you only want to see a smaller subset or you want to further aggregate your data. You have the option to do this inside your visualization tool:

Figure 7.9 – Column aggregations in Looker Studio

Creating the right visualizations for your BigQuery data is essential to extract meaningful insights and effectively communicate findings to others. By understanding your data and objectives, matching visualization types to data types, and keeping visualizations clear and concise, you can create visuals that bring your data to life. Through an interactive process of refining and iterating, you can fine-tune your visualizations to achieve maximum impact and enable stakeholders to derive valuable insights from your BigQuery analysis efforts. In the next section, we'll explore how to integrate other visualization tools with BigQuery data. This is useful when have had previous experience or a current preference with another tool. You have the flexibility to choose how to present your data in BigQuery.

Data quality discovery while creating visualizations

As you create visualizations, you will notice data characteristics and begin to understand your data better. Charts and visualizations are an easier way to spot trends and perform data discovery and quality checking. You will learn more about your data through visualizations. For example, if you are creating a visualization and notice you are missing data from the current year, as displayed in *Figure 7.10*, you may have a data quality issue:

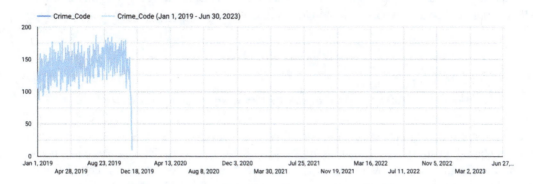

Figure 7.10 – Missing data on a line chart identifying a possible problem with the data source

The preceding line chart shows missing `Crime_Code` data from 2019 onward. This may indicate a data quality issue as `Crime_Code` data may be missing. You can return to BigQuery to validate this and check the `max` value on a date column:

```
SELECT
MAX(Date_Reported) AS max
FROM `data-exploration-and-prep-w-bq.collisions.data`
```

The results also show and confirm that data is only available through **2019-11-30**:

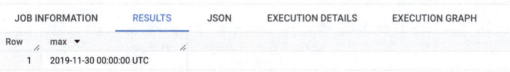

Figure 7.11 – Verifying that data is missing in our table

The identified data may indicate a data source or data load issue if you were expecting data from 2023 to be included in this table. At this point, you will want to check your data source, re-upload files, and reload the data into BigQuery. If you have a streaming source or a pipeline setup, you may want to check for any failed executions.

Filtering data in visualizations

You can apply filters to charts to adjust the information that's displayed. You can do this within the chart settings in Looker Studio. A common filter you may choose to apply is to exclude null values:

Figure 7.12 – Filtering null values from the Victim_Age column in Looker Studio

Other common filtering methods may include time-based filters, which allow you to narrow down the data based on specific time periods, numerical filters, which restrict data based on specific numerical conditions, and categorical filters, which can filter based on attributes such as product categories, customer segments, regions, or any other categorical variables available in your dataset. You may also combine multiple filters simultaneously to refine your visualizations further. The choice of filters depends on the data being analyzed and the objectives of the analysis. Applying appropriate filters helps focus the visualization on the relevant data subsets, enabling deeper insights and more accurate interpretations.

Integrating other visualization tools with BigQuery

BigQuery integrates easily with popular visualization tools, such as Looker Studio, Tableau, Power BI, and QlikView. These tools have their own approach for enabling you to create visually appealing dashboards, charts, and reports. By connecting BigQuery to these tools, you can take advantage of a current visualization tool standard in your organization or explore a tool that works best for your needs. For example, if your company already uses Microsoft collaboration tools, you may consider doing your visualizations in PowerBI.

The integration process with visualization tools typically involves connecting the tool to BigQuery, selecting the desired datasets, and designing interactive dashboards or reports. The most common tools will have integrations with BigQuery built in and they will guide you through connecting to your datasets in a wizard-type setup. For other tools, you may need to create a service account (`https://cloud.google.com/iam/docs/service-accounts-create`) or use **Open Database Connectivity (ODBC)** or **Java Database Connectivity (JDBC)** drivers (`https://cloud.google.com/bigquery/docs/reference/odbc-jdbc-drivers`).

Visualization tool integration expands your options, enhances interactivity, and enables collaboration and sharing of insights with stakeholders. As BigQuery is a data warehouse standard across various industries, you will find that integrating other tools can be very easy. Any visualization tool you choose will help you explore and present your data excitingly and compellingly so that you can communicate your findings.

Summary

In this chapter, we explored the power of continued data exploration and visualization with BigQuery. We learned how to explore data distributions and uncover relationships so that we can understand our data and gain insights. We also explored different visualization techniques and approaches. By mastering the art of visualization, you will be equipped to extract meaningful insights and effectively communicate your findings from large datasets using BigQuery. The next few chapters will enable you to use tools to prepare and clean datasets so that you can make your data more meaningful.

Further reading

To learn more about the topics that were covered in this chapter, take a look at the following resources:

- *Aggregate functions*: `https://cloud.google.com/bigquery/docs/reference/standard-sql/aggregate_functions`

- *Create service accounts*: `https://cloud.google.com/iam/docs/service-accounts-create`

- *ODBC and JDBC drivers for BigQuery*: `https://cloud.google.com/bigquery/docs/reference/odbc-jdbc-drivers`

Part 3:
Data Preparation
with BigQuery

This section of the book will focus on data preparation and transformation. Approaches to improve data quality to enhance exploration efforts will be covered. Finally, best practices for optimization and cost control in BigQuery will be reviewed, teaching you how to utilize BigQuery efficiently.

This part has the following chapters:

- *Chapter 8, An Overview of Data Preparation Tools*
- *Chapter 9, Cleansing and Transforming Data*
- *Chapter 10, Best Practices for Data Preparation, Optimization, and Cost Control*

8

An Overview of Data Preparation Tools

Data preparation involves transforming, cleaning, and structuring data to ensure its quality and suitability for analysis. Taking the time to learn about the options and perform data preparation on your BigQuery data will enhance the accuracy of your analysis. In this chapter, we will explore various approaches and tools that can be used in conjunction with BigQuery to streamline your data preparation workflow and improve data quality.

The tools we will go over in this chapter have capabilities for data transformation, cleaning, and enrichment, enabling you to unlock the greatest potential of your data and derive meaningful insights for decision-making. By understanding and utilizing these data preparation tools, you will be equipped with the necessary techniques to handle diverse data sources, address data quality issues, and prepare your data, setting yourself up for the most effective possible analysis in BigQuery.

In this chapter, we are going to go over the following main topics:

- Getting started with data preparation
- Data preparation approaches
- Data preparation tools

Technical requirements

In this chapter, we will discuss the different data preparation approaches and tools at a high level. You will need access to the Cloud console for exploration and testing as you follow along.

Getting started with data preparation

Before getting started with the process of data preparation, it is essential to establish a strong foundation and understand the key principles and approaches involved. Let's explore the fundamental steps, presented in chronological order, to get started with data preparation.

Clearly defining your data preparation goals

Begin by clearly defining your data preparation and analysis goals. What insights are you looking to gain from your data? What specific questions do you want to answer? By having a clear understanding of your objectives you can focus your efforts on preparing the data in a way that aligns with your analysis goals. There may be cases where your raw data is sufficient for good analysis and little to no preparation is required. Conversely, there may be situations where your data is missing values or needs to be updated or enriched during the preparation phase.

Evaluating your current data quality

Data quality is critical for accurate analysis. Evaluate the quality of your data by examining factors such as completeness, consistency, occurrence of values, accuracy, and integrity. This practice is also known as **data profiling**.

You can evaluate data quality manually by scanning your table's rows by using the table preview feature in the BigQuery console or by executing some basic queries described previously in *Chapter 3, Exploring Data in BigQuery*. Your goal with evaluating data quality is to assess issues such as missing values (null values), duplicate records, top common values, and other inconsistencies and patterns in your data that may impact your analysis.

Automated data quality and profiling can be performed with Dataplex. **Dataplex** is a Google Cloud service that can help discover, manage, and govern data in BigQuery as well as on-premises and hybrid environments. Dataplex can help improve data quality with data profiling scans that allow you to understand and analyze data more efficiently. Dataplex can help identify information such as common data values, data distribution, and null values that will your improve analysis efforts. Read more about the data profiling scan in BigQuery using Dataplex in the official documentation at `https://cloud.google.com/dataplex/docs/data-profiling-overview`.

In addition to data profiling, Dataplex can provide data-quality information automatically. You can automate the scanning of your data, validate data against rules you set, and configure alerts for data that does not meet quality requirements. Dataplex allows you to manage your data quality rules as code, which can improve the integrity of data production pipelines. For mature data engineering and analysis teams, Dataplex supports regular quality checking for automated data pipelines. Learn more about the automatic data quality features in the Dataplex official documentation at `https://cloud.google.com/dataplex/docs/auto-data-quality-overview`.

Taking the time to evaluate data quality in your tables will help you determine the data cleaning and transformation steps needed.

Data cleansing and transformation

Execute the data cleansing and transformation tasks according to the plan you established during the initial exploration and analysis of your table's data quality. Leverage the data preparation tools and techniques described in this chapter such as SQL transformation queries, dataflow pipelines, or visual preparation tools to cleanse, transform, and enrich your data. Ensure that the data is standardized, properly formatted, and ready for analysis.

Validating prepared data

Once the data cleansing and transformation steps are complete, you next need to validate your prepared data. Perform data quality checks to confirm the accuracy and consistency of the transformed data. Validate that the data aligns with your goals and requirements and its completeness will allow good results with analysis. Validation can be done by exporting data to Sheets to create charts or by visualizing the data in tools such as Looker Studio, as described in *Chapter 7, Further Exploring and Visualizing Data*.

By following these foundational steps you can establish a good data preparation practice for your data in BigQuery. This process sets the stage for high-value exploration and analysis. By defining goals, evaluating the quality of your data, performing data cleansing, and validating your prepared data you will be better equipped to gain more accurate insights and value from your BigQuery data. Next up, we'll introduce the different data preparation approaches and get more into their details in *Chapter 9, Cleansing and Transforming Data*.

Data preparation approaches

When getting ready to begin data preparation, you benefit most from a systematic approach to handling the complexities and potential challenges associated with raw data. We previously discussed the fundamental foundational steps to get started with data preparation. In this section, we will discuss the different data preparation approaches that can be taken with data preparation tools that we will discuss later in this chapter. These approaches will assist you in selecting a route for transforming and preparing your data for analysis.

There are a number of different approaches to data preparation. The best approach for a particular project will depend on the specific needs of the project. It is important to understand the options available so you can apply an approach that works best for you and your unique needs:

- **Manual data preparation (ad hoc)**: This involves manually cleaning, transforming, and integrating data. This approach can be time-consuming and error-prone but it can be effective for small datasets or datasets with simple requirements. Manual data preparation can be done using SQL in the BigQuery console.

- **Automated data preparation**: This involves using a data preparation tool to automate the cleaning, transforming, and integration of data. This approach can be more efficient than manual data preparation, but it can be more complex to set up and use.

- **Hybrid data preparation**: This involves using a combination of manual and automated data preparation techniques. This approach can be the most effective, as it allows you to take advantage of the strengths of both manual and automated data preparation.

In addition to manual, automated, and hybrid preparation, there are **focus areas** that you can consider when determining what steps to take to prepare your data.

Data sampling involves selecting a representative subset of data from a larger dataset for exploratory analysis. Sampling helps to reduce compute costs and expedite the analysis process. You can create data samples in BigQuery based on specific criteria, and in some cases, this can enable faster and more efficient data exploration. Consider running a query and saving it as a new table to quickly create a data sample. For example, this query would create a table with three columns called `cohort1`. You could add a `WHERE` clause to specify the data in the sample even further:

```
CREATE TABLE collisions.cohort1 AS (
SELECT victim_age, date_occured, area_name
FROM data-exploration-and-prep-w-bq.collisions.data)
```

Data integration involves combining data from multiple sources and disparate systems to create a unified dataset for analysis. It includes tasks such as data merging, data deduplication, and data transformation to ensure consistency and compatibility across different data sources. By integrating data from various sources, you can gain a comprehensive view and uncover new insights. Tools such as BigQuery Data Transfer Service and Google Cloud Dataflow simplify the process of ingesting and integrating data from different sources and can enable seamless data integration.

Data cleaning is the process of identifying and rectifying errors, inconsistencies, and inaccuracies in the dataset. It involves tasks such as handling missing values, resolving duplicates, and addressing outliers. The data-cleaning process ensures the accuracy and completeness of the data, which is crucial for meaningful analysis. Data preparation tools such as Cloud Dataprep provide features specifically designed for data cleaning, making the process more efficient and intuitive.

Data transformation involves converting data from one format to another or restructuring it to meet specific analysis requirements. This process often includes tasks such as aggregating data, creating calculated fields, and applying data normalization techniques. Data preparation tools such as Cloud Dataprep and Python libraries such as pandas provide a range of transformation functions and operations to allow you to perform data transformation tasks efficiently.

> **Important note**
>
> Data preparation can be a complex and time-consuming process. It can be done at different times during data analysis. You may choose to perform data preparation prior to loading data into BigQuery for exploration. Alternatively, you may choose to prepare, cleanse, and transform data after understanding your data and doing exploration. These steps are not always performed in a linear fashion – it is important to be flexible and iterative!

By adopting one or many of the previously described data preparation approaches in conjunction with a data preparation tool, you can ensure that your data is sampled, integrated, cleansed, and transformed effectively. These approaches lay the foundation for reliable data analysis, enabling you to derive accurate insights from properly prepared datasets. Now, we will shift from introducing approaches to introducing tools for data preparation.

Data preparation tools

BigQuery integrates with various data preparation tools, allowing you to enhance your data preparation workflow. In this section, we will explore some of the popular data preparation tools that can be used with BigQuery. These tools can help to reduce the time and effort required to prepare data, along with improving the accuracy of the data preparation process.

Visual data preparation tools

Google Cloud Dataprep (`https://cloud.google.com/dataprep`) is a visual, web-based data preparation tool that enables you to explore, clean, and transform data. It offers a wide range of data transformation capabilities allowing you to perform tasks such as data cleansing, deduplication, and data enrichment. Dataprep is easy for you to navigate through the data preparation process without the need for coding. Dataprep has native integration with Google Cloud services such as Google Cloud Storage, Dataflow, Sheets, and BigQuery. The native integrations enable you to import data from files and tables, perform data transformations, and export the cleaned data back to BigQuery or other services for further analysis or retention.

In Dataprep, you create a **flow**, which is a visual pipeline to connect, transform, and export your data. You can easily connect to data Google Cloud Storage, Sheets, and BigQuery to preview and import data and add to a flow. After creating a flow, you can edit the **recipe**. The recipe is where you visually analyze and identify preparation and manipulation opportunities across your tables. Within the recipe view, you can browse column details such as unique values, distribution, and patterns; replace, standardize, and change column types; add columns, and much more. After the recipe is created, you can run it and publish results back to Cloud Storage or a BigQuery table. Cloud Dataprep's integration makes it easy to import, manipulate, prepare, and publish data back to BigQuery for analysis and exploration. We will explore Dataprep more in *Chapter 9, Cleansing and Transforming Data*.

Another visual preparation tool available in the Cloud console is **Cloud Data Fusion** (`https://cloud.google.com/data-fusion`). Cloud Data Fusion is a powerful data integration and preparation tool that enables you to build data pipelines and perform data preparation tasks. With Cloud Data Fusion you can extract data from various sources, transform it, and load it into BigQuery for analysis. Different from Cloud Dataprep, Data Fusion provides more capabilities for building ETL pipelines (as we covered in *Chapter 4, Loading and Transforming Data*) and connecting external data sources.

Cloud Data Fusion has a collection of pre-built connectors for various data sources, including databases, cloud storage, and streaming platforms [2]. These connectors make it easy to access a wide range of databases and platforms allowing you to integrate and combine data from multiple sources. Data Fusion also includes built-in transformations and functions to manipulate and transform data. These transformations include cleansing, filtering, aggregation, joining, and more. The tool provides a visual interface to define and configure these transformations, making it easy to utilize API-based services, standardize data formats, and enrich your data. The ability to visually set up a full ETL pipeline without code can be very appealing to accelerate integrations and get data into BigQuery faster. For the complete list of Data Fusion plugins that can help integrate and transform data for BigQuery, review the plugin page (`https://cloud.google.com/data-fusion/plugins`).

Query and code-based tools

In addition to visual preparation tools, there are query and code-based tools that enable a more advanced and flexible data preparation option for specific users. These tools provide data analysts and data engineers the ability to use SQL skills and coding expertise to perform data transformations and integrations.

SQL queries serve as the foundation and entry point for data preparation at times. SQL DML statements enable you to perform a wide range of operations, such as `INSERT`, `DELETE`, `UPDATE`, and `MERGE`, enabling data cleaning, filtering, aggregation, and joining within SQL. You can leverage various DML statements and SQL functions and operators to handle data quality issues, perform calculations, and apply transformations. For example, imagine a scenario where you wanted to remove rows from a table where there were null values in an age column:

```
DELETE FROM `data-exploration-and-prep-w-bq.collisions.data_2`
WHERE victim_age IS NULL
```

This query would remove all rows where there is a `NULL` value in the `victim_age` column, reducing the number of rows in your table if any `NULL` values exist, using the `DELETE` DML statement [3].

Automated data preparation

Cloud Dataflow, based on the open source Apache Beam software [4], is a powerful tool for batch and stream data processing and preparation for BigQuery. Dataflow provides a programming model that allows you to express transformations in Java, Python, and other supported languages. With Dataflow you can create automated data pipelines that perform complex transformations and aggregations on your BigQuery data. Dataflow supports large-scale data preparation tasks and real-time data processing. In Apache Beam, a pipeline is a graph of transformations applied to collections of data. A collection is called a **Pcollection** and transforms are called **Ptransforms** [1]. You can write Ptransforms or use the Apache Beam SDK's library. Some of the available Ptransforms in Apache Beam include filtering out elements that do not match, grouping elements by key, and counting elements in a collection. Dataflow is a service that should be considered for large-scale integration and streaming scenarios.

Dataplex is a data fabric that can bring together distributed data sources and automate data governance and management. Dataplex simplifies data management by automating the tasks involved including data quality checks, data profiling, and data lineage tracking. This service can automate many of the data quality and integrity validation tasks that should be performed on data prior to analysis. Dataplex can run on a schedule and enforce governance policies to make sure data meets quality rules, compliance, and data security requirements.

Google Cloud Functions and **Cloud Run** are serverless environments that enable you to run code in response to events or HTTP requests. These tools can be utilized for data loading and preparation tasks in BigQuery. For example, when a new file (perhaps a CSV containing rows of data) is uploaded to a Cloud Storage bucket, a Cloud Function or Cloud Run container can be triggered to load the data into BigQuery, perform transformations, and update the relevant tables.

Python is a common programming language for data analysis and manipulation and is widely used in data science. Libraries such as pandas and NumPy provide tools for data cleansing, transformation, and manipulation. With the ability to use the BigQuery Python client library, you can leverage the extensive capabilities of Python libraries to prepare your data. Using Python, you can write custom scripts to perform complex data transformations, handle missing values, perform statistical computations, and more. Python offers a flexible code-based option for preprocessing and preparing data before and after querying it from BigQuery, and its ecosystem of data analysis and visualization libraries can further enhance the data preparation process for BigQuery.

Summary

In this chapter, we outlined the different approaches and considerations for getting started with data preparation. We went over the various tools that can support you in your data preparation process. By understanding the available options for data preparation, you are now more equipped to process and interpret large, complex, raw data. As you have seen, the options for data preparation range from visual web-based to code-based variants to fit all analyst skill and experience levels.

In the next chapter, we will go in depth into data preparation using SQL and visual tools to ready you with repeatable approaches for cleansing and preparing your data.

Further reading

1. *Cloud Data Fusion*: https://cloud.google.com/data-fusion

2. *Cloud Data Fusion Plugins*: https://cloud.google.com/data-fusion/plugins

3. *BigQuery explained: How to run data manipulation statements to add, modify and delete data stored in BigQuery*: https://cloud.google.com/blog/topics/developers-practitioners/bigquery-explained-data-manipulation-dml

4. *About data profiling*: https://cloud.google.com/dataplex/docs/data-profiling-overview

5. *Programming model for Apache Beam*: https://cloud.google.com/dataflow/docs/concepts/beam-programming-model

6. *Auto data quality overview*: https://cloud.google.com/dataplex/docs/auto-data-quality-overview

9
Cleansing and Transforming Data

Data engineers and analysts can spend massive amounts of time transforming, cleaning, and preparing data. They know it is not possible to generate accurate reporting and models with corrupted or incomplete data. With the variability of systems reports, you will likely encounter datasets that need to be manipulated in your future as a data analyst. In this chapter, we will dive deeper into data preparation. We will focus on cleansing and transforming data and provide you with approaches, strategies, and repeatable code and guidance that will help you improve the quality of your data in BigQuery.

Cleansing and transforming data can be done at various times in the data life cycle. Also known as data pre-processing, the goal of cleansing and transforming data is to enhance the performance of your data. We touched on transforming data alongside the loading process in *Chapter 4, Loading and Transforming Data*. Now, we will continue and discuss cleansing and transforming data in greater detail for optimizing table data after data loading and initial exploration. This chapter will prepare you with the necessary skills to handle situations that you will encounter as you work to refine your query results and data visualization accuracy. This chapter will build upon the previous chapter, *Chapter 8, An Overview of Data Preparation Tools*, and specifically outline how to clean and transform data to accelerate and execute specific data preparation efforts.

In this chapter, we will go over the following topics:

- Using ELT for cleansing and transforming data
- Assessing dataset integrity
- Using SQL for data cleansing and transformation
- Using Cloud Dataprep for visual cleansing and transformation

At the end of this chapter, you will better understand how to fit data cleansing and transformation into your workflow as a data analyst. You will understand how to assess your dataset's quality and integrity and how to perform specific cleansing and transformation on your data using SQL and other tools. Let's get started!

Technical requirements

In this chapter, we will use the NYPD (Police Department) Motor Vehicle Collisions – Crashes dataset (`https://data.cityofnewyork.us/Public-Safety/Motor-Vehicle-Collisions-Crashes/h9gi-nx95`) provided by the New York Open Data Catalog: `https://opendata.cityofnewyork.us`.

You may wish to load this data into BigQuery to work through the cleansing and transformation examples provided in this chapter as being hands-on with this chapter's content will help reinforce the concepts. You may reference the hands-on exercise loading data guide in *Chapter 4, Loading and Transforming Data*. The raw data is available at the preceding link, as well as this book's GitHub repository: `https://github.com/PacktPublishing/Data-Exploration-and-Preparation-with-BigQuery/releases`. You can download the dataset locally, upload it to a **Google Cloud Storage** (**GCS**) bucket, then create a new table in BigQuery using the GCS bucket and file as a source.

Using ELT for cleansing and transforming data

ELT is the modern approach to the older process of **extract, transform, and load** (ETL), where transformations take place *before* the data is loaded into the data warehouse. The difference with the **extract, load, and transform** (ELT) approach is that it allows for cleansing and transformation to happen *inside* the data warehouse. In this section, we will focus on transformation and cleansing *after* your data has already been loaded.

> **Why has ELT gained in popularity over ETL?**
>
> ELT is being adopted more frequently due to several advancements in data processing and computing infrastructure. ELT is less complex to manage and can deliver the same results as ETL. Compute resources have become much more accessible, flexible, and cheaper in the past decade, with cloud computing allowing for more data transformation work to be done within the data warehouse. Analytics infrastructure and enterprise data warehouses now run on hyperscaler providers' data centers instead of within companies' owned and operated facilities. Today's modern data warehouses are very easy to bring online and fully operationalize and they can process petabytes of data rapidly. The democratization of compute and analytics resources has made it easier to run data transformations and execute machine learning pipelines with a few lines of SQL.

The ELT process starts with extracting data from the source, loading it into the target database, and then transforming and cleaning data *within* the data warehouse. Data is transferred once, from source to target. The extract and load steps can be simplified and bundled together with automation and tools. When done manually, the extract and load steps are typically decoupled. The transformation steps will help you reach higher levels of accuracy with reporting and visualizations. Transformations may perform data integrations, aggregation, data conversion, and quality checking.

Transforms in BigQuery for ELT can be accomplished by stored procedures or scheduled queries, as covered in *Chapter 4, Loading and Transforming Data*, that automatically perform common data transformations (for example, dropping null columns, joining tables, and flattening nested data) with no coding required beyond SQL. ELT is great if you are migrating to BigQuery and do not have experience with other ETL tools such as Dataflow (Apache Beam) or Spark for data processing. It is especially useful for regular data preparation tasks in automatically updating tables. Implementing an automated ELT approach can help data scientists and engineers who may not want to spend time developing code for common data engineering tasks.

Automating ELT can be done in various ways with BigQuery. In *Chapter 4, Loading and Transforming Data*, we introduced **BigQuery Data Transfer Service** (**BQDTS**), a managed ingestion service for BigQuery that eliminates the need for manual source data extraction. This service handles the extract and load steps in ELT and can greatly simplify your data ingestion processes if your source is supported. To review supported data sources, visit the BQDTS documentation page at `https://cloud.google.com/bigquery/docs/dts-introduction`. If you have determined that your data source is supported by BQDTS, you can set up a managed ELT pipeline with BQDTS and use scheduled queries or stored procedures to perform data cleansing and transformation tasks.

> **Important note**
>
> There are third-party transfer services that can help with extracting, ingesting, and loading data in BigQuery. You can view the available option in the Google Cloud Marketplace: `https://cloud.google.com/bigquery/docs/third-party-transfer`. Beyond Google-provided services, other SaaS ETL/ELT services offer managed data pipelines and integrate seamlessly with BigQuery. These services simplify the integration of source and target data by offering pre-built connectors for common data services. Consider these options to accelerate your data analysis efforts and regularly rehydrate your data to create a streaming near real-time enterprise data warehouse.

See the following diagram for a visual representation of managed automated ELT using BQDTS. After data is transferred from the source table, you will have a target raw data table in BigQuery. This can be your master table, protected and only accessed by the data team. Scheduled queries and stored procedures can create additional new transformed tables for use cases such as removing **personally identifiable information** (**PII**) from customer records, correcting data types and missing values, or creating custom views or reports for different business users:

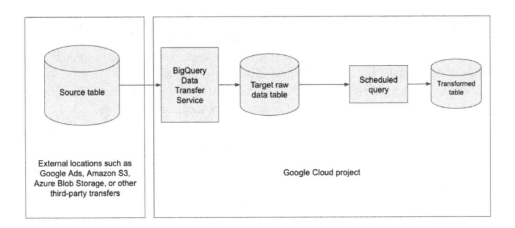

Figure 9.1 – Automated ELT in BigQuery using scheduled queries

For more complex automated ELT pipelines in BigQuery, you may want to consider using BigQuery stored procedures. Each stored procedure is self-contained and allows you to modularize a transformation pipeline. The automated ELT approach of using stored procedures is more extensible as it allows you to call as many or as few stored procedures that may be required for data transformation. You can prebuild and combine various stored procedures and they can be run manually, programmatically, or scheduled. This approach opens opportunities to script and automate the pipeline to run according to your needs. For example, you can call a stored procedure through a scheduled query in the BigQuery console, through the BigQuery command line using a Bash script, or via the BigQuery API.

See the following diagram for an example of a scalable advanced automated ELT pipeline in BigQuery. This approach also uses BQDTS to extract and load an external data source and uses stored procedures to join tables and prepare data cleansing, dropping null values in the table:

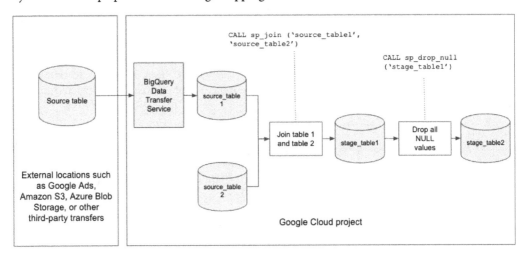

Figure 9.2 – A more scalable advanced automated ELT pipeline in BigQuery using stored procedures

Dataform is another option for creating data transformations and preparation workflows. Dataform uses Dataform Core, an open source SQL-based language for managing transformations. Dataform is fully managed and integrates with GitHub and GitLab for version-controlled repositories for data engineering teams to collaborate on transformation pipelines. You can learn more about Dataform by reading the official docs: `https://cloud.google.com/dataform`.

In this section, we reviewed the ELT approach and its value for cleansing and transforming data in BigQuery. By using ELT in your data preparation workflow, you can start transforming data with your existing SQL experience. Automated tasks for data transformation can be executed in a self-contained flexible manner using features such as stored procedures, scheduled queries, and Dataform all within the BigQuery console. Next up, we'll review dataset integrity and provide some methods for determining the level and frequency of data preparation that may be required on your datasets in BigQuery.

Assessing dataset integrity

Dataset integrity refers to the quality and consistency of data within a dataset. It is the assurance that the data is accurate, complete, reliable, and free from errors or inconsistencies. Understanding your data's integrity is important for ensuring the quality and usability of data and determining to what degree you will need to cleanse or transform data. A dataset with poor integrity can lead to incorrect analysis, inaccurate reports, and misinformed business decisions. There are several ways to assess dataset integrity. In this section, we will discuss techniques and considerations for assessing dataset integrity in BigQuery.

The shape of the dataset

Understanding your dataset's shape helps you form a baseline expectation for the quality of results you will receive from queries. Consider *Figure 9.3*. Your dataset may be taller than wide, indicating a lot of rows and few columns. This may present a situation where you want to join your tall table to expand the number of rows in your query. A wide but short dataset means you have many columns but not a lot of rows or records to analyze. In the case of a wide shape, you would want to seek more data to append or transform your table for better insights [1]:

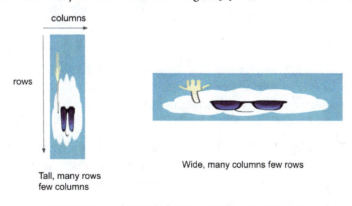

Figure 9.3 – A dataset's shape – visual representation

Skew of the dataset

Dataset skew is an important concept to understand when cleansing and preparing data for analysis. **Skew** refers to the asymmetry of the distribution of values in a dataset. A dataset is said to be skewed if most of the values are clustered around one side of the distribution, while the remaining values are spread out on the other side. This can be caused by several factors, such as outliers, errors in data entry, or the natural distribution of the data.

Data profiling

Data profiling is an approach to analyzing the dataset and understanding its characteristics. It provides insights into the structure, content, and quality of your data. BigQuery has functions that can help with data profiling. Functions such as COUNT, AVG, MIN, MAX, and SUM can be used to calculate basis statistics on numerical columns. These statistics can reveal the distribution and variability of the data. Data profiling can also be done with visual data preparation tools, as we will discuss later in this chapter.

Data validation

Data validation involves verifying the accuracy, correctness, and consistency of the data against specific rules or constraints. Validation makes sure that your data adheres to specific requirements and business rules. In BigQuery, you can perform data validation using SQL operators such as NOT NULL and the DISTINCT function. For example, you can filter out rows with NULL in the age column and count users from unique or distinct countries:

```
-- Select all columns where column age has data
SELECT *
FROM project.dataset.table
WHERE age IS NOT NULL;
-- Count unique country records from user table
SELECT COUNT(DISTINCT country)
FROM project.dataset.users
```

Data visualization

Data visualizations can also help assess the quality of your datasets. Visualizations such as histograms and scatter plots can uncover patterns, trends, and outliers in your data. Consider using a visualization tool to determine your data quality before embarking on a journey of data cleaning and transformation. We discussed visualization tools in *Chapter 7, Further Exploring and Visualizing Data*.

It is important to know the quality of your data as a data analyst. By applying these approaches and checking your dataset's integrity, you can identify and address data issues, ensure the reliability of the data, and lay a strong foundation for your subsequent data cleansing and transformation tasks.

Using SQL for data cleansing and transformation

Data cleansing and data transformation are two main steps in the data preparation process. Data cleansing is the process of identifying and correcting errors in data, while data transformation is the process of converting data from one format or structure into another.

Here are some common examples of data cleansing tasks:

- Identifying and correcting typos
- Filling in missing values
- Formatting data consistently
- Removing duplicate records

Here are some examples of data transformation tasks:

- Converting data from one format to another
- Aggregating data (for example, summing sales figures by month)
- Normalizing data (for example, converting all dates into the same format)
- Formatting data for visualizations or machine learning

Now that you understand some scenarios where data cleansing and transformation would be useful, let's look into some examples using SQL so that you understand approaches and where to get started.

SQL data cleansing strategies and examples

Data cleansing involves identifying and resolving data quality issues, inconsistencies, and inaccuracies to ensure accurate and reliable analysis. Let's explore various data cleansing techniques using SQL in BigQuery, followed by examples for you to try on your own.

Removing duplicates

Duplicates in a dataset can distort analysis results and lead to inaccurate insights. BigQuery provides SQL functions and statements to identify and remove records:

```
## Identify duplicate records based on specific columns
SELECT column1, column2, COUNT(*)
FROM project.dataset.table
GROUP BY column1, column2
HAVING COUNT(*) > 1 ;
## Remove duplicates based on specific columns
DELETE FROM dataset.table
WHERE (column1, column2) IN (
```

```
SELECT column1, column2
FROM project.dataset.table
GROUP BY column1, column2
HAVING COUNT(*) > 1)
```

You can run these queries independently or together. These examples show how to identify duplicate records by grouping columns of interest and how to use the HAVING clause to filter records with a count greater than one. The second query shows how to remove duplicates by deleting the identified duplicate records.

Handling missing values

Missing values are a common data quality issue that needs to be addressed during data cleansing. BigQuery has SQL functions to handle missing values effectively. In the first example, the COALESCE function replaces missing values in column1 with the specified string value, Unknown:

```
## Replace missing values with a default value Unknown
SELECT COALESCE (column1, 'Unknown') AS column1

FROM project.dataset.table;
```

The second example demonstrates removing rows with missing values using the DELETE statement and the IS NULL condition:

```
## Remove rows with missing values
DELETE FROM project.dataset.table

WHERE column1 IS NULL
```

The third example uses the LAST VALUE function with the IGNORE NULLS clause to fill missing values in column1 with the previous non-null value based on a specified sorting column:

```
## Fill missing values with the previous non-null value in a column
SELECT column1,
    LAST_VALUE (column1 IGNORE NULLS) OVER (ORDER BY       sorting_
column) AS filled_column1
FROM project.dataset.table
```

These examples can help with common data cleansing tasks when rows are missing values.

Standardizing and formatting data

Standardizing and formatting data is essential to ensure consistency and accuracy in your datasets. SQL provides functions and expressions to achieve data standardization and formatting.

Consider the following examples:

```
## Convert text to lowercase or uppercase
SELECT LOWER(column1) as columns1_lower,
UPPER (column2) as columns2_upper
FROM project.dataset.table;
```

You can use the LOWER function to convert all characters in a string into lowercase. This may be helpful when you're dealing with case-insensitive data searches or comparisons:

```
## Format date column to a specific pattern
SELECT FORMAT_DATETIME ('%Y-%m-%d', date_column) AS formatted_date
FROM project.dataset.table
```

In these examples, the LOWER and UPPER functions convert text columns into lowercase and uppercase. The FORMAT_DATETIME function formats date_column with the specified pattern (YYYY-MM-DD). There are many different DATETIME functions; for more information, check out the BigQuery docs: https://cloud.google.com/bigquery/docs/reference/standard-sql/datetime_functions.

The following code snippet shows how you can use the CONCAT function to combine data from multiple columns into a single column, including columns of different data types. It can be used for creating new attributes or exporting data:

```
## Combine first and last name columns in a table
SELECT CONCAT(first_name,' ' last_name) AS full_name
FROM project.dataset.table
```

Correcting inconsistent values

Inconsistent values can negatively impact accurate analysis, and SQL in BigQuery offers various ways to correct them. One common approach is using conditional statements or expressions to correct values based on an allowable range. Consider the following example:

```
## Correct inconsistent values using a CASE statement
SELECT columns1,
CASE
WHEN column1 = 'ValueA' THEN 'ValueX'
WHEN column1 = 'ValueB' THEN 'ValueY'
ELSE column1
END AS corrected_column1
FROM project.datatset.table
```

In this example, the CASE statement checks the value of column1 and assigns a corrected value based on specific conditions. Any values not specified in the WHEN clauses remain unchanged.

SQL data transformation strategies and examples

As mentioned previously, data transformation involves modifying the structure, format, or values of the dataset to meet specific requirements and support your analysis. In this section, we will explore a few data transformation techniques using SQL in BigQuery.

Aggregation and grouping

This involves grouping data and summarizing it. You can use the GROUP BY clause to group data by a common value, and the SUM function to calculate the sum of the values in a group. This allows you to summarize data and derive insights per group of data:

```
## Summarize data by grouping and calculating totals
SELECT category, SUM(quantity) AS total_quantity
FROM project.dataset.table
GROUP BY category;
## Count records by grouping
SELECT country, COUNT(*) AS record_count
FROM project.dataset.table
GROUP BY country
```

Joins and combining tables

Combining data from multiple tables is sometimes necessary for comprehensive analysis. Joins are common for enriching data, bringing in another perspective, and extending dataset usability and value. SQL provides various join operations to merge tables based on shared columns or relationships.

In this example, the first query demonstrates an inner join, combining records from table1 and table2 based on shared_column. Only the matching records are returned:

```
## Perform an inner join
SELECT t1.column1, t2.column2
FROM table1 AS t1
INNER JOIN table2 AS t2
ON t1.shared_column = t2.shared_column;
```

The second query shows a left join, which receives all records from table1 and matching records from table2 based on the shared column. If no match is found, NULL values are returned for the table2 columns:

```
## Perform a left join
SELECT t1.column1, t2.column2
```

```
FROM table1 AS t1
LEFT JOIN table2 as t2
ON t1.shared_column = t2.shared_column
```

These are two different joins that give you options for matching and returning data.

Conditional transformations

SQL allows you to apply conditional transformations to create new values based on specific conditions. This is useful when you're creating calculated columns or transforming data based on specific criteria.

In this first example, a calculated column called `category` is created using a `CASE` statement. The `column2` values are evaluated and `category` is assigned based on specific conditions. This SQL conditional transformation is like conditional formatting in spreadsheets in Google Sheets or Microsoft Excel:

```
## Create a calculated column using a CASE statement
SELECT column1,
CASE
WHEN column2 > 100 THEN 'High'
WHEN column2 > 50 THEN 'Medium'
ELSE 'Low'
END as category
FROM project.dataset.table;
```

The second example shows a math expression by multiplying `column2` by the `conversion_rate` column to create a new column called `converted_value`:

```
## Perform mathematical expressions
SELECT column1, (column2 * converstion_rate) AS converted_value
FROM project.dataset.table
```

Data type conversion

Data type conversion may be necessary to ensure compatibility or facilitate specific operations in your queries. If you wish to perform string manipulations or calculations, your column data types need to be set correctly:

```
## Convert a string column to a numeric data type
SELECT column1,
CAST(column2 AS INT64) AS numeric_column
FROM project.dataset.table;
## Convert a numeric column to a string data type
SELECT column1,
CAST(column2 AS STRING) AS string_column
FROM project.dataset.table
```

The CAST function converts the data type of `column2` into `INT64` and `STRING`, allowing for integer and text manipulation and aggregation. The CAST function can convert strings and integers and also strings into datetime data types and vice versa.

Writing query results

Now that you understand the different data cleansing and transformation opportunities in BigQuery using SQL, you have options to write these results to new or existing tables. In your query, you can include your query in the CREATE TABLE function to create a new table in your dataset that contains the query results. Here's an example:

```
## Create a new table with query results
CREATE TABLE nyc_collisions.smaller_table AS (
  SELECT CRASH_DATE, CRASH_TIME, BOROUGH, CONTRIBUTING_FACTOR_
VEHICLE_1, VEHICLE_TYPE_CODE_1
FROM `data-exploration-and-prep-w-bq.nyc_collisions.raw_data`
);
```

This query will create a smaller table in the `nyc_collisions` dataset. This may allow for more refined analysis and reporting.

Using the UPDATE command, you can modify and standardize row data. For example, if your table data contained mixed full and abbreviated street details, you may consider using the UPDATE command to standardize on a common value:

```
## Change all occurrences of 'RICHMOND AVENUE' to 'RICHMOND AVE'
UPDATE `data-exploration-and-prep-w-bq.nyc_collisions.raw_data`
SET ON_STREET_NAME = 'RICHMOND AVE' WHERE ON_STREET_NAME ='RICHMOND
AVENUE'
```

For more on writing query results, review the BigQuery documentation: `https://cloud.google.com/bigquery/docs/writing-results`.

By understanding and using these data transformation techniques with SQL in BigQuery, you can reshape and restructure your data, combine and join tables, derive new calculated columns, and ensure data compatibility enabling strong analysis and rich insights. As a data analyst, you have options and flexibility for your data life cycle activities. In the next section, we will review visual cleansing and transformation using Cloud Dataprep.

Using Cloud Dataprep for visual cleansing and transformation

Visual data preparation tools provide an alternative to SQL-driven data preparation. These tools offer a **graphical user interface** (**GUI**) that allows data analysts and business users to interactively visualize, clean, and transform data without extensive SQL knowledge. In this section, we will go over Cloud Dataprep so that you have an additional option to clean and transform your data in BigQuery.

Previously introduced in *Chapter 8, An Overview of Data Preparation Tools*, Cloud Dataprep, by Trifacta, is a data preparation tool that simplifies the process of cleaning and transforming data. It provides a visual interface that automatically suggests transformations, detects data quality issues, and offers smart recommendations to enhance the data cleansing process. Users can interactively explore the data, apply wrangling steps, and preview the transformed data in real time before committing to existing or new tables. Let's look at the process of transforming data in Cloud Dataprep.

Cloud Dataprep calls the process of transforming data a **flow**. This flow includes a dataset, a recipe with transformation actions, and an output. Cloud Dataprep's native integration with BigQuery makes it easy to connect data and import datasets from Google Cloud Storage, Google Sheets, and BigQuery:

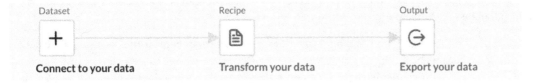

Figure 9.4 – Cloud Dataprep's flow process for data transformation

Regarding the flow process in Cloud Dataprep, note that this tool is essentially performing ETL, the data transformation approach we discussed earlier in this chapter and *Chapter 4, Loading and Transforming Data*. Using Cloud Dataprep, you can see how a visual tool can greatly simplify the ETL process and be a very powerful option and an alternative approach to the ELT and transformations within BigQuery in SQL that were suggested earlier in this chapter.

Once you have connected your BigQuery dataset, you can preview data and edit and create recipes (see *Figure 9.5*). **Recipes** are fundamental components that drive the data preparation process in this tool. A recipe represents a series of data transformation steps that are applied to the raw data to clean, enrich, and shape it into a more structured and useful format. Transformations such as statistical operations, aggregations, and data manipulations can be done in a drag-and-drop approach, making it accessible to both technical and non-technical users:

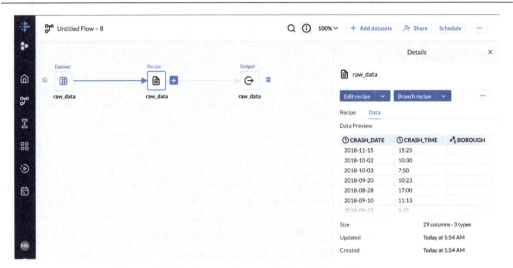

Figure 9.5 – Previewing imported data in Cloud Dataprep

With recipes, you can quickly explore BigQuery data, identify patterns, handle missing values, remove duplicates, and perform various data cleansing and transformation tasks without the need for any complex coding or SQL. Additionally, recipes can be saved, shared, and reused, allowing for consistent and automated data preparation workflows.

Before creating a recipe, Cloud Dataprep makes it easy to perform **data profiling** on your source data so that you can gain insights into its quality. As seen in *Figure 9.6*, The initial data view before creating transformations with recipes lets you see column data types and value distribution and ranges for your columns, giving you an idea of the shape and skew of your data:

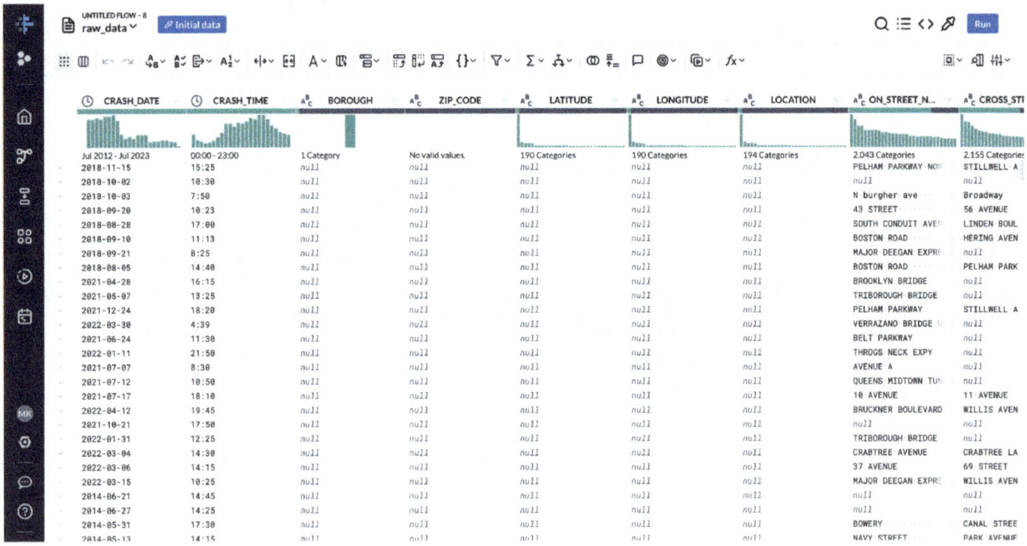

Figure 9.6 – An overview of exploring the distribution of values in Cloud Dataprep

Upon review of the initial data, you can see that Cloud Dataprep only takes a limited initial sample (about 10,000 rows) for you to determine what type of transformations may be required for your data. This is intended to be a snapshot of the overall quality and patterns in your dataset. There may be cases where you want to collect an additional sample of your dataset before creating transformations so that Cloud Dataprep can better understand your data. Within the tool, you can collect a new sample with various methods such as random, first rows, filter-based, anomaly-based, stratified or distinct value layers, or cluster-based. In some cases, collecting additional samples may give you more insights into the quality of your data before you build your recipe:

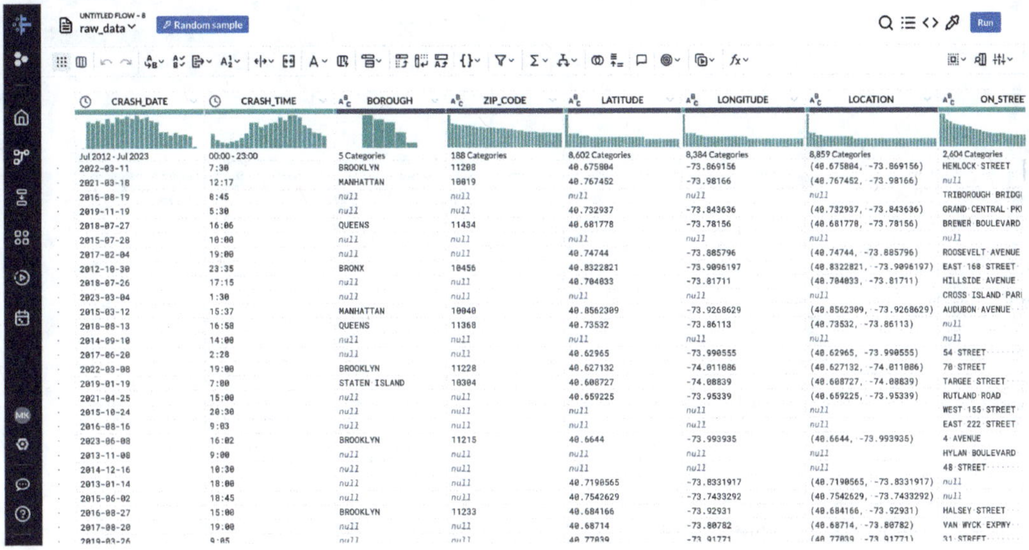

Figure 9.7 – An overview of data profiling in Cloud Dataprep using a random sample

Taking a second sample of the NYC Collison data provides a better snapshot of the quality of the dataset, showing that there are values in every column, only missing data in rows. In the first sample, ZIP_CODE showed no valid values, which was an indicator that there may be a data quality issue. By taking a second sample of data, you can see there are values in every column. This dataset has over 2 million rows and the sample that was taken in Cloud DataPrep was only around 10,000, so the first sample was misrepresentative of the entire dataset.

> **Note**
>
> Behind the scenes of Cloud Dataprep, the tool uses Cloud Dataflow (Apache Beam) to extract data, take a sample for preparation, and ultimately execute transformation and processing tasks.

Figure 9.8 shows how Cloud Dataprep allows you to select a column and perform more data profiling, revealing more detail about your data quality and value distributions:

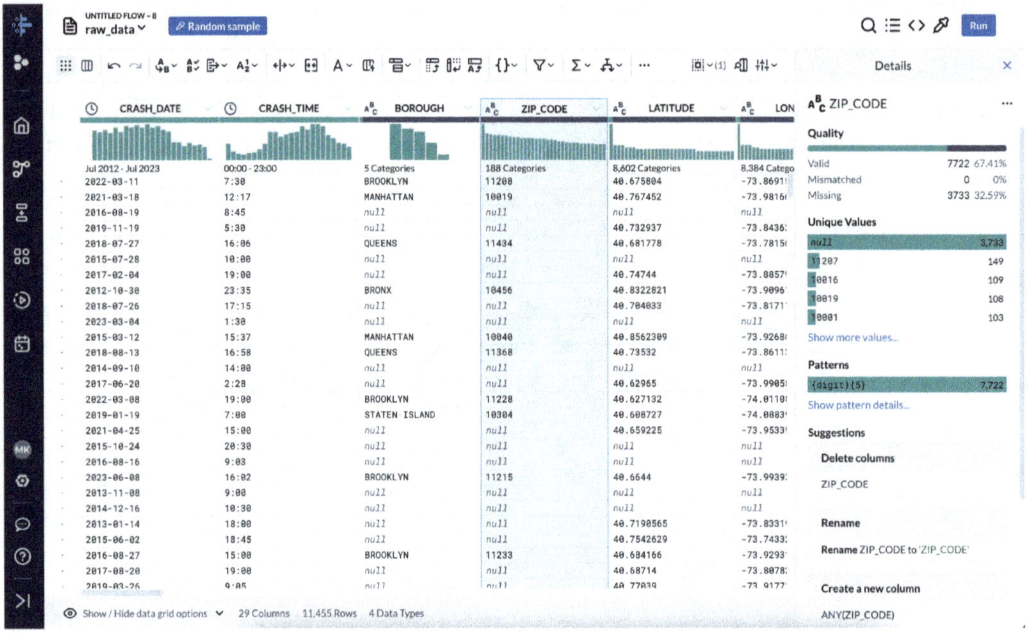

Figure 9.8 – An overview of selecting a column to do more granular data profiling

After data profiling and determining our data quality, we are ready to create a recipe to begin transforming our data. One common transformation step is replacing null values with a specified value. In Cloud Dataprep, you can specify a custom value and preview how the new value will look in your table data. In this transformation, we are only transforming STRING (ABC) columns with the new value, NA:

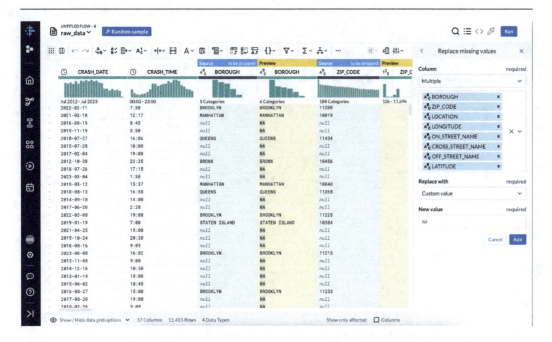

Figure 9.9 – An overview of data cleansing in Cloud Dataprep, replacing null values

It is important to note this text transformation was done only on STRING columns. When creating cleansing and transformation recipes in Cloud Dataprep, you will want to decide if you want to create a standard replacement for all NULL values, such as 0, that can span STRING and INT columns, or use something such as NA for STRING columns and 0 for INT columns.

Cloud Dataprep gives you a formula, schema, comment, condition, find and replace, filter, extract, format, combine, merge, pivot, split, standardize, and many other functions that can be performed on individual or multiple columns. As you create steps in a recipe, Cloud Dataprep lets you preview what the changes will look like in your table. After your recipe is complete, it contains all of the steps and transformations that may be needed, and you are then ready to run the recipe on your imported data:

Figure 9.10 – An overview of finalized recipe in Cloud Dataflow

After completing your recipe and clicking **Run**, you will be presented with several options. The default running environment for the transformations is Dataflow and BigQuery. There are also options for profiling the job results, validating schema match, ignoring errors, and failing if the schema has changed since import. The default option for publishing your transformed data is using GCS with the CSV file format. This would require you to import the transformed data in the BigQuery console. Instead, you can change the publishing action to **Append-BigQuery**, after which Cloud Dataflow can create a new table and write dataset changes to that new table:

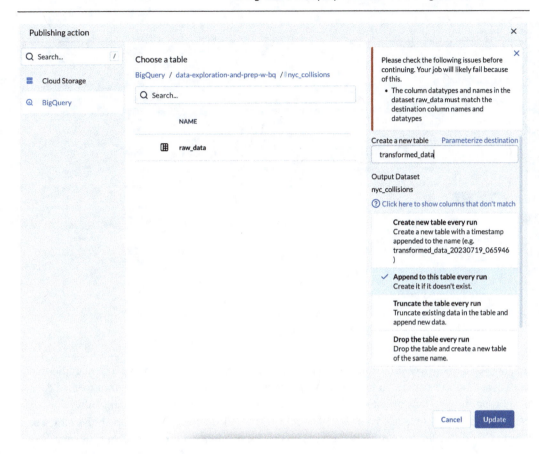

Figure 9.11 – Modifying the publishing action in Cloud Dataprep to create a new BigQuery table

After the publishing action has been updated, the job is ready to run. On the **Job** page in Cloud Dataprep, you can monitor the execution stages and progress during execution. After the job is complete, you can preview the output data and verify your transformations:

Figure 9.12 – An overview of Cloud Dataprep completed job

There may be cases where your transformations do not complete, or you wish to perform additional cleansing and transformation. In this case, you can go back, create a new flow on the transformed data, and apply additional transformations. You may have missed a column when replacing null values or determined that you would like your data to be transformed in another way. You can always return to a flow in Cloud Dataflow and modify the steps in a recipe or adjust and rerun your transformations.

After completing data cleansing and transformation in Cloud Dataprep, you can continue to assess additional transformation tasks that are necessary for your datasets. You may determine that you need to modify table column names so that they match other datasets so that you can perform JOINs to enrich data. You may decide that you want to drop columns and create a smaller dataset for analysis. You may return to data preparation with Cloud Dataprep after creating queries or visualizations to continue to refine and improve your data quality for better insights and reporting:

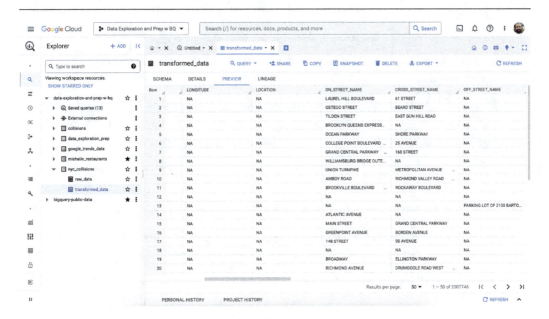

Figure 9.13 – An overview of previewing transformed data in BigQuery after publishing in Cloud Dataprep

Like many steps with exploring and preparing data, data cleansing and transformation is an iterative process and more of a practice. Data preparation can be an ongoing effort. You should continue to work to make sure your data is accurate and reliable so that you can deliver the most impactful results in your data reporting and analysis. BigQuery and Cloud Dataprep enable you to easily execute data cleansing and transformation tasks and manage ETL in a visual no-code way. As you are starting to see, you have options as a data analyst and engineer and BigQuery integrations and services such as Cloud Dataprep make it easy to operationalize data life cycle events such as cleansing and transformations.

Summary

In this chapter, we covered data cleansing and transformation, two critical data preparation steps for data analysis and reporting. We discussed the importance of data quality and introduced several data cleansing and transformation techniques. Then, we demonstrated how to use SQL to cleanse and transform data in BigQuery and introduced Cloud Dataprep as an alternative approach for visual data preparation.

The following are the key takeaways from this chapter:

- Data cleansing and transformation are important steps in the data preparation process
- Data quality issues can negatively impact data analysis and reporting, so it is important to determine the integrity of your data

- SQL is powerful for data cleansing and transformation in BigQuery

- Cloud Dataprep is a visual data preparation tool that simplifies the process of cleaning and transforming data

In the next chapter, we will discuss data preparation best practices and cost control for BigQuery. You will learn about optimizing data preparation and query execution to minimize costs. You will also gain strategies for maximizing the overall value of BigQuery for data preparation.

Further reading

To learn more about the topics that were covered in this chapter, take a look at the following resources:

- *Exploring and Preparing your Data with BigQuery*: `https://www.coursera.org/learn/gcp-exploring-preparing-data-bigquery`

- *What is BigQuery Data Transfer Service?*: `https://cloud.google.com/bigquery/docs/dts-introduction`

- *Datetime functions*: `https://cloud.google.com/bigquery/docs/reference/standard-sql/datetime_functions`

- *Writing query results*: `https://cloud.google.com/bigquery/docs/writing-results`

10

Best Practices for Data Preparation, Optimization, and Cost Control

At a time when compute and storage access is abundant and organizational budgets are slim, knowledge of optimization and cost control practices is critical. In this chapter, we will review best practices for data preparation by focusing on optimizing for data efficiency and performance. We will review best practices and optimization techniques for BigQuery storage and compute analysis, as well as monitoring and controlling costs. We will introduce the many unique cost control and optimization features of BigQuery. The goal of this chapter is to teach you how to use BigQuery cost-effectively.

In this chapter, we will go over the following topics:

- Data preparation best practices
- Best practices for optimizing storage
- Best practices for optimizing compute
- Monitoring and controlling costs

This chapter will serve as a reference for best practices for data preparation as well as cost control for any usage level in BigQuery. Upon completing this chapter, you will be able to implement strategies for optimization and cost control so that you can use BigQuery efficiently.

Technical requirements

In this chapter, we will go over cost optimizations for BigQuery with examples. To get the most out of this chapter, you should have the BigQuery console (`https://console.cloud.google.com/bigquery`) open as you read to test some of the best practices and optimizations to reinforce your learning.

Data preparation best practices

As discussed in previous chapters, data preparation is a critical step to make sure your data is well organized, clean, and optimized for analysis in BigQuery. By following the data preparation best practices listed in this section, you will be ready to perform cost-effective regular operations on BigQuery.

Understanding your data and business requirements

Before doing any data preparation or analysis, you want to have a good understanding of your data and the business questions you wish to answer. It is recommended to have a good idea of your requirements and the opportunities in the data for business insights. Make it your mission to gain insights into the specific identified area of your business and data. This will guide you in designing an appropriate schema and choosing the right data types, which will allow you to operate efficiently and cost-effectively.

Denormalizing your data

Storing related data in the same table can improve performance for queries that access multiple related tables. In older data strategies, when storage was expensive, **database analysts** (**DBAs**) would normalize data or split it into multiple tables to reduce redundant data. We still strive to reduce redundant storage but not so much for cost reasons, mostly for operational reasons such as business agility. The cloud has eliminated the previous need to procure physical **hard disk drives** (**HDDs**) or **solid-state drives** (**SSDs**) in a time when storage was limited. In modern data warehouses, where storage is relatively cheap, denormalization has advantages, such as faster data retrieval, improved read performance, and easier queries (fewer joins).

Optimizing schema design

It is important to thoughtfully design your schema and carefully validate data types and column names when importing data. A well-designed schema is important for efficient and effective data management in BigQuery as it directly impacts query performance, data organization, and overall usability. Use the schema design to enforce data consistency and define appropriate data types. This helps prevent data inconsistencies, reduces data entry errors, and ensures that the data is accurate and reliable.

Considering nested and repeated fields

You may consider nested and repeated fields to preserve the structure of your data and plan for optimized queries. Nested and repeated fields in BigQuery are advanced features that allow you to structure your data in more complex ways than traditional flat tables. They can be incredibly useful in certain scenarios, offering flexibility and efficiency for storing and querying data. Nested fields can help you organize data more efficiently. This structure works well with hierarchical data such as JSON or XML, one-to-many relationships, and data with different attributes. Repeated fields can work well with lists or arrays (items in an order) or aggregated data such as historical price changes. Repeated fields can efficiently store and enable querying of collections without the need for additional tables or joins. Nested and repeated fields can introduce complexities such as more complex queries, and data loading and transformation may require extra steps.

Using correct data types

BigQuery supports a variety of data types and each type has its advantages and disadvantages. Choosing the right data type for each column will improve query performance and results and reduce costs. When loading data into BigQuery, think about the type of queries that you will want to run, match data types with the appropriate columns, and perform data cleansing when necessary.

Data cleansing and validation

Validate your data for accuracy and completeness before loading it into BigQuery if possible. Deal with missing or incorrect values, outliers, and duplicates. *Chapter 9, Cleansing and Transforming Data* can be your guide for this best practice. More on data types can be found in the documentation at `https://cloud.google.com/bigquery/docs/reference/standard-sql/data-types`.

Partitioning and clustering

For large datasets, consider using table partitioning and clustering. Leveraging BigQuery's partitioning and clustering features can significantly boost query performance. Partitioning involves dividing large tables into smaller, manageable portions based on a specific column (for example, a date or timestamp). Clustering organizes data within each partition based on similar values in a designated column. By partitioning and clustering, BigQuery will only scan relevant partitions and clusters. This reduces the amount of data that's processed during queries, which leads to faster and more cost-effective operations. Partition the data based on time or based on ranges of values in `INTEGER` columns for the best performance.

Optimizing data loading

Use batch loading whenever possible as it is more cost-effective than streaming. If you need to stream data, batch the streaming inserts to reduce costs and avoid excessive streaming API calls. Batch loading is free; streaming inserts are charged for rows that are inserted.

By following these data preparation best practices, you will set a foundation for effective exploration and preparation in BigQuery. Next, we will review how to optimize storage and computing layers, which are the main service components of BigQuery.

Best practices for optimizing storage

After preparing and setting up your data, a good area to begin optimizing BigQuery usage is at the **storage layer**. BigQuery storage is relatively low cost, starting at $0.02 per GB per month (comparable to Cloud Storage or Amazon S3 storage costs) with *the first 10 GB of storage per month free*. When getting started with BigQuery, the first 10 GB of storage at no cost is a great advantage and creates a frictionless entry point for cost-conscious individuals and businesses. As you begin to load more data, you will want to be aware of the best practices for optimizing storage to operate efficiently and cost-effectively. In this section, we will highlight some of the best practices for managing your data storage in BigQuery.

When you create a dataset, you can set the default table expiration (refer to *Figure 10.1*). This allows you to set the number of days after creation that the table will be automatically deleted. This is useful for temporary data that does not need to be preserved. You will want to think about how long you need to keep your data, and if the data does not need to be kept indefinitely, then consider setting a table expiration. One scenario could be to set temporary staging tables between the source and target tables during data cleansing or transformation with a standard expiration. If you know the data that's being stored during transformation is temporary, the expiration setting removes the need to manually remove columns once processing has completed and reduces redundant unused table storage. This could be an alternate approach to automation and a best practice set by data engineering teams:

> **Note**
>
> Default table expiration can be set at the dataset level or when the table is created. You can also set expiration on a dataset's default partition. This affects all newly created partitioned tables. Partition expiration time for individual tables can be set when partitioned tables are created.

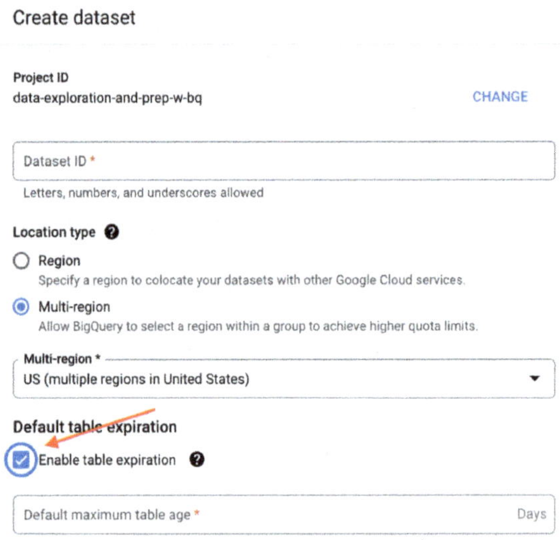

Figure 10.1 – Creating a dataset workflow with the option to set a default table expiration

Setting a table expiration can create an ephemeral life cycle for your data preparation or data management practices. Consider using table expirations on temporary datasets where the data will not need to be preserved.

Long-term and compressed storage

BigQuery has two storage tiers for table data. **Active storage** is the default storage type and includes any table or table partition that has been modified in the last 90 days. This storage is priced as per the actual storage pricing. **Long-term storage** is the storage type for any table or table partition that has not been modified for 90 consecutive days. If you have tables that have not changed for 90 days, the storage price automatically drops by 50% using long-term storage. If a non-partitioned table or table partition is edited, the price reverts to the original storage pricing and the 90-day timer starts again.

Storage pricing happens automatically within BigQuery, so you do not have to set or manage the table storage life cycle. Still, there are some best practices to follow to optimize your usage:

- **Actions that reset the 90-day storage tier timer**: Loading data into a table, copying data into a table, writing query results to a table, using DML or DDL, and streaming data into the table

- **Actions that do not reset the 90-day storage tier timer**: Table queries, creating a view that queries a table, exporting data from a table, and copying a table

BigQuery Compressed Storage, also known as the physical storage billing model, is a pricing model that charges you for the actual amount of storage your data uses after it has been compressed. Compressed Storage can save you money on your BigQuery bills if you have a lot of data that is compressible. This is because many types of data, such as text data and numerical data, can be compressed significantly. To use Compressed Storage, you must enable it for your dataset. Once you have enabled Compressed Storage, your data will be compressed automatically. You will not need to make any changes to your queries or applications.

Cross-cloud data analytics with federated access model and BigQuery Omni

Consider using *external data sources* and federated queries instead of duplicating your data in BigQuery. BigQuery has a *federated data access model* for Google services such as Drive BigTable, Cloud Storage, and Cloud SQL. This option is useful for infrequently changing datasets and allows you to keep the table data and storage where it is currently and only utilize BigQuery's analysis layer to query and return results. External tables are contained in a dataset and you manage them the same way you manage a regular BigQuery table. Federated queries send a query to Cloud SQL or Cloud Spanner and return the results as a temporary table. To determine if you have data in accessible external data sources, review the external data source docs (`https://cloud.google.com/bigquery/docs/external-data-sources`). For accessing data outside of Google services, **BigQuery Omni** allows you to run BigQuery analysis on data stored in Amazon S3 or Azure Blob Storage using BigLake tables.

> **Note**
>
> BigLake tables are an extension of the BigQuery storage layer across clouds (S3, Azure) and open formats. It enables interoperability between data warehouses and data lakes. BigLake lets you manage all data as tables and keep a single copy of your data while still using the powerful management and processing capabilities of BigQuery.

BigQuery Omni is a multi-cloud data tool that allows you to use the same familiar BigQuery interface to access data across clouds. This feature is most useful for organizations that have data in multiple cloud services and can help increase accessibility and insights across organizational data. To further evolve the BigQuery architecture of decoupled compute and storage, BigQuery Omni enables a multi-cloud data warehouse with a data plane performing processing on other clouds. With BigQuery Omni, you do not need to physically move data into BigQuery storage, as analysis and processing happen where the data resides:

> **Note**
>
> With BigQuery Omni, you can use cross-cloud join to query data across clouds in a single SQL statement. This means you do not need to copy data from different cloud platforms or data lakes in AWS S3 or Azure to BigQuery.

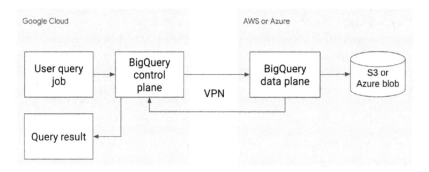

Figure 10.2 – BigQuery Omni data movement for queries

In *Figure 10.2* the diagram shows data movement between Google Cloud and AWS or Azure when using SELECT or CREATE EXTERNAL TABLE statements. The BigQuery console on Google Cloud, also known as the control plane in this architecture, sends a query job for processing to the BigQuery data plane on AWS or Azure. The data plane reads table data from S3 or Azure Blob Storage and runs a query job on the table data. The query result is sent from the data plane back to the control plane via a VPN connection and the query result is returned to the console.

> **Note**
>
> If you wish to automate the transfer of large data files from Amazon S3 to BigQuery regularly, you will want to consider using BigQuery Data Transfer Service, as we covered in *Chapter 4, Loading and Transforming Data*.

BigQuery also supports **cross-cloud operations**, which let you load or copy data from S3 or Azure Blob Storage into BigQuery tables. This is another method to transfer data from other clouds into BigQuery tables. In comparison to BigQuery Omni, where your data stays on other clouds, cross-cloud operations use the LOAD DATA statement to move data to native BigQuery tables.

With federated queries, BigQuery Omni, and cross-cloud operations, you have multiple options and the ability to enable cross-cloud data analytics practices. If your organization's applications or systems run in other clouds, you can export data to their cloud storage service and keep your data warehouse in BigQuery. Multi-cloud data warehousing is an advantage that can accelerate your time to insights and break down data silos.

Backup and recovery

BigQuery has some powerful features for data retention and copying table data:

- **Time travel**: It helps you recover from mistakes such as accidentally changing or deleting data in tables. By default, you can access table data from any point from the past 7 days with this feature. Time travel lets you query table data that was updated or deleted and gives you the ability to restore a table that was deleted or a table that expired. Time travel is a built-in type of column and table retention feature that can be useful during analysis and especially during exploration or preparation of your tables. At the time of writing, you can go back 7 days.

  To use time travel, simply query a table stored in BigQuery using the SYSTEM_TIME AS OF filter. For example, to query time travel data on a table from 1 day ago, do the following:

  ```
  SELECT *
  FROM `project.dataset.table`
  FOR SYSTEM_TIME AS OF TIMESTAMP_SUB(CURRENT_TIMESTAMP(),
  INTERVAL 1 DAY)
  ```

- **Table clones**: Consider using table clones for modifiable copies of production data. You are only charged for the data in a table clone that differs from the clone's base table. This can be a useful cost-saving option for accessing and modifying table data that is used by business-critical applications or dashboards. To clone a table, use the CREATE TABLE CLONE statement. In the query editor in BigQuery, enter and run the following statement:

  ```
  CREATE TABLE
  project.dataset_backup.table_clone
  CLONE project.dataset.table
  ```

- **Table snapshots**: BigQuery table snapshots preserve the contents of a table at a particular time. This allows you to keep a record of a table for longer than 7 days with time travel. You can capture a table's data from a specified time within the past 7 days or the current time and retain it for as long as you want. You can set a table expiration for snapshots as well. You query a table's snapshot the same way you would query a regular table. Snapshots can be created in the cloud console by using the snapshot option on a table view:

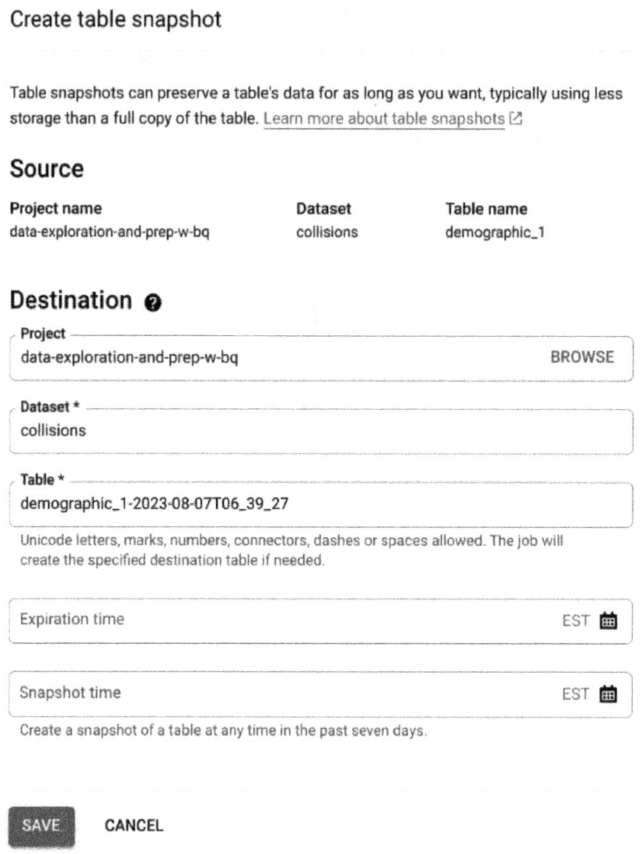

Create table snapshot

Table snapshots can preserve a table's data for as long as you want, typically using less storage than a full copy of the table. Learn more about table snapshots ☑

Source

Project name	Dataset	Table name
data-exploration-and-prep-w-bq	collisions	demographic_1

Destination ❓

Project

data-exploration-and-prep-w-bq   BROWSE

Dataset *

collisions

Table *

demographic_1-2023-08-07T06_39_27

Unicode letters, marks, numbers, connectors, dashes or spaces allowed. The job will create the specified destination table if needed.

Expiration time   EST 📅

Snapshot time   EST 📅

Create a snapshot of a table at any time in the past seven days.

SAVE   CANCEL

Figure 10.3 – BigQuery table snapshot workflow

- **Archive to Cloud Storage**: If you do not want to use time travel, table clones, or snapshots, you can move archival "cold data" from BigQuery to Cloud Storage. You can move data from BigQuery to Cloud Storage from the BigQuery console using the `bq extract` CLI command, export a data SQL statement, or implement BigQuery API. This option can give you an automated way to tier data from BigQuery to Cloud Storage. If your data compresses well, the compressed storage billing model in BigQuery Editions may allow you to reduce your storage cost enough that it does not make sense to move data out of BigQuery.

Now that we have covered storage optimization and best practices, we will cover compute analysis optimization. In the next section, we will give you guidance on how to restructure and refine your queries and choose the right pricing model for your data analysis workflows.

Best practices for optimizing compute

This section covers analysis optimization. Here, you will learn how to plan, adjust, and utilize the greatest amount of cost efficiency in BigQuery. Referred to as compute, analysis, or processing, you have various options and strategies to leverage and consider as you utilize and optimize BigQuery to process your table data.

Analysis cost options

Because of its accessibility and capabilities, BigQuery has been adopted as the primary data platform for users from various data backgrounds and experience levels. Initially, the service was entirely an on-demand pay-as-you-go pricing model. This means you are only billed for what you use and there is a standard service level and features for everyone. Now, in addition to on-demand pricing, with BigQuery Editions, there are options for more demanding and predictable data analytics workloads.

As mentioned previously, query processing costs in BigQuery can be billed in two different ways – on-demand and Editions pricing. With on-demand, you are charged for the number of bytes processed by each query. *The first 1 TB of query data processed per month is free*. With Editions pricing, you leverage slots, which are dedicated processing capacities that you can use to run queries. Slots are worker nodes; they execute a part of an active query, read data from a source with external tables, and perform aggregations. You have a limit or reservation on how many slots can be in use at any time.

> **Note**
>
> A BigQuery slot is Google's proprietary unit of compute, RAM, and network throughput required to execute SQL queries.

The easiest way to get started with BigQuery is to use the *on-demand pricing model*. On-demand offers pay-as-you-go pricing based on the number of bytes processed in each query. This model is easy to use but relies on you to manage your query budgets. As you mature on the platform, your usage increases, or you need a fixed cost, BigQuery Editions offers predictable and performance-based pricing for consistent workloads. BigQuery Editions has *capacity-based pricing*, where you pay for dedicated or autoscaled query processing capabilities instead of paying for each query individually with on-demand. With autoscaling features, BigQuery dynamically adjusts your available capacity in response to changes in demand. By using BigQuery Editions and autoscaling, you can specify a top-line capacity budget, at which point BigQuery automatically adjusts your compute capacity based on the workload.

Refer to *Table 10.1* for a comparison between on-demand analysis features and BigQuery Editions features:

On-Demand	BigQuery Editions
A consumption-based model where you pay per query	A capacity-based model where you pay for processing capacity or slots
Based on the amount of data your query scans	Performance-based pricing; there are three options based on workload
Access up to 2,000 concurrent slots	Auto-provision capacity based on demand or pending work
The first 1 TB per month is free	Autoscaling
	Only pay for what you use
	Supports slot sharing between reservations within the model
	1- or 3-year commitment (with discounts)
	Billed per second with a 1-minute minimum

Table 10.1 – BigQuery's compute and analysis options

BigQuery Editions includes **Standard**, **Enterprise**, and **Enterprise Plus** service levels:

- Standard provides a predictable price option and is a great choice for proof of concepts and ad hoc SQL workloads, with a maximum of 1,600 slots.

- Enterprise includes increased security features such as row- and column-level security, VPC service controls, and advanced functionality including integrated ML models and ML on object tables, as well as BI Engine and Autoscaling baseline.

- Enterprise Plus, the highest level of BigQuery Editions, is for demanding data analytics workloads and supports the highest level of resilience with regional disaster recovery and includes high and specific regulatory compliance through the Assured Workloads service. With Enterprise and Enterprise Plus, you have an option for 1- or 3-year commitments to save on cost for steady-state regular workloads:

> **Note**
> You can use the slot estimator and recommender that we will discuss in the *Monitoring and controlling costs* section to determine how many slots to use when transitioning from BigQuery on-demand to Editions pricing models.

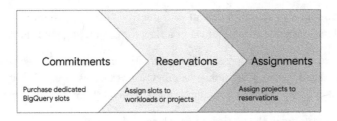

Figure 10.4 – BigQuery Editions capacity-based pricing features

BigQuery **commitments** allocate dedicated resources (slots) and reserved capacity within BigQuery. By opting for commitments, users with business-critical analysis needs can ensure consistent performance for their data analytics processing work. These commitments allow you to reserve a specific amount of query processing, ensuring that your workloads always have the necessary resources available. BigQuery slots can be reserved in increments of 100 in a commitment. This approach can provide a more cost-effective solution for businesses with consistent or high-volume data processing requirements as it offers both enhanced performance and predictable performance compared to a purely on-demand usage model.

Reservations allow businesses to balance performance optimization and cost management. Reservations are reserved capacity and allow you to assign the committed slots to critical data analytics workloads, leading to enhanced query processing speed and highly reliable insights. This resource allocation is important in data warehouse financial planning as it provides cost predictability and potential savings, which is beneficial for enterprises looking to optimize their cloud expenses. You manually assigned projects, folders, or organizations to a reservation. Any projects, folders, or organizations not assigned will use on-demand billing.

> **Note**
>
> You can programmatically perform workload management using reservations. With the BigQuery API, you can create and delete reservations, move projects between reservations, and move slots between reservations.

Slot **assignments** enable you to assign a project, folder, or organization to a slot reservation. They let you specify any job types for the assignment, query jobs, load and extract jobs, or background jobs, such as BigQuery search index management, change data capture background jobs, or replicating source databases to BigQuery. Background job types are only available in BigQuery's Enterprise and Enterprise Plus editions. We will discuss more about slots and the slot estimator tool in the last section of this chapter, *Monitoring and controlling costs*.

Query optimization

The remainder of this chapter is geared toward giving you practical ways to improve query efficiency and cost monitoring and controls. You will want to take advantage of query optimization techniques as they will reduce your analysis costs, speed up your queries, and give you more accurate results. In this section, we will outline some common best practices for optimizing your queries.

When building queries, you will want to keep this best practice in mind: *the less work a query performs, the faster it will respond and the less it will cost*. When BigQuery executes a query job, it converts the SQL query into a graph of execution broken into query stages, which are composed of execution steps [8].

To define work, let's break down the work-intensive stages of a query:

1. **I/O (READ)**: How many bytes were read.

2. **Shuffle (JOINs, aggregations, analytic operations)**: How many bytes were passed onto the next stage. This happens in memory.

3. **Grouping**: How many bytes were passed onto each group.

4. **Materialization (WRITE)**: How many bytes the query wrote.

5. **Compute**: SQL functions and expression evaluation.

By better understanding the work your query is doing, the better you will be able to prioritize query and compute optimization. Before you start optimizing, it's good to learn how to properly interpret the **query plan**. We will look at this in more detail later when we review query insights or the query plan in the *Monitoring and controlling costs* section.

Query optimization cheat sheet

The following best practices can optimize your queries and analysis costs in BigQuery:

- Using `SELECT *` in your queries is the most expensive way to query data. When you use `SELECT *`, BigQuery does a full scan of every column in the table. An alternate is to use `SELECT * EXCEPT` to exclude unnecessary columns. This can save you time typing a long list of column names in a `SELECT` statement:

```
SELECT * EXCEPT (column1, column2, column3)
    FROM `project.dataset.table`
```

- Use a `WHERE` clause to limit the bytes that are processed. `WHERE` clauses should be executed earlier in queries, especially with joins so that the table joins are as small as possible. Review the query plan to see if filtering is happening as early as possible.

- Use `LIKE` over `REGEXP_CONTAINS` when possible. `LIKE` can provide similar results in queries when you do not need the full power of regex pattern matching. `LIKE` works well in cases where there's less complex string comparison such as wildcard matching. Use approximate functions such as `APPROX_COUNT_DISTINCT()` instead of `COUNT()` for faster query performance. Approximate functions provide high-accuracy results that are within 1% of the exact number.

- Use query cache on duplicate queries. BigQuery automatically caches query results to a temporary table for 24 hours. When you run a query, BigQuery writes the results to a temporary table. This table can be a destination table specified by you or a Google-managed temporary cached results table. Temporary cached results tables are stored per user and project and there are no storage costs associated with temporary tables. You can create a cached query from BigQuery Explorer. To cache a query, under **Query settings**, enable **Use cached results**. This attempts to use results from a previous run of this query, so long as the referenced tables are unmodified. More on cached queries can be found in the docs (`https://cloud.google.com/bigquery/docs/cached-results`).

This list is a non-exhaustive sampling of query optimization techniques. Combining these approaches with the monitoring and controlling techniques we will outline in the next section will empower cost-efficient practices in BigQuery.

Monitoring and controlling costs

As organizations deal with increasingly large volumes of data, optimizing cost becomes a fundamental aspect of data processing. In this section, we will explore best practices for monitoring and controlling costs in BigQuery to help you make the most of your data exploration and preparation efforts without overspending.

Query plan and query performance insights

After a query is complete, you can review the query plan in the cloud console. The query plan provides details about query stages and steps to complete that can help you identify ways to improve performance. After running a query, click **EXECUTION DETAILS** to view the query plan, as shown in *Figure 10.5*:

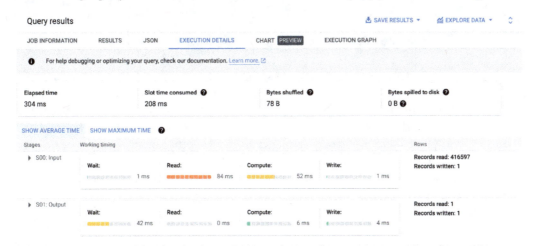

Figure 10.5 – Query plan details in the cloud console

In the query plan, you can view the longest execution time steps to troubleshoot any bottlenecks. In the preceding example, the longest time was spent reading the input. The query was counting columns and finding averages and minimum and maximum values in a single column. The query plan detail can help with understanding long-running recurring queries that you may use to generate and run regular reports or visualizations. You may also use the query plan to troubleshoot queries that are taking too long.

In addition to the query plan, you can use the **EXECUTION GRAPH** option to see a graphical representation of each stage of the query, as well as query insights for specific stages:

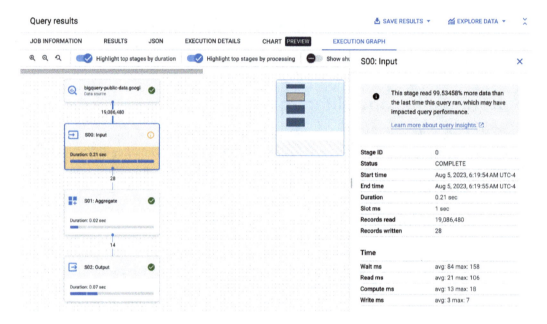

Figure 10.6 – Query insights in BigQuery's execution graph view

Query insights can provide you with information such as overall query performance versus prior execution. This can reveal insufficient slots allocated to a query or comparatively more data processed in the current query than the last time the table was queried. Query insights can let you know why a query that was previously run may be running slower and will give you tips on how to improve its performance. Analysts and data warehouse administrators will benefit from using the information in the BigQuery performance plan and insights to gain a better understanding of how to optimize queries or increase analysis usage. For more on query insights, you can check out the documentation at https://cloud.google.com/bigquery/docs/query-insights.

Monitoring, estimating, and optimizing costs

When you reach the usage level in BigQuery where you need predictable performance and costs, you may purchase reserved slots. At this point, you will need to estimate the right number of slots for your analysis workload. The slot estimator helps you manage slot capacity based on historical performance metrics [9].

BigQuery's slot estimator is a tool that helps you estimate your slot capacity requirements in BigQuery Editions capacity-based commitment pricing. It uses historical data to model your workload and predict how many slots you will need in the future. You can use the slot estimator to do the following:

- View slot capacity and utilization data for the past 30 days and identify periods of peak utilization when the most slots are used.
- Get recommendations for the number of slots you need to purchase. This helps you identify how many slots to use when moving from on-demand to Editions pricing.
- Model the impact of different slot configurations on your workload.

You can use the table's **PREVIEW** view to explore your data for free (refer to *Figure 10.7*). It may give you ideas on how to refine and structure queries and build smaller tables for more precise cost-effective analysis. It allows you to browse your table data without running queries:

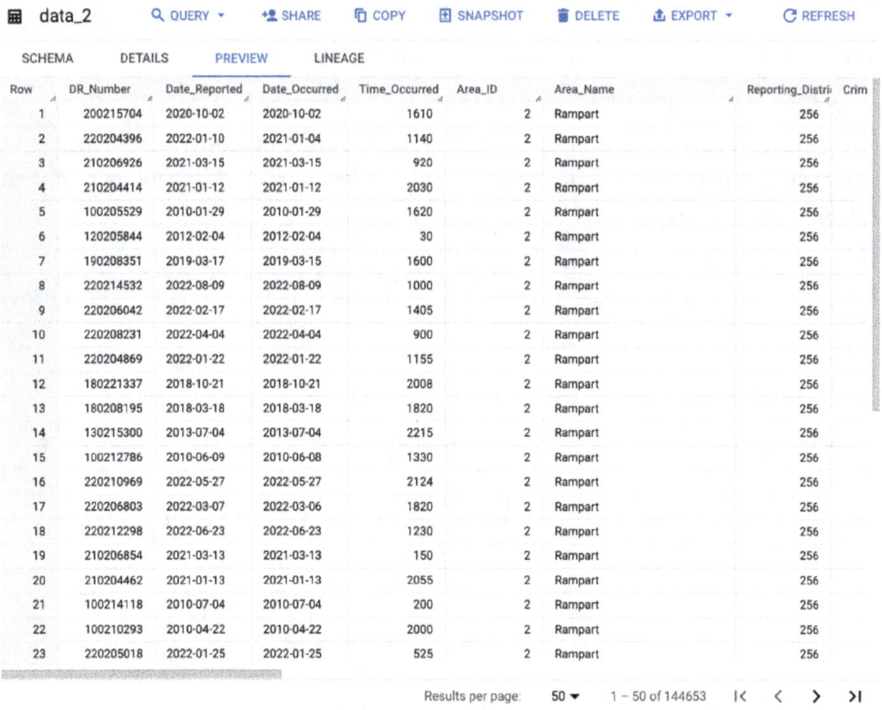

Row	DR_Number	Date_Reported	Date_Occurred	Time_Occurred	Area_ID	Area_Name	Reporting_Distri	Crim
1	200215704	2020-10-02	2020-10-02	1610	2	Rampart	256	
2	220204396	2022-01-10	2021-01-04	1140	2	Rampart	256	
3	210206926	2021-03-15	2021-03-15	920	2	Rampart	256	
4	210204414	2021-01-12	2021-01-12	2030	2	Rampart	256	
5	100205529	2010-01-29	2010-01-29	1620	2	Rampart	256	
6	120205844	2012-02-04	2012-02-04	30	2	Rampart	256	
7	190208351	2019-03-17	2019-03-15	1600	2	Rampart	256	
8	220214532	2022-08-09	2022-08-09	1000	2	Rampart	256	
9	220206042	2022-02-17	2022-02-17	1405	2	Rampart	256	
10	220208231	2022-04-04	2022-04-04	900	2	Rampart	256	
11	220204869	2022-01-22	2022-01-22	1155	2	Rampart	256	
12	180221337	2018-10-21	2018-10-21	2008	2	Rampart	256	
13	180208195	2018-03-18	2018-03-18	1820	2	Rampart	256	
14	130215300	2013-07-04	2013-07-04	2215	2	Rampart	256	
15	100212786	2010-06-09	2010-06-08	1330	2	Rampart	256	
16	220210969	2022-05-27	2022-05-27	2124	2	Rampart	256	
17	220206803	2022-03-07	2022-03-06	1820	2	Rampart	256	
18	220212298	2022-06-23	2022-06-23	1230	2	Rampart	256	
19	210206854	2021-03-13	2021-03-13	150	2	Rampart	256	
20	210204462	2021-01-13	2021-01-13	2055	2	Rampart	256	
21	100214118	2010-07-04	2010-07-04	200	2	Rampart	256	
22	100210293	2010-04-22	2010-04-22	2000	2	Rampart	256	
23	220205018	2022-01-25	2022-01-25	525	2	Rampart	256	

Results per page: 50 1 – 50 of 144653

Figure 10.7 – Table preview in the BigQuery SQL workspace

After typing a query, BigQuery will let you know how much processing it will use. This feature is called the **query validator** or **dry run**. The query validator gives you an estimate of the amount of processing required to execute your query:

Figure 10.8 – Query validator estimate

In addition to the query validator in the cloud console, you can also use the bq command line with the --dry_run flag and the query to estimate your processing charges. For example, the **victim_age** table is a view from a larger table. The view only has only three columns:

```
bq query --use_legacy_sql=false --dry_run 'SELECT *
FROM `data-exploration-and-prep-w-bq.collisions.victim_age` LIMIT
1000'
```

The preceding bq command returns the following response:

Query successfully validated. Assuming the tables are not modified, running this query will process 3816839 bytes of data.

This is a very inexpensive query since it's only processing 3.8 MB.

After viewing your table preview and estimated query costs, check your table storage size in BigQuery Explorer (refer to *Figure 10.9*). In the table's **DETAILS** section, you can browse details such as the last modified date, which will let you know if cached queries can be utilized, table expiration settings, and table storage information:

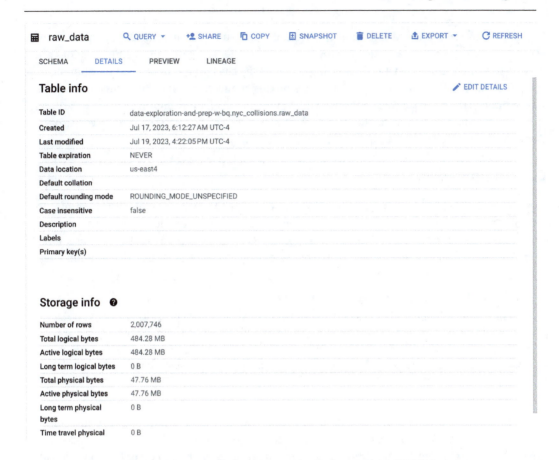

Figure 10.9 – Table storage information in the BigQuery table's DETAILS section

To estimate your possible BigQuery costs, take the amount processed from the query validator and the table storage cost and add it to the pricing calculator. This will allow you to do some cost basic projection. Review the pricing calculator (`https://cloud.google.com/products/calculator`) for a cost estimation before executing regular or scheduling queries that may require a lot of processing.

Google Cloud has a service called **Recommender** (`https://cloud.google.com/recommender`) that provides recommendations and insights for using resources based on ML and resource usage. Recommender for BigQuery is powered by **Active Assist**, an intelligent tool that helps you optimize operations to reduce cost, improve performance, and improve security in Google Cloud.

In BigQuery, there are partition and cluster recommendations to optimize your BigQuery tables. Recommender analyzes workflows on tables and provides recommendations to better optimize workflow and query costs using either table partitioning or table clustering [10].

Recommender uses workload execution data from the past 30 days to analyze BigQuery tables for partition and clustering configuration improvements. The cluster and partition recommendations can provide you with recommendations on saving slot hours by clustering columns and partitioning by date range, integer, time-unit, or ingestion time. The cluster and partition recommendations can be viewed through the cloud console, the gcloud CLI, or the REST API. More information about partition and cluster recommendations can be found at `https://cloud.google.com/bigquery/docs/view-partition-cluster-recommendations`.

Controlling costs

As you expand your BigQuery usage, you may want to set some guardrails **with custom quotas** to control costs. You can set or modify custom quotas on the quotas page in the cloud console (`https://console.cloud.google.com/quotas/`). Quotas can be set at the project level or user level. User-level quotas can be applied to service accounts for external services such as visualization tools.

> **Limit visualization or processing tool expenses**
>
> To control costs for internal or external visualization services or data processing tools, you can set a user-level or service account quota. To find a suitable quota, you can use the dry run and pricing calculator described previously. Quotas can be set according to team or organizational cost budgets. This strategy can be useful for IT departments that have a charge-back model for other departments.

To set custom quotas, the Google Cloud organization admin will need to grant you the Quota Administrator IAM role (`role/servicemanagement.quotaAdmin`) on a project or folder. The project-level and user-level quota options enable you to organize and budget according to workload, project, or individual roles. When a project or user exceeds a quota, BigQuery stops working for everyone in that project.

In addition to custom quotas to limit usage, you can set up **budgets** and **alerts** for billing accounts. A billing account is a billing profile associated with a payment method. With budgets, you can set threshold rules for notifications. For example, you can specify if you reach 50% of a $1,000 budget, giving you an alert as an early notice before reaching that budget amount. You can modify the percentage and budget amount for any percentage and any amount. More on budgets and alerts can be found in the Cloud Billing documentation (`https://cloud.google.com/billing/docs/how-to/budgets`).

Summary

Google Cloud provides intelligent recommendations and service features in BigQuery to enable you to operate a modern data warehouse cost-effectively. With its free tier, you can store and process data at no cost, and with BigQuery Editions, you can take advantage of capacity-based pricing for business-critical data analytics workloads. In this chapter, we went over various methods for preparing and optimizing data and provided best practices for cost-effectively using BigQuery.

By taking advantage of ML recommendations based on your specific workloads, rich SQL functions and capabilities, and thoughtful setup and regular querying practices, you can run a highly efficient data warehouse to unlock insights at any usage level. In the next chapter, we will start covering this book's end-to-end use cases with advertising data.

Further reading

Explore the resources in this section for more information on optimizing costs in BigQuery:

1. *Data types*: https://cloud.google.com/bigquery/docs/reference/standard-sql/data-types

2. *Clustered tables*: https://cloud.google.com/bigquery/docs/clustered-tables#combinine-clustered-partitioned-tables

3. *External data sources*: https://cloud.google.com/bigquery/docs/external-data-sources

4. *External federated data sources*: https://cloud.google.com/blog/products/gcp/accessing-external-federated-data-sources-with-bigquerys-data-access-layer

5. *Table clones*: https://cloud.google.com/bigquery/docs/table-clones-intro

6. *Pricing calculator*: https://cloud.google.com/bigquery/docs/best-practices-costs#use-pricing-calculator

7. *Cached results*: https://cloud.google.com/bigquery/docs/cached-results

8. *Query plan*: https://cloud.google.com/bigquery/docs/query-plan-explanation#background

9. *Slot estimator*: https://cloud.google.com/bigquery/docs/slot-estimator

10. *Partition and cluster recommendations*: https://cloud.google.com/bigquery/docs/view-partition-cluster-recommendations

Part 4: Hands-On and Conclusion

In the final part of this book, three hands-on exercises and use cases will be presented. These exercises are modeled from common, real-life data analytics challenges and data sources that teams have used to start a data analytics function. The use cases and approaches can be utilized with your own company data. This part is intended to accelerate your ability to gain insights, deliver value, and begin building a strong data analytics practice. Finally, the book will conclude with future directions to explore and be aware of in the rapidly evolving field of data analytics.

This part has the following chapters:

- *Chapter 11, Hands-On Exercise – Analyzing Advertising Data*
- *Chapter 12, Hands-On Exercise – Analyzing Transportation Data*
- *Chapter 13, Hands-On Exercise – Analyzing Customer Support Data*
- *Chapter 14, Summary and Future Directions*

11

Hands-On Exercise – Analyzing Advertising Data

In this chapter, we will walk through a hands-on exercise analyzing advertising data in BigQuery. We will cover some of the common challenges and approaches for handling sales, marketing, and advertising data in BigQuery. In this chapter, we intend to show you a repeatable process for handling advertising data in BigQuery that can be replicated with real data sources.

This chapter will cover the following sections:

- Exercise and use case overview
- Loading CSV data files from a local upload
- Data preparation
- Data exploration, analysis, and visualization

By the end of this chapter, you will understand specific approaches to handle advertising data in BigQuery. Following along this with chapter will give you hands-on experience and experience prior to trying out these steps with real data. Using this chapter as a reference can help you as a process guide to explore your own advertising data in BigQuery.

Technical requirements

There are three datasets used in this hands-on example. They are sample data and synthetic data, intended to replicate real-life scenarios, and they are based on industry advertising analytics use cases.

You may wish to use your existing Google Cloud project for this exercise or create a new one. If you wish to create a new project, follow these steps:

1. Within the console, click the project selector on the top menu bar to open the **Select a project** dialog box.

2.   From within the project selection window, you can create a new project for this exercise.

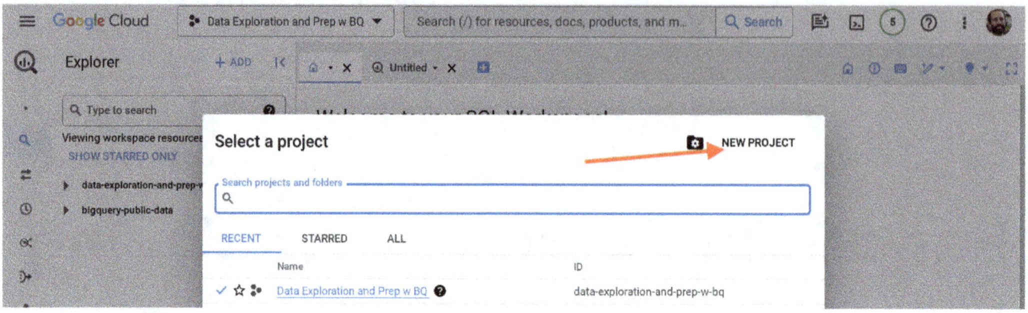

Figure 11.1 – The project selection dialog box

To follow along with this chapter, bring each of these data sources into your BigQuery project. Each dataset can be downloaded from the following links below or the book's GitHub repository (`https://github.com/PacktPublishing/Data-Exploration-and-Preparation-with-BigQuery/tree/main`). We will review step by step how to load these datasets into BigQuery later in this chapter. For now, you can download each file locally onto your computer:

- **Jewelry Store Ads Data**: `https://storage.googleapis.com/depwbq-uploads/jewelry_ads_data`

- **Jewelry Store Google Analytics Data**: `https://storage.googleapis.com/depwbq-uploads/jewelry_ga_data`

- **Jewelry Store eCommerce Sales Data**: `https://storage.googleapis.com/depwbq-uploads/jewelry_sales_data`

The preceding files are hosted on a publicly accessible cloud storage bucket for you to download.

When loading data into a table, make sure to select **File Format: CSV** and **Schema: Autodetect**. We will go over this in more detail in the *Loading CSV data files from a local upload* section.

The preceding datasets were modified from sources on Kaggle [1] [2]. The Google Analytics synthetic data was created using a Python script in the book's GitHub repository [3].

> **Attribution**
>
> The eCommerce purchase history dataset usage was approved by its owner Michael Kechinov (`https://www.linkedin.com/in/mkechinov/`). *Thank you, Michael.*

Exercise and use case overview

These sample data sources outlined in the technical requirement section are representative of data sources you would use in marketing and advertising analytics. The three data sources contain jewelry store advertising, analytics, and sales data. The queries and approaches in this solution can be replicated and used for similar use cases, with actual business data. See the following diagram of the tables and some of the column associations.

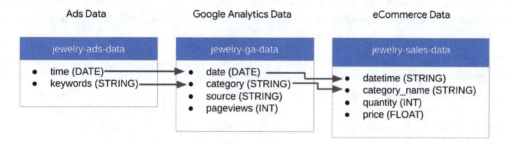

Figure 11.2 – The advertising and sales datasets and their relationships

Reviewing *Figure 11.2*, you can see some of the possible relationships between the tables. The **Ads Data** and **Google Analytics Data** tables both have a DATE column (time and date, respectively). This can help us correlate ad keywords and site visits, possibly showing the effectiveness of advertising campaigns. The datetime column on the **eCommerce Data** table could then be used to determine whether an ad placement, followed by a website visit, translates into a sale. The keywords, category, and category_name columns in each table could provide insights into product marketing effectiveness. In this exercise, we will attempt to find the following insights:

- **Advertising campaign effectiveness**: Optimize advertising performance by measuring elements of a campaign such as durations, keywords, search tags, channels, impressions, and clicks

- **Return on ad spend (ROAS)**: Determine what ad campaigns are most effective by combining ad data with analytics data and sales data

- **Attribution**: Track the customer journey, and identify each touchpoint up to a purchase

- **Sales trends**: Determine how most sold products correlate with advertising data

To begin with this solution, we will first load data. In a real-life scenario, your data sources would come in various shapes and forms, meaning you would have a different data output from source systems. This exercise assumes you can export data as a CSV from source systems, as this is commonly found in most services and tools. Throughout the next section, we will share pointers on other ways to integrate data sources beyond CSV exports.

Loading CSV data files from local upload

In this example scenario, we will load three advertising and sales data sources into a dataset in BigQuery for analysis. Each data source CSV file will be loaded manually through a single batch job. Loading CSV files has the advantage of being an easy process, as they can be loaded from local upload or Google Cloud Storage.

This approach has disadvantages as well. First, the data will only be from a snapshot or a moment in time, and second, it is a manual operation – it needs to be done by an individual. Beyond this example, with moment-in-time data, you may consider setting up streaming ingestion when possible for automated data loading. Many common advertising or marketing services support integration with BigQuery to handle data loading and updates for you. For additional information on loading data into BigQuery, review *Chapter 4, Loading and Transforming Data*.

> **Google Analytics BigQuery linking**
>
> In **Google Analytics** (**GA**) you can set up BigQuery linking to bring your GA data into BigQuery. This will automatically export your GA data either daily, through streaming, or both. This is a simple way to create a data ingest pipeline with little configuration and setup. Review the GA BigQuery linking article on the Google Analytics BigQuery docs at `https://developers.google.com/analytics/bigquery`.

Within the BigQuery console (`https://console.cloud.google.com/bigquery`), select the three dots next to your project ID, and select **Create dataset**.

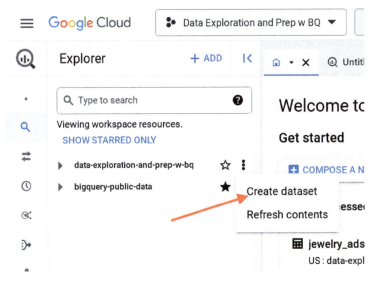

Figure 11.3 – Create dataset in the BigQuery console

For this example, give your dataset a name or dataset ID such as `ch11`, and choose the **Region** location type. From the drop-down list, you can select a region closest to you. Keep all settings as default, and click **Create dataset**.

Your dataset should now be available in the BigQuery explorer resource view:

data-exploration-and-prep-w-bq
Saved queries (18)
External connections
ch11

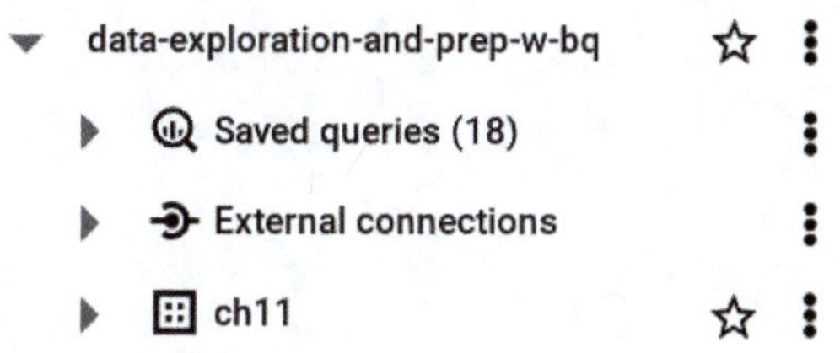

Figure 11.4 – The BigQuery explorer resource view, showing the newly created dataset

Now that your dataset is created, you can begin loading tables into it. If you have not already, download the three data sources provided in this chapter's *Technical requirements* section to your local workstation.

> **Google Ads transfers**
>
> You can automatically schedule and manage recurring load jobs for your Google Ads reporting data. This is a convenient way to automatically bring your Ads data into BigQuery and always have updated data. Find out more in the BigQuery docs: `https://cloud.google.com/bigquery/docs/google-ads-transfer`.

Similar to creating a dataset in the console, we will now create a new table and load our data sources. This process will be repeated three times, once for each data source.

data-exploration-and-prep-w-bq
Saved queries (18)
External connections
ch11
collisions
data_exploration_prep
google_trends_data
nyc_collisions
COMPOS
Recently acc
Open
Open in
Create table

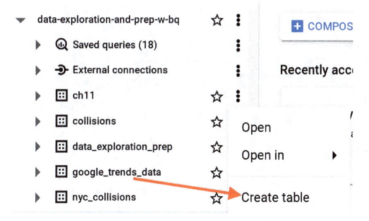

Figure 11.5 – The Create table option in the BigQuery explorer

After selecting the **Create table** option within your newly created dataset, you will be presented with the **Create table** dialog box.

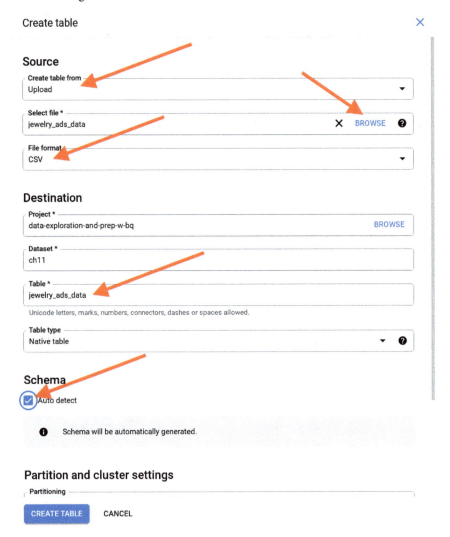

Figure 11.6 – The Create table dialog box

Within the **Create table** dialog, as shown in the preceding screenshot, choose and update the following and leave everything else as default:

- **Create table from**: **Upload**
- **Select file**: Locate the locally downloaded file
- **File format**: **CSV**

- **Table**: Give the table a name related to the data source or similar to the filename – in this case, `jewelry_ads_data`

- **Schema**: Enable **Auto detect**

After this is done, click **CREATE TABLE**. Repeat this process for the three data sources listed in the *Technical requirements* section of this chapter.

We now have loaded three different data sources into BigQuery, as shown in *Figure 11.7* – the sample dataset of ads data (`jewelry_ads_data`), the Google Analytics data (`jewelry_ga_data`), and the e-commerce data (`jewelry_sales_data`). Together, these data sources can give you an idea of how your ad campaigns translate into website visits and purchases of your online goods.

Figure 11.7 – Three advertising and sales data sources loaded into BigQuery

Now that all the sample datasets are loaded, let's prepare and clean them to ensure we can join and explore them together.

Data preparation

To derive meaningful insights from these three different datasets, proper data preparation is crucial. In this section, we will explore a few ways to prepare and harmonize data from Google Analytics, Google Ads, and e-commerce sales sources for effective analysis and reporting. We will use the **data definition language (DDL)** and **data manipulation language (DML)**. We introduced DDL and DML in *Chapter 4*, *Loading and Transforming Data*, and explored these concepts further in *Chapter 8*, *An Overview of Data Preparation Tools*.

To prepare our datasets for insights and exploration, we will standardize date formats across our data sources. Let's get started!

Standardizing date formats

Across our three data sources, there are three different date columns. This is an opportunity for us to standardize, making querying and joining data easier later. In the following table, you can see the three columns and the unique way they are named, as well as their data types. It is common when working with different sources to have different column names and data types.

By reviewing the preceding figure, you can see the three tables and their different column names and data types:

Table	Column name	Data type	Example
`jewelry_ads_data`	`time`	DATE	2022-10-26
`jewelry_ga_data`	`date`	DATE	2022-01-02
`jewelry_sales_data`	`datetime`	TIMESTAMP	2020-12-31 03:36:13 UTC

Table 11.1 – Three different columns and their data types

Our goal should be to have a standard date format and name so that we can filter and query across all three data sources with ease.

Changing column names

Let's use DDL to modify column names. The following SQL query will modify the `time` column name to `date` in our `jewelry_ads_data` table:

```
ALTER TABLE `ch11.jewelry_ads_data`
RENAME COLUMN time TO date
```

> **Note**
>
> Make sure to update `data-exploration-and-prep-w-bq` in the following examples with your project ID. You can find your project ID on the cloud overview dashboard page of the Cloud Console: `https://console.cloud.google.com/`.

Now, we have two of our tables with the same column name and data type. Next up, the `jewelry_sales_data` table requires a change in the data type from TIMESTAMP to DATE. This will allow us to query date ranges across our three tables.

Changing column data type from datetime to date

To change a table's column data type, at this stage, you must create a new table and copy results over from the source table.

First, we will use DDL in a SQL query to create a new table. Make sure to have the right data types in this query. Note that in the new table, we call our date column `date`, with the DATE data type:

```
CREATE TABLE `ch11.jewelry_sales_data2` (date DATE, order_id INT,
product_id INT, quantity INT, category_id INT, category_name STRING,
brand_id INT, price FLOAT64, gender STRING, metal STRING, stone
STRING)
```

After this query completes, you will have a new empty table called `jewelry_sales_data2`.

Next, we'll use DML to insert data from our source table into our newly created table. We will use the CAST function to change the `datetime` column to the DATE data type, and select all columns from the source dataset:

```
INSERT `ch11.jewelry_sales_data2`(date, order_id, product_id,
quantity,category_id, category_name, brand_id, price, gender, metal,
stone)
(
SELECT
CAST(datetime AS DATE) AS date, order_id, product_id,
quantity,category_id, category_name, brand_id, price, gender, metal,
stone
FROM
`ch11.jewelry_sales_data`
)
```

After this completes, you will have populated the new table with all rows and changed the data type for the `date` column. Now, we have an extra table, our original `jewelry_sales_data` and `jewelry_sales_data2`.

Figure 11.8 – This exercise's data sources with the newly populated table

Before removing the old sales table, verify the table schema, and check the newly created table and the date column with a simple query:

```
SELECT date FROM `ch11.jewelry_sales_data2`
```

Now, let's remove our old sales data table:

```
DROP TABLE `ch11.jewelry_sales_data`
```

Finally, rename the new sales data table:

```
ALTER TABLE ch11.jewelry_sales_data2
RENAME TO jewelry_sales_data
```

Now, we have three tables, all with the same name column, `date`, and all with the same data type, DATE. We have just standardized date columns with DDL and DML in BigQuery. Now, we can proceed to do some data exploration and visualization and unlock some insights into our data.

Data exploration, analysis, and visualization

In this section, we will begin by exploring our data sources, doing some initial analysis, and then creating some visualizations. We will show you how to create meaningful insights from advertising, analytics, and sales data.

Let's begin by finding the minimum and maximum date in each of our tables. This will let us know what date range we can compare across our three data sources:

```
SELECT min(date), max(date)
FROM `ch11.jewelry_sales_data`
```

We get the following result:

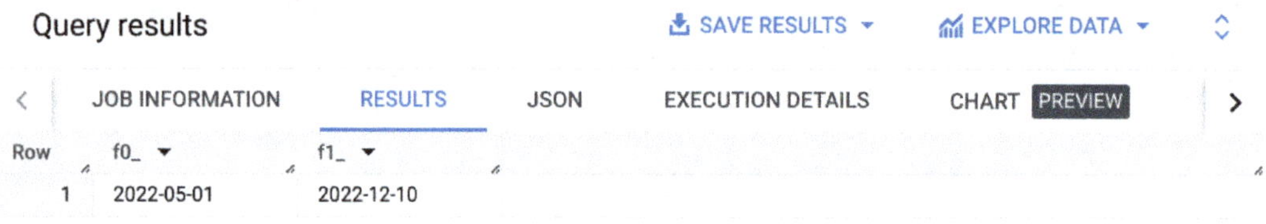

Figure 11.9 – Date range analysis

Running this query across our three tables shows the three datasets have a date range overlap between 2022-05-01 and 2022-12-10. We will use this window to correlate and measure ads, website visits, and sales data.

Continuing our exploration, the following query will return the unique keywords that we are using in our advertising campaigns:

```
SELECT DISTINCT(keywords)
FROM `ch11.jewelry_ads_data`
```

We get the following result:

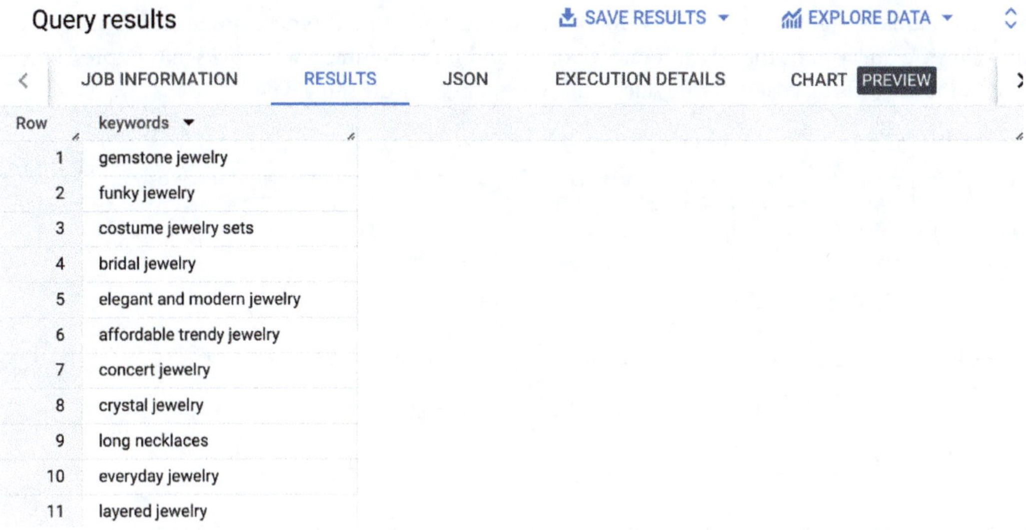

Figure 11.10 – Unique keywords in the ads data source

Next, the following query will return unique categories from our e-commerce sales data.

```
SELECT distinct(category_name)
FROM `ch11.jewelry_sales_data`
WHERE category_name LIKE '%jewelry%'
```

We get the following result:

Figure 11.11 – Unique categories from the sales data source

Analyzing ads and sales data

Now that we have done some initial exploration, we are ready to do some more in-depth analysis. The following query joins the ads and sales datasets and finds the amount of clicks and impressions per day, the advertising cost with the sales, and the revenue for the same day:

```
SELECT ads.date, ads.keywords, ads.clicks, ads.impressions,
IF((ads.impressions >=1000),ads.media_cost_usd * ads.impressions, 0)
AS vCPM_cost, ads.media_cost_usd, sales.category_name, sales.price *
sales.quantity as revenue
FROM `ch11.jewelry_ads_data` as ads
JOIN `ch11.jewelry_sales_data` as sales
ON ads.date = sales.date
WHERE sales.date BETWEEN "2022-05-01" AND "2022-12-01"
ORDER by revenue DESC
```

https://tinyurl.com/34htspsm

The previous query brings together ad data and sales data, showing the advertising cost per day and revenue on that specific day. It finds the advertising cost per day for any keywords that had over 1,000 impressions, or the **cost per thousand viewable impressions bidding (vCPM)**.

> **Cost-per-thousand viewable impressions bidding (vCPM)**
>
> When an advertising campaign targets a display network, you pay for the number of times your ad is visibly shown. Advertisers pay for every 1,000 times the ad appears and is viewable. A better understanding of the cost and budget fields in advertising datasets will help you to write more accurate queries and generate more useful reports.

Return on ad spend

Return on Ad Spend (ROAS) is an important metric in digital advertising that measures the effectiveness of advertising campaigns, by evaluating the revenue generated compared to the amount spent on advertising. ROAS is expressed as a ratio or percentage, often calculated as: ROAS = (Revenue from Ads) / (Cost of Ads).

ROAS provides advertisers with insights into the efficiency and profitability of their marketing efforts, helping them make data-driven decisions about allocating their advertising budget and optimizing their strategies to maximize returns. It is an important KPI for businesses seeking to achieve a positive impact on their bottom line through digital advertising campaigns.

The following query can be used to find ROAS:

```
SELECT ads.date, ads.keywords, ads.impressions,
IF((ads.impressions >=1000),ads.media_cost_usd * ads.impressions, 0)
```

```
AS vCPM_cost, ads.media_cost_usd, sales.category_name, sales.price *
sales.quantity as revenue,
SAFE_DIVIDE((sales.price * sales.quantity),(ads.media_cost_usd * ads.
impressions))AS ROAS
FROM `ch11.jewelry_ads_data` as ads
JOIN `ch11.jewelry_sales_data` as sales
ON ads.date = sales.date
WHERE sales.date BETWEEN "2022-05-01" AND "2022-12-01"
ORDER BY sales.date
```

https://tinyurl.com/5n6hjk57

This query builds upon this section's initial advertising and sales query, finding the vCPM cost (cost of the advertising campaign), and it uses the SAFE_DIVIDE function to take sales.price * sales_quantity for that day (or the revenue) and divide it by ads.media_cost_usd * ads. impressions (or vCPM cost). This query can help us better understand what ad keywords may or may not be leading to revenue. This can be an indicator to change keywords or increase a budget.

When working with advertising datasets in a business scenario, it can be helpful for data teams to work with someone from the marketing department to better understand their specific objectives, as they are industry-specific.

Visualizations

One quick way to create visualizations with data in BigQuery is through native integration with Looker Studio, as described in *Chapter 7, Further Exploring and Visualizing Data*. A Looker Studio report can be created from query results and enable you to quickly create visual representations of your data for executive audiences, business users, and teams that want to better understand their departmental data. To initiate a Looker Studio dashboard, run a query and click **Explore Data**. You will be presented with the **Explore with Looker Studio** option, which you need to select.

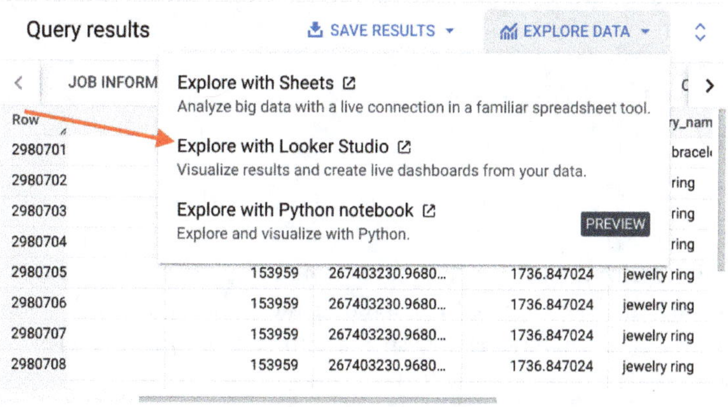

Figure 11.12 – Exploring data with Looker Studio from the query results

Once you are in Looker Studio, you can add a chart. After adding a chart, you are prompted to configure chart settings. For our ROAS chart, we will use keywords as the dimension and average of the ROAS column.

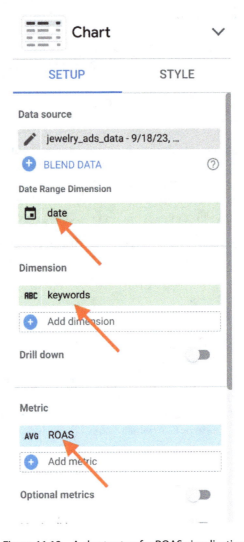

Figure 11.13 – A chart setup for ROAS visualization

After creating a few visualizations in Looker Studio from our previous queries on your own, you can create a dashboard that can be used by marketing and advertising teams to track campaign effectiveness. This dashboard can be saved and shared with anyone with a personal Google account or a Workspace account.

Jewelry Advertising Dashboard

Ads Data

	keywords	ROAS ▾			keywords	impressions ▾
1.	personalized jewelry	1,830.48		1.	minimalistic jewelry	28,844
2.	layered bracelets	966.65		2.	jewelry sets	28,243
3.	stud earrings	49		3.	layered jewelry	27,726
4.	arm cuffs	11.03		4.	hair accessories	27,594
5.	fall jewelry	9.52		5.	initial jewelry	27,585
6.	gemstone jewelry	7.45		6.	hoop earrings	27,409
7.	layered earrings	7.3		7.	casual chic jewelry	27,406
8.	threader earrings	7.26		8.	fashion jewelry for women	27,399
9.	summer jewelry	6.65		9.	stud earrings	27,317
10.	concert jewelry	6.49		10.	midi rings	27,131

1 - 100 / 118   ‹ ›   1 - 50 / 118   ‹ ›

Sales Data

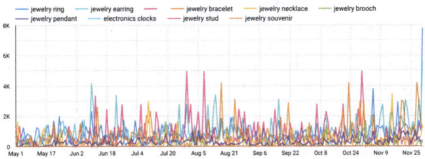

Figure 11.14 – A Looker Studio dashboard with advertising data

You can view this dashboard example here: `https://tinyurl.com/2p88dvcw`. This dashboard allows the viewer to understand advertising spend and performance, the most active search keywords, as well as sales trends and volume. A dashboard like this could be useful to various functions within a business interested in marketing trends and progress. This data can empower business decisions, sales, marketing, and product team performance.

In this section, we explored data exploration, analysis, and visualization for advertising data. Concepts such as budgets, vCPM, and ROAS were presented, and solutions were examined to report on these areas of advertising insights in BigQuery.

Summary

In this chapter, we examined an end-to-end example to load, analyze, and report on advertising data in BigQuery. This chapter can be used as a reference or walk-through, preparing you to utilize data analysis practices on corporate advertising data. By completing this chapter, you have gained experience in the common practices that are performed by data analysts and data engineers assisting marketing and advertising business teams. Moving forward from this foundational example of data analysis for advertising data, you are now enabled to create more advanced specific analyses and visualizations for real-life advertising data requests.

In the next chapter, we will present another hands-on example, using transportation data. You will explore the use of geospatial analytics and visualizations on GPS data.

References

Following are the sources used throughout the chapter:

1. *Jewelry Store eCommerce Sales Data*: https://www.kaggle.com/datasets/mkechinov/ecommerce-purchase-history-from-jewelry-store

2. *Jewelry Store Ads Data*: https://www.kaggle.com/datasets/rahulchavan99/marketing-campaign-dataset

3. *Google Analytics Data Generator*: https://github.com/PacktPublishing/Data-Exploration-and-Preparation-with-BigQuery/blob/main/ch11/ga_data_gen.py

12

Hands-On Exercise – Analyzing Transportation Data

In this chapter, we will walk through a hands-on exercise analyzing transportation data in BigQuery. We intend to show you a repeatable process for handling transportation data in BigQuery that can be replicated with real data sources.

This chapter will cover the following sections:

- Exercise and use case overview
- Loading data from GCS to BigQuery
- Data preparation
- Data exploration, analysis, and visualization

By the end of this chapter, you will understand specific approaches for handling transportation data in BigQuery. Following along with this chapter will give you hands-on experience prior to trying out these steps with real data. Using this chapter as a reference can help you as a guide to the process for exploring your own transportation data in BigQuery.

Technical requirements

The dataset we use in this exercise is the *Historic Vehicle GPS Data: Department of Public Services (2016)* dataset. This hands-on example is intended to replicate a real-life scenario based on vehicle location data and a transportation data use case.

You may wish to use your existing Google Cloud project for this exercise or create a new one. If you wish to use a new project, do the following:

1. Within the Cloud console, click the project selector on the top menu bar to open the project selection dialog box.

2.   From within the project selection window, you can create a new project for this exercise.

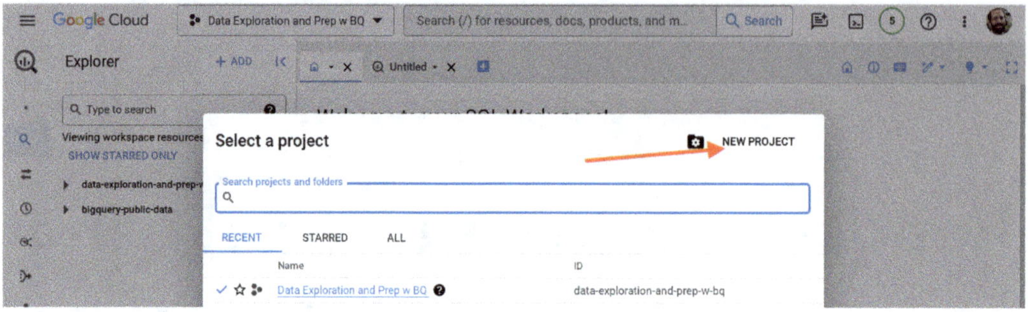

Figure 12.1 – The project selection dialog box

To follow along with this chapter you will need to bring the following data source into your BigQuery project. We will review step by step how to load the dataset into BigQuery later in this chapter. For now, you can download each file locally to your computer so it will be ready.

Historic Vehicle GPS Data: Department of Public Services (2016):

https://data.cincinnati-oh.gov/Thriving-Neighborhoods/Historic-
Vehicle-GPS-Data-Department-of-Public-Ser/qswr-c7y6 (Short URL: https://
tinyurl.com/3uhv8z4p)

Click **Export** then **CSV** to download the data locally to your workstation. Later in this chapter, in the *Data loading* section, we will upload this file to Google Cloud Storage to load it into BigQuery. If you wish to revisit loading data in detail, you may review *Chapter 4, Loading and Transforming Data*.

Exercise and use case overview

The sample data in this exercise is representative of data sources that would be used in transportation or fleet usage data analytics. The queries in this chapter can be replicated and reused with actual business data. As transportation data is rich in location and geography information, we will use the BigQuery GIS and geospatial analytics (https://cloud.google.com/bigquery/docs/geospatial-intro) approaches described in the Google Cloud docs [2]. See the following diagram for our example data source and some of the columns that will be used to derive insights.

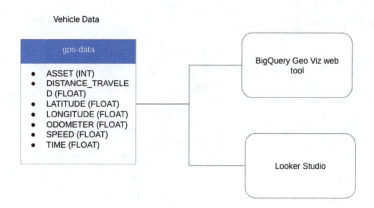

Figure 12.2 – Transportation data and visualization tool approaches

Reviewing *Figure 12.2*, you can see the gps-data table and the columns that we will use in this hands-on example. We will do some basic data preparation in this example to get to the insights quicker and will change the TIME column to DATE data type so it can be more easily displayed in charts. We will change the FLOAT datatype to DATE in the *Data preparation section* later in this chapter. In this solution, we will attempt to find the following insights with our queries and visualizations:

- Assets with the highest ODOMETER readings

- Assets with longest trips (DISTANCE_TRAVELED)

- Most common vehicle events (REASONS_TEXT)

- Plot vehicle location (LATITUDE, LONGITUDE) on a map

- Most active days for vehicle data (TIME)

Before we are able to get to these insights from our transportation dataset, we need to load and then prepare the data. The next sections will take you through these steps.

Loading data from GCS to BigQuery

In the previous chapter, we loaded data into BigQuery from a local file. This time, we will upload our data source into **Google Cloud Storage** (**GCS**) and load it into BigQuery from GCS.

Uploading data files to Google Cloud Storage

If you do not already have a Cloud Storage bucket, create one now:

1. Visit Cloud Storage in the Cloud console: https://console.cloud.google.com/storage/browser.

2.   Click **CREATE** to create a new bucket.

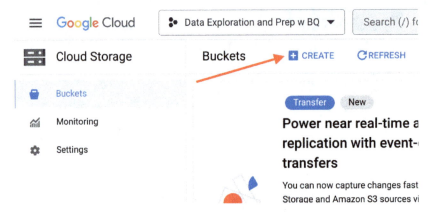

Figure 12.3 – Create a Cloud Storage bucket

3.   Give the bucket a name and location type, set the storage class and protection tools, and click **CREATE**.

> **Note**
>
> During this step of creating a storage bucket, you can accept all the defaults. Keep in mind it is best to keep your storage bucket in the same region as your BigQuery dataset.

4.   After your bucket has been created, add the data files by clicking **UPLOAD FILES**.

5.   Select the dataset CSV file we are using in this example. If you have not yet downloaded it, do so now.

Historic Vehicle GPS Data: Department of Public Services (2016):

`https://data.cincinnati-oh.gov/Thriving-Neighborhoods/Historic-Vehicle-GPS-Data-Department-of-Public-Ser/qswr-c7y6`

Here's a short URL: `https://tinyurl.com/3uhv8z4p`

> **Note**
>
> If you are just now downloading the file from the preceding URL, click **Export** then **CSV** to download it locally to your workstation. Repeat *steps 4 and 5*.

6.   Verify your file has been uploaded to Google Cloud Storage.

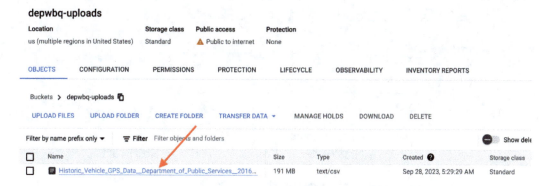

Figure 12.4 – Dataset CSV uploaded to Google Cloud Storage

Now that our file is uploaded to Google Cloud Storage, we can load it into BigQuery.

Loading data into BigQuery

Let's go through the following steps to load our file into BigQuery:

1.   Open the BigQuery console at `https://console.cloud.google.com/bigquery`.

2.   If it's not already selected, select your project, and create a new dataset.

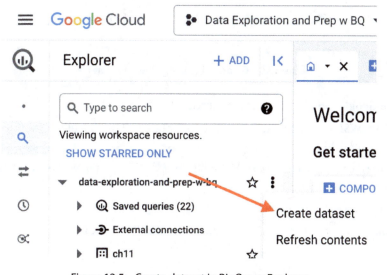

Figure 12.5 – Create dataset in BigQuery Explorer

3.   Give the dataset an ID of `ch12`, specify the location type, and click **CREATE DATASET**.

4. Select your new dataset and click on **Create table**.

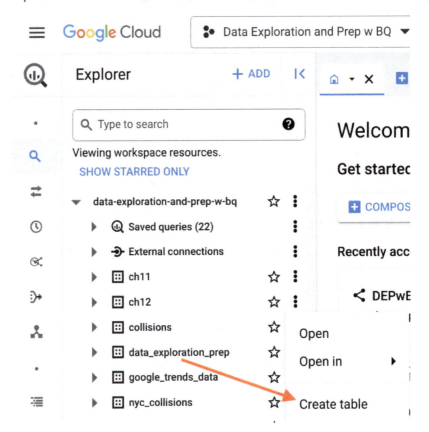

Figure 12.6 – Create table in BigQuery Explorer

5. Choose **Google Cloud Storage** as the source.

6. Click **BROWSE** to select a file from your GCS buckets. Find the file in your newly created bucket and click **SELECT**.

7. Make sure the file format is set to **CSV** and that the destination project and dataset are correct, and name the table gps-data.

8. For **Schema**, select **Auto detect**.

9. Leave all other options on the defaults and click **CREATE TABLE** to load the data.

Now you can browse your dataset schema, and preview and query your data in BigQuery.

Figure 12.7 – Historical vehicle GPS data loaded into BigQuery

Now that we have created a Google Cloud Storage bucket, uploaded our file, and loaded our dataset into BigQuery, we can move on to preparing our data for analysis.

Data preparation

By examining *Figure 12.7*, you can see that many of the columns in our dataset are of the data type FLOAT. While FLOAT is a legacy SQL data type, the GoogleSQL modern datatype is FLOAT64. FLOAT64 provides higher precision than FLOAT as FLOAT64 uses 64 bits to represent floating-point numbers, while FLOAT uses 32 bits.

For this hands-on example, we will leave most of the FLOAT and other data types and only modify the TIME column. We will be able to gain the insights we need from our dataset by leaving most of the data types as they are.

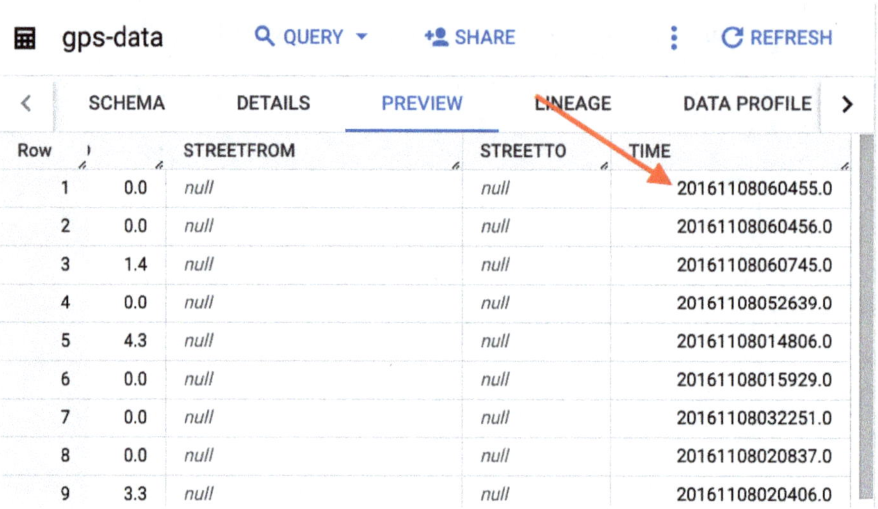

Figure 12.8 – Previewing our GPS data set to examine the TIME column

Note in *Figure 12.7* that the **TIME** column is FLOAT, has a decimal point, and is not very readable. Upon loading, the **TIME** column is formatted YYYYMMDDHHMMSS (14 digits). To prepare our dataset, we will convert this column into YYYY-MM-DD format (8 digits).

To convert the **TIME** column, we will use BigQuery **Data Definition Language** (**DDL**). First, we will create a new table and CAST our FLOAT column as a STRING. Next, we will trim the data in the column to 8 digits using the LEFT function and convert it to YYYY-MM-DD format:

```
#cast FLOAT as STRING and create new table
CREATE OR REPLACE TABLE `ch12.gps-data2` AS
SELECT asset, assetnhood, distance_traveled, heading, id_ham_pvmnt_
plygn, latitude, loadts, longitude, odometer, ppolylabel, reasons,
reasons_text, speed, streetfrom, streetto, CAST(time AS STRING) as
datetime
FROM `ch12.gps-data`
;
#trim STRING to YYYY-MM-DD and convert to DATE
CREATE OR REPLACE TABLE `ch12.gps-data2` AS
SELECT asset, assetnhood, distance_traveled, heading, id_ham_pvmnt_
plygn, latitude, loadts, longitude, odometer, ppolylabel, reasons,
reasons_text, speed, streetfrom, streetto,
PARSE_DATE('%Y%m%d', LEFT(datetime, 8)) AS date
FROM `ch12.gps-data2`
```

https://tinyurl.com/ypxvvvbf

After running this query, you will have a new table in your dataset called `gps-data2`. Examine `gps-data2` and you will see the `TIME` column has been changed to `date` and the data type has been changed to `DATE`.

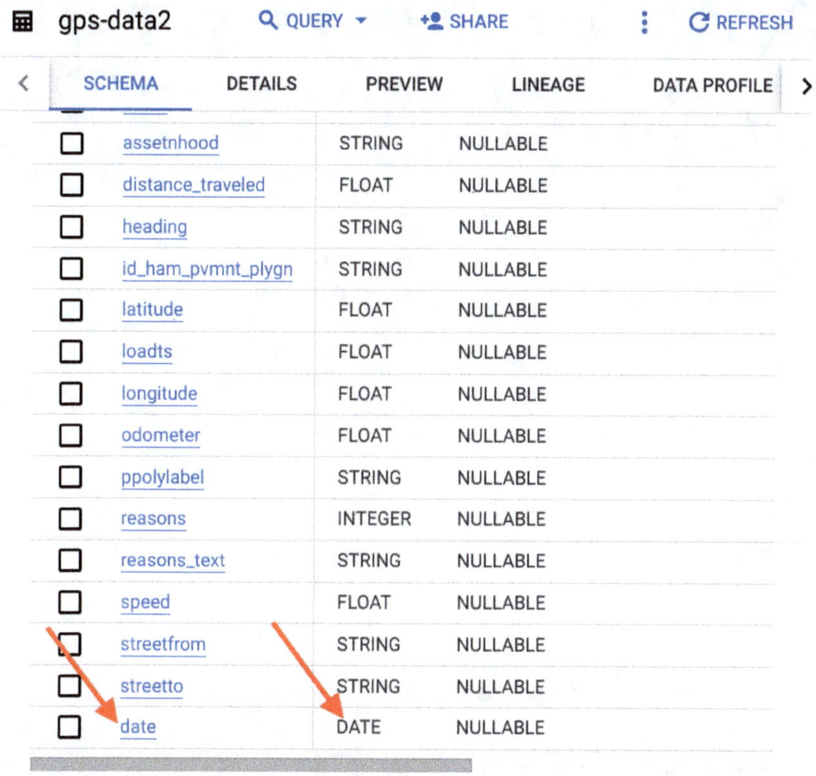
gps-data2
QUERY
SHARE
REFRESH
SCHEMA
DETAILS
PREVIEW
LINEAGE
DATA PROFILE
assetnhood STRING NULLABLE
distance_traveled FLOAT NULLABLE
heading STRING NULLABLE
id_ham_pvmnt_plygn STRING NULLABLE
latitude FLOAT NULLABLE
loadts FLOAT NULLABLE
longitude FLOAT NULLABLE
odometer FLOAT NULLABLE
ppolylabel STRING NULLABLE
reasons INTEGER NULLABLE
reasons_text STRING NULLABLE
speed FLOAT NULLABLE
streetfrom STRING NULLABLE
streetto STRING NULLABLE
date DATE NULLABLE

Figure 12.9 – Our data source after the TIME column has been transformed to date

Review the data further by clicking the **PREVIEW** view in the table browser. You will see the date column is in our desired YYYY-MM-DD format. The `LEFT` function with the `8` argument removed the HHMMSS time data in the original column, retaining only the YYYY-MM-DD elements.

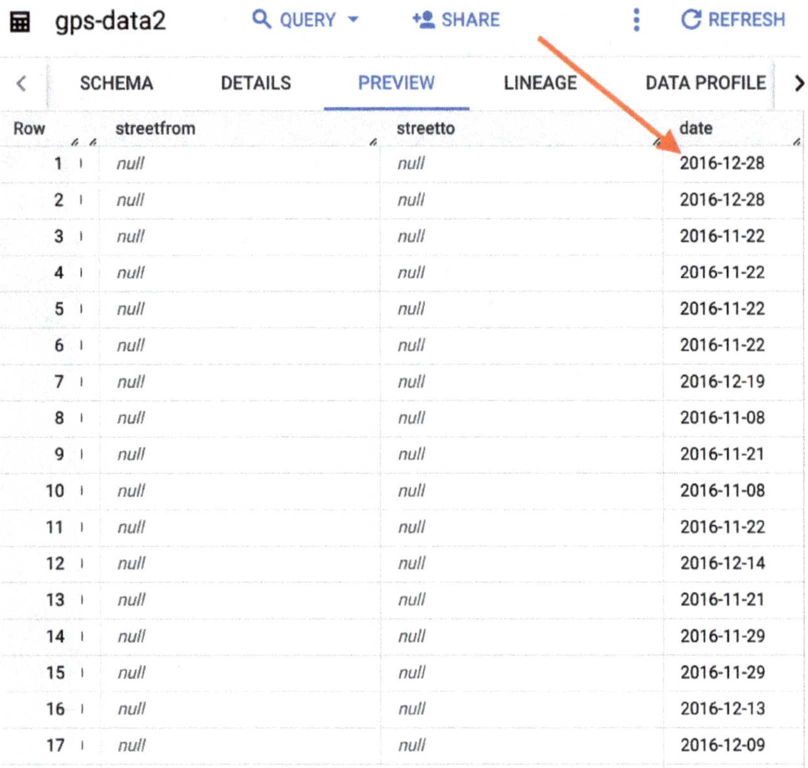

Figure 12.10 – gps-data2 with formatted date column

In this section, we used BigQuery DDL, CAST, PARSE_DATE, and LEFT functions to convert a DATE data type, trim a column, and convert the data into a readable format. Now that we have prepared our date column, we will go ahead to explore, query, and analyze our dataset to gain insights into our transportation GPS data.

Data exploration and analysis

Let's do some exploration and analysis on our gps-data2 table.

Assets with the highest ODOMETER readings:

```
#find assets (vehicles) with highest amount of miles
SELECT asset, assetnhood, MAX(odometer) as odometer
FROM `ch12.gps-data2`
GROUP BY asset, assetnhood
ORDER BY odometer desc
```

https://tinyurl.com/557zt6px

As displayed in the following screenshot, the preceding query displays the assets or vehicles with the highest odometer readings. This can be used to inform the business of vehicles reaching their end of life or requiring maintenance.

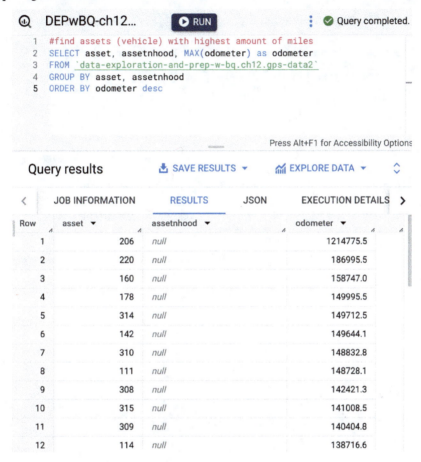

Figure 12.11 – Query results finding vehicles with the most miles

Assets with the longest trips (DISTANCE_TRAVELED):

```
#find longest trips per assets
SELECT asset, MAX(distance_traveled) as longest_trip
FROM `ch12.gps-data2`
GROUP BY asset, distance_traveled
ORDER BY distance_traveled DESC
```

https://tinyurl.com/2peyv773

The preceding query finds the longest trips made by given vehicles. This data can be used to identify patterns for certain vehicles and provide insights into regular trips, creating the opportunity to optimize routes.

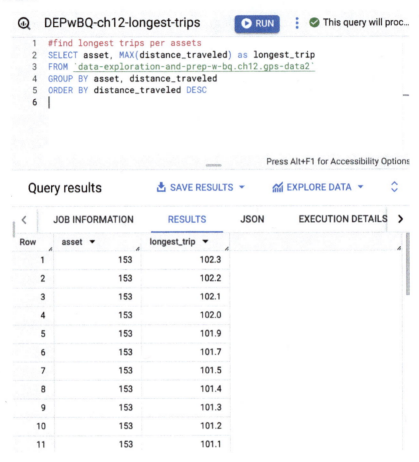

Figure 12.12 – Query results finding vehicles with the longest trips

Most common vehicle events (REASONS_TEXT):

```
#find most common reasons for data log
SELECT reasons_text, count(reasons)
FROM `ch12.gps-data2`
GROUP BY reasons_text
ORDER BY count(reasons) DESC
```

https://tinyurl.com/mwxzkv72

Sensor data can provide some of the most interesting metrics and data points on vehicles. The preceding query finds the most recorded events for vehicles in the fleet. This data can be used to identify the use of assets (e.g., driving patterns) and can provide details into situation and maintenance analysis.

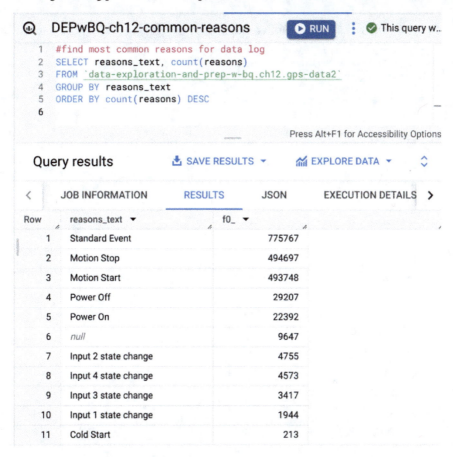

Figure 12.13 – Query results finding the most common reasons for data logged by GPS

Most active days for vehicle data (TIME):

```
#find most active days for vehicles
SELECT date, COUNT(date) as amount
FROM `ch12.gps-data2`
GROUP BY date
ORDER BY count(date) DESC
```

https://tinyurl.com/4d69e4pu

The preceding query shows the most active days in terms of data received from vehicles. This data could be correlated with other business data such as service calls to identify periods of high demand and enable the business to perform predictive and trend analysis for planning and resourcing.

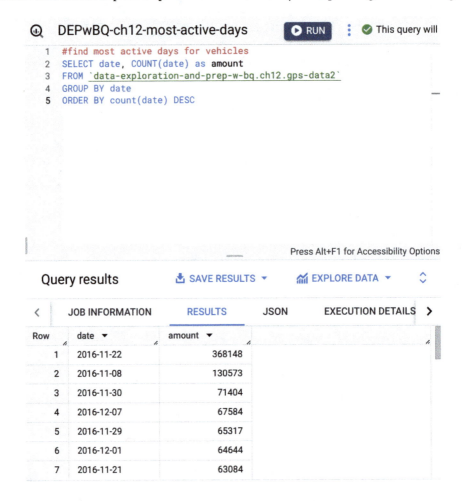

Figure 12.14 – Query showing most active dates with data logged

After running these queries, we now have some basic insights into our transportation dataset. By running these queries we have learned that many vehicles have over 100,000 miles, all vehicles have trips under 100 miles, and standard events such as start, stop, and power on/off are the most common reasons for data logged. The most active dates for vehicle data were in November and December 2016. This data gives basic information to better understand the vehicles monitored and may also encourage data teams to improve source data so the data can be more insightful to the business.

Visualizing data with BigQuery geography functions

In this section, we will use BigQuery geography functions to plot data using BigQuery Geo Viz (https://bigquerygeoviz.appspot.com).

In this query, we will find the location of vehicles that had a cold start recorded in the reason_text column. Run the following query in the BigQuery console:

```
#find vehicles and their location that had a cold start
SELECT
ST_GeogPoint(longitude, latitude) AS WKT,
asset
FROM `ch12.gps-data2`
WHERE reasons_text = "Cold Start"
```

https://tinyurl.com/38t7xhd5

After running the preceding query, in the query results click **EXPLORE DATA** and then **Explore with GeoViz**.

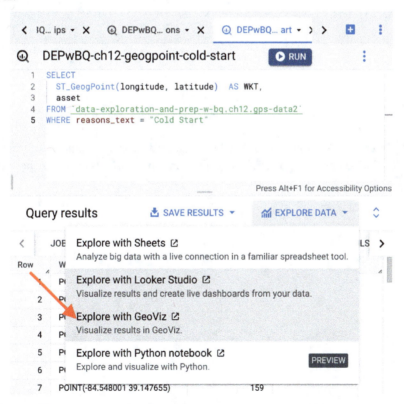

Figure 12.15 – The Explore with GeoViz option after running a query with a BigQuery geography function

The BigQuery Geo Viz page will load, displaying your project ID as well as the query from BigQuery.

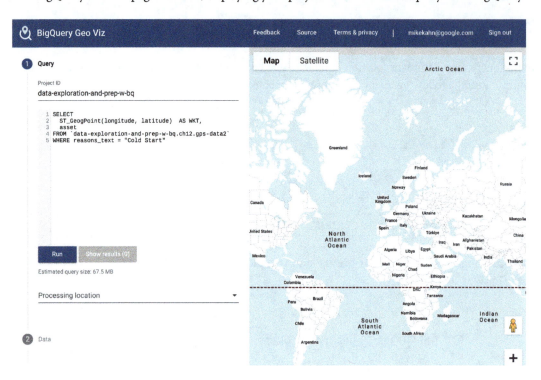

Figure 12.16 – BigQuery GeoViz with our project ID and query from BigQuery

Click **Run**. BigQuery Geo Viz will plot your table and query data on a map and allow you to browse the table results. This can provide powerful and easy-to-interpret insights from transportation data.

Figure 12.17 – BigQuery Geo Viz with transportation GPS data plotted on a map

In *Figure 12.17*, we can see the locations of vehicles that reported a cold start from their GPS. This indicates that vehicles started at a low temperature. This example demonstrated one way to show vehicle locations on a map for service and usage insights.

Other scenarios could include tracking delivery drop-offs, anticipating vehicle service needs, and tracking highly valuable vehicles or liabilities to protect sensitive fleets and business operations. If the GPS and sensor data report events accurately, analyzing the data with location information can help to map any event related to vehicle operations. Vehicles are important assets to the livelihood of many service businesses, and by analyzing the data they produce, businesses may be able to keep them running and servicing customers more efficiently for longer.

Summary

Using BigQuery to analyze transportation data can be highly insightful for business data needs. In this hands-on exercise, we analyzed a transportation dataset including GPS data. We gained basic insight into fleet and vehicle data using BigQuery functions and explored using BigQuery GIS functions to plot data on a map. This hands-on example gave a basic look at the high value that BigQuery can produce with transportation data, fleet management data, and GPS data.

Further reading

Following are a few resources for you to read further:

- *Creating Cloud Storage Buckets*: `https://cloud.google.com/storage/docs/creating-buckets`

- *BigQuery GIS*: `https://cloud.google.com/bigquery/docs/geospatial-intro`

- *BigQuery GIS Functions*: `https://cloud.google.com/bigquery/docs/reference/standard-sql/geography_functions`

13

Hands-On Exercise – Analyzing Customer Support Data

In this chapter, we will walk through a hands-on exercise analyzing customer support data in BigQuery. This chapter is intended to show you a repeatable process for handling customer support data in BigQuery that can be replicated with real data sources.

This chapter will cover the following sections:

- Exercise and use case overview
- Data loading from CSV upload
- Data preparation
- Data exploration and analysis
- Analyzing emotions with sentiment analysis

By the end of this chapter, you will understand specific approaches for handling customer support data in BigQuery. Following along with this chapter will give you hands-on experience prior to trying out these steps with real data. Using this chapter as a reference will help you as a process guide for exploring your own customer support data in BigQuery.

Technical requirements

The datasets we use in this exercise are *Customer Support Ticket* datasets. This hands-on example is intended to replicate a real-life scenario where a business is looking to gain insights from its customer support data.

You may wish to use your existing Google Cloud project for this exercise or create a new one. If you wish to use a new project, within the console, click the project selector on the top menu bar to open the project selection dialog box.

From within the project selection window, you can create a new project for this exercise.

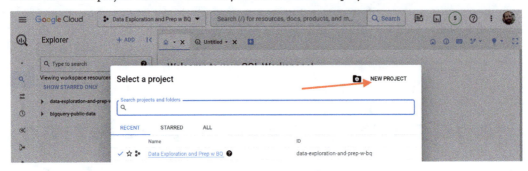

Figure 13.1 – The project selection dialog box

To follow along with this chapter, you will need to bring the following data sources into your BigQuery project. We will review, step by step, how to load the datasets into BigQuery later in this chapter. For now, you can download each file locally to your computer so they will be ready:

- **Customer Support Ticket Dataset**

  `https://www.kaggle.com/datasets/suraj520/customer-support-ticket-dataset`

  Short URL: `https://tinyurl.com/33w85cw9`

- **Bitext Customer Support Training Dataset**

  `https://github.com/bitext/customer-support-llm-chatbot-training-dataset`

  Short URL: `https://tinyurl.com/mwnsntkt`

> **Attribution**
>
> The Bitext customer support dataset usage was approved by its owner Antonio Valderrabanos, the founder of Bitext (`https://www.linkedin.com/in/asvbitext/`). *Thank you, Antonio.*

Exercise and use case overview

For this exercise, we will use two different customer support data sources to better understand how to analyze customer support data for insights. The sample data sources in this exercise are representative of data sources you would use in customer support data analytics. The queries in this chapter can be replicated and reused with actual business data.

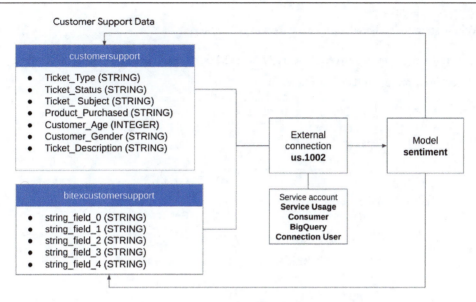

Figure 13.2 – Customer support data solution overview

Figure 13.2 shows our two data sources with the columns we will use in this chapter. The diagram also shows an external connection with a service account and the identity and access management roles attached, along with a sentiment **BigQuery Machine Learning** (**BQML**) model. You may notice the column names are missing on the `bitextcustomersupport` table (`string_field_x`). During the data preparation process, we will fix these column names. In this exercise, we will attempt to find the following insights in queries and visualizations:

- Count of `ticket_type` across both datasets

- Most common support issues using `ticket_subject` data

- Average resolution time per `ticket_type`

- Customer demographics using `customer_age` and `customer_gender`

- Customer sentiment analysis

Before we are able to get to these insights in our customer support datasets, we will need to load and then prepare data. The next sections will take you through these steps.

Data loading from CSV upload

In the previous two chapters, we loaded data from a local file and from Google Cloud Storage. For this example, we will load data again using local CSV files. If you have not already, download the two datasets in the *Technical requirements* section to your local workstation so you can load them into BigQuery.

Follow these steps to load our example datasets into BigQuery:

1. Open the BigQuery console: `https://console.cloud.google.com/bigquery`.

2. Select your project and create a new dataset:

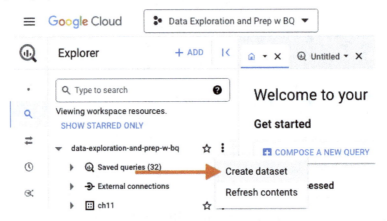

Figure 13.3 – Create a new dataset in an expanded project in the BigQuery console

3. Give the dataset the dataset ID `ch13`, keep it set to multi-region US, and leave all options as the default. Click **Create dataset**.

4. Click the three dots on your newly created dataset and click **Create table**, as shown in the following screenshot.

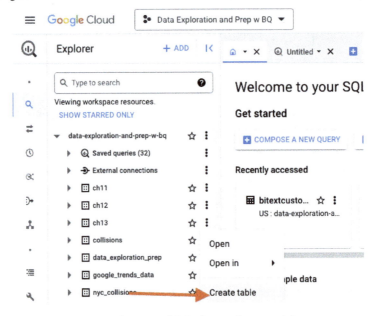

Figure 13.4 – Create a table in the newly created dataset

5.   You'll get the **Create table** dialog, as seen in the following screenshot:

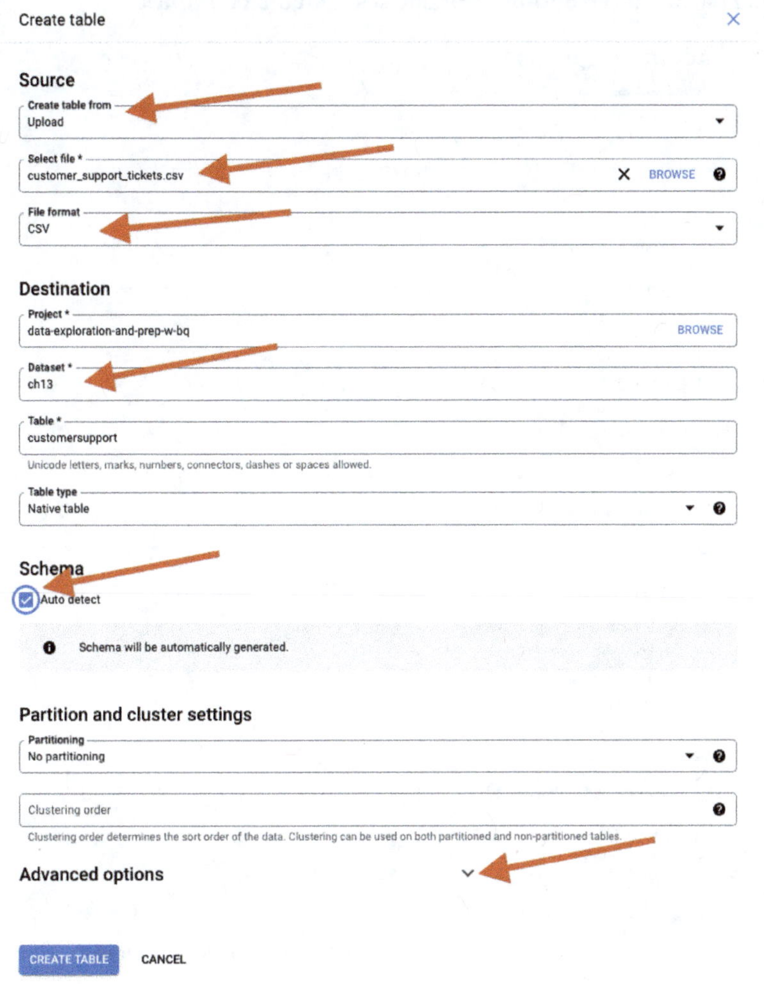

Figure 13.5 – Create table workflow

Within it, choose and update the following and leave everything else as the defaults:

- **Upload** under **Create table from**.

- In **Select file**, locate the locally downloaded file. For the first dataset, use the Customer Support Ticket dataset `customer_support_tickets.csv` file.

- **File format: CSV**.

- **Table** – give the table a name related to the data source or similar to the filename – in this case, `customersupport`. Do not include any hyphens or underscores in this table name.

- **Schema**: **Auto detect**.

- Expand the **Advanced options** pane and select **Quoted newlines**:

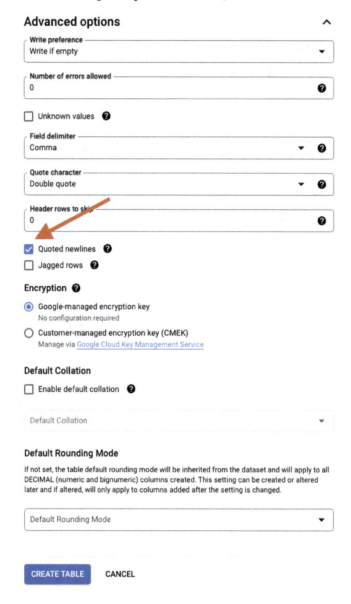

Figure 13.6 – Advanced options within the Create table workflow

6.   Click **CREATE TABLE** to load the data.

Repeat this process for the second dataset. Review the *step 5* with the second downloaded dataset CSV.

In **Select file**, locate the locally downloaded file. For the first pass, use the Bitext Customer Support Training dataset `Bitext_Sample_Customer_Support_Training_Dataset_27K_responses-v11.csv` file.

Now that we have our two datasets loaded into BigQuery, let's do some basic preparation to get them ready for analysis.

Data preparation

In this section, we will perform data preparation to correct column names in our Bitext Customer Support Training dataset. At this time, the Cloud console bq CLI tool and API do not support renaming column names. To do this, we will run the following query to give columns different names in the results, and we will set the query results to override the existing table data.

Type the `rename column names` query in the BigQuery SQL console – *do not run the query yet*:

```
#rename column names
SELECT string_field_0 AS flags, string_field_1 as instruction, string_
field_2 as category, string_field_3 as intent, string_field_4 as
response
FROM `ch13.bitextcustomersupport`
```

https://tinyurl.com/5ccw3nwa

Before running the query, click **More** and then **Query settings**.

Figure 13.7 – Query settings menu in the BigQuery console

Within the **Query settings** menu, select the following options:

- Select the destination as **Set a destination table for query results**
- Select the tables dataset
- Provide the table ID or table name

- Set **Destination table write preference** to **Overwrite table** and click **SAVE**

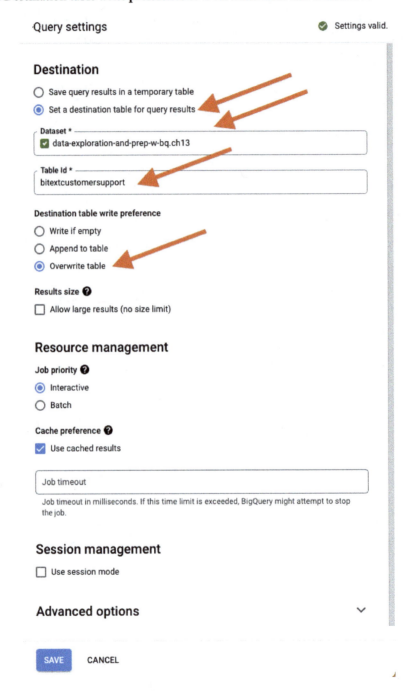

Figure 13.8 – Table query settings in BigQuery

After completing the query destination settings, you can see at the bottom of the query in *Figure 13.9* that the destination table is set and there is a setting to overwrite the table.

Figure 13.9 – The query with destination table and overwrite settings

Now run the query by clicking **RUN**. Now the table has updated column names to better reflect their details:

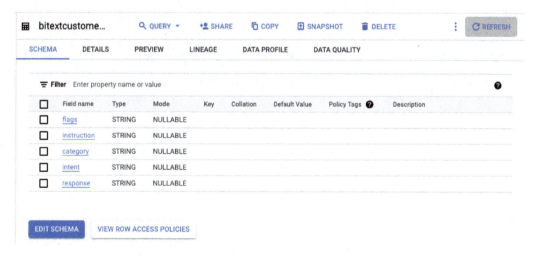

Figure 13.10 – Table with updated column names

In this section, we just renamed column names. This is one approach in data preparation to make data sources easier to understand and work with. Next, we will move on to exploring our tables, running queries, and doing visualizations.

Data exploration and analysis

Let's do some exploration and analysis of our customer support datasets. The following queries will allow us to unlock some insights and better understand what is happening with customer support.

Count of ticket_type across both datasets

This query uses the UNION DISTINCT function to list all of the category and ticket_type records across both of our customer support datasets. This data could be helpful to better understand the most common and least common ticket types for improvements and prioritization:

```
#ticket types and their counts across both datasets
SELECT category, count(category) as count
FROM `ch13.bitextcustomersupport`
GROUP BY category
UNION DISTINCT
SELECT ticket_type, count(ticket_type) as count
FROM `ch13.customersupport`
GROUP by ticket_type
ORDER BY count desc
```

https://tinyurl.com/5brcxzy3

The following query results show the top ticket types across both support data sources.

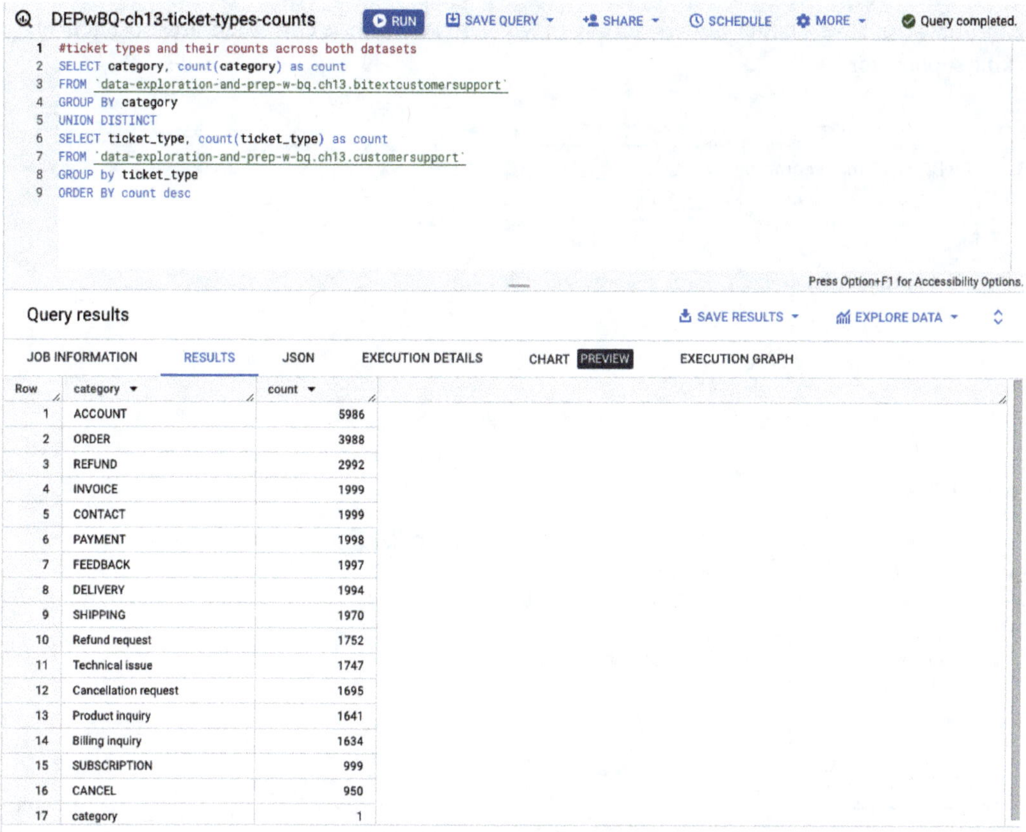

Figure 13.11 – Query results finding ticket counts across two datasets

The most common support issues using ticket_subject data

This basic query uses the DISTINCT and COUNT functions to find the top ticket subjects. Like the previous query, this query could also identify areas of improvement in documentation or resources to improve customer processes and satisfaction around specific subject areas:

```
#most common ticket subjects
SELECT distinct(ticket_subject), count(ticket_subject) as amount_of_
tickets
FROM `ch13.customersupport`
GROUP BY ticket_subject
ORDER BY amount_of_tickets DESC
```

https://tinyurl.com/46z8zc63

This query shows the most common ticket subjects. This data can point to product or process improvement areas and can show the most common pain points for customers. With this information, the business can have a better understanding of which product areas customers are most actively seeking support for.

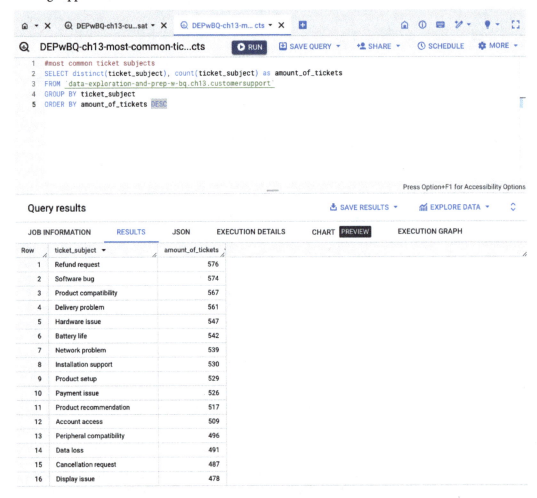

Figure 13.12 – The most common ticket subjects

Average resolution time per ticket_type

This query finds the average ticket resolution time for each ticket type. These insights tell us that from our data, **Product inquiry** and **Refund request** tickets take the longest to resolve (13 and 14 hours on average). This information may lead us to improvements in product team responsiveness or staffing, to improve product inquiry turnaround times for customers, supporting more sales. The following query also finds that **Technical issues** were resolved in under 4 hours on average. This may be a **key performance indicator** (**KPI**) for that specific team – to keep the average response time under 4 hours for technical support issues:

```
#average resolution time by ticket_type
SELECT ticket_type, AVG(time_to_resolution- first_response_time) as
avg_resolve_time, AVG(customer_satisfaction_rating) as avg_cust_sat_
rating
FROM `ch13.customersupport`
GROUP BY ticket_type
ORDER BY avg_resolve_time desc
```

https://tinyurl.com/ycksdkj5

The following query results show technical issues had the fastest average response time. This is helpful data to support team managers and operation leads.

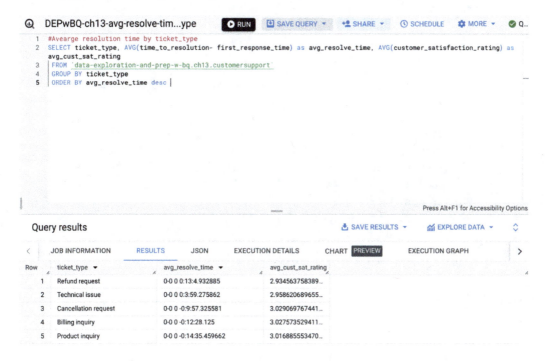

Figure 13.13 – Average resolve time per ticket type

Customer demographics using customer_age and customer_gender

The customer demographic query has two parts – the first part uses the MIN, MAX, and AVG functions as well as the COUNT function to find the minimum, maximum, and average age of our customers as well as the number of customers using customer support. The second part of the query uses the CASE conditional expression to segment our customers into age groups:

```
#customer demographics
#min,max,avg and count of ages
min(customer_age) as min_age, max(customer_age) as max_age,
avg(customer_age) as avg_age, customer_gender, count(customer_age) as
count FROM `ch13.customersupport`
GROUP by customer_gender;
#age_range break down
SELECT
    customer_age AS age_range,
    COUNT(*) AS customer_count
FROM (
    SELECT
        CASE
            WHEN customer_age >= 0 AND customer_age < 18 THEN '0-17'
            WHEN customer_age >= 18 AND customer_age < 25 THEN '18-24'
            WHEN customer_age >= 25 AND customer_age < 35 THEN '25-34'
            WHEN customer_age >= 35 AND customer_age < 45 THEN '35-44'
            WHEN customer_age >= 45 AND customer_age < 55 THEN '45-54'
            WHEN customer_age >= 55 AND customer_age < 65 THEN '55-64'
            ELSE '65+'
        END AS customer_age,
        FROM `ch13.customersupport`
)
GROUP BY age_range
ORDER BY age_range;
```

https://tinyurl.com/2rd9vhwn

The preceding query is actually two queries. After running them, you can click **VIEW RESULTS** and see the results of each one.

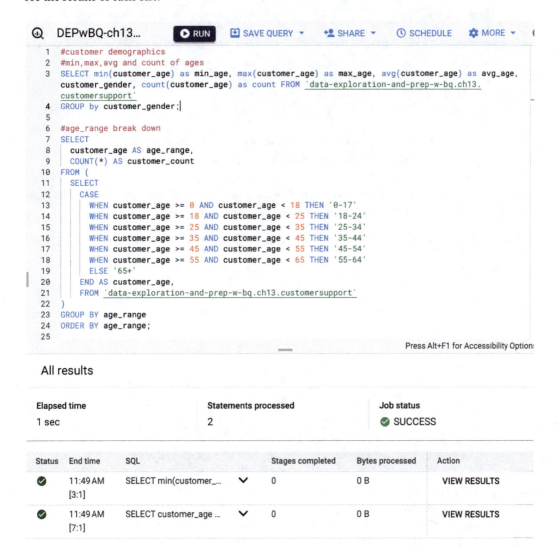

Figure 13.14 – Customer demographic query

The following screenshot shows the results of the query for grouping by gender:

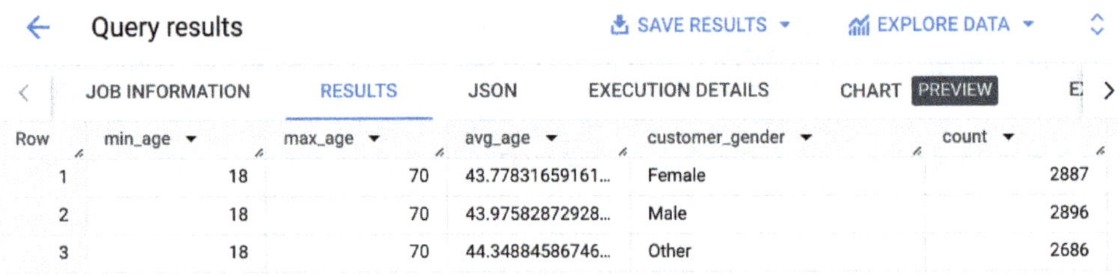

Row	min_age	max_age	avg_age	customer_gender	count
1	18	70	43.77831659161...	Female	2887
2	18	70	43.97582872928...	Male	2896
3	18	70	44.34884586746...	Other	2686

Figure 13.15 – Customer demographics results – minimum, maximum, average, and count of ages per gender

Grouping customers by gender shows a very equal distribution in our data sources. Average ages are also very close. More useful demographic information can be found in the age range query.

The following screenshot shows the results of the query for grouping by age range:

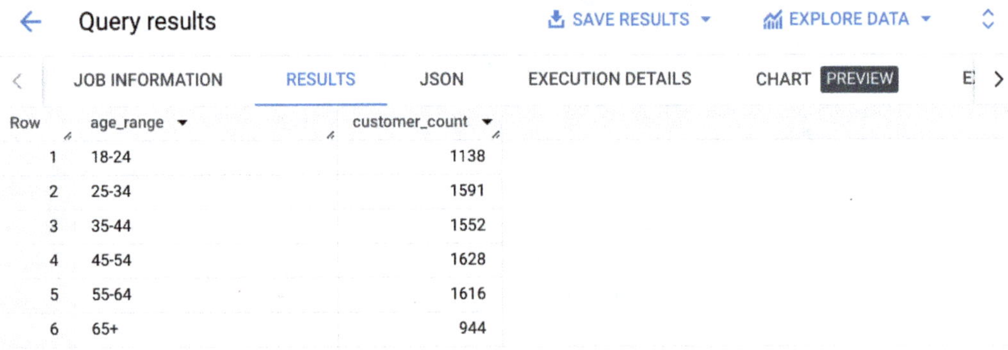

Row	age_range	customer_count
1	18-24	1138
2	25-34	1591
3	35-44	1552
4	45-54	1628
5	55-64	1616
6	65+	944

Figure 13.16 – Customer demographic age results grouped by age range

By observing these results, we can see that our customer support dataset has the highest concentration of users in the 45-54 age range. The average age of users is 44. The customer demographics queries on the customer support datasets provide insights to better target, market to, and understand customers. This data can be used by marketing and support teams to better reach and correspond with customers.

Analyzing emotions with sentiment analysis

In this section, we will use the `ML.UNDERSTAND.TEXT` function [2] and a remote model to perform natural language text analysis on our customer support data. Sentiment analysis attempts to determine positive or negative attitudes expressed within text. Sentiment is represented by numerical magnitude and score values. These functions are delivered by **BigQuery ML** (**BQML**) and make it possible to analyze text in BigQuery tables, SQL, and Google's **Large Language Models** (**LLMs**).

We will analyze the STRING column instruction in the bitextcustomersupport table to determine the feelings and attitudes of our customers.

Creating a connection

Enable the BigQuery Connection API by searching for this API in the console or visiting https://console.cloud.google.com/marketplace/product/google/bigqueryconnection.googleapis.com and also visit the BigQuery console https://console.cloud.google.com/bigquery. Next, let's get started with the steps:

1. Click + **ADD** then click **Connections to external data sources**.

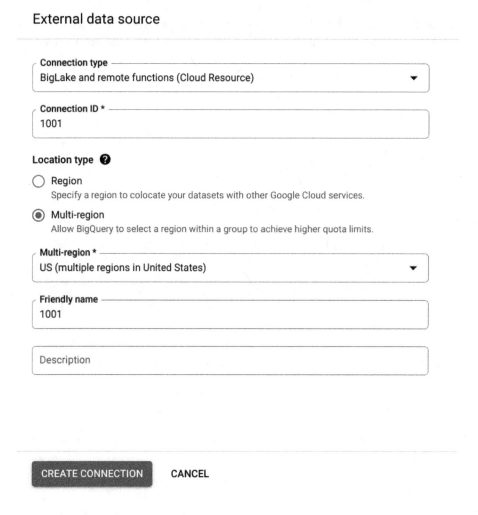

Figure 13.17 – Create a BigQuery external connection

2.   In the **Connection type** list, select **BigLake and remote functions (Cloud Resource)**.

3.   In the **Connection ID** field, give your connection the name 1001.

4.   Select the location type.

> **Important note**
>
> It is very important that your connection matches the same location as your BigQuery dataset. If you are unsure where you created your dataset, open the dataset in the BigQuery Explorer, click **Details**, and verify the location listed under **Data Location**.

5.   Click **Create Connection**.

After you create a connection resource, BigQuery creates a system service account and associates it with the connection. You will need to grant that service account IAM permissions to access the model.

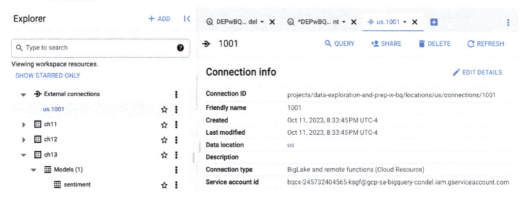

Figure 13.18 – BigQuery external connection info

6.   Open the connection in the BigQuery console and obtain the service account ID.

Granting access to the external connection service account

After creating a connection, a service account will be created. We need to give that service account and the connection the ability to access our BigQuery table with IAM roles:

1.   Visit the **IAM & Admin** page: https://console.cloud.google.com/project/_/iam-admin.

2.   Click **+ Grant Access**.

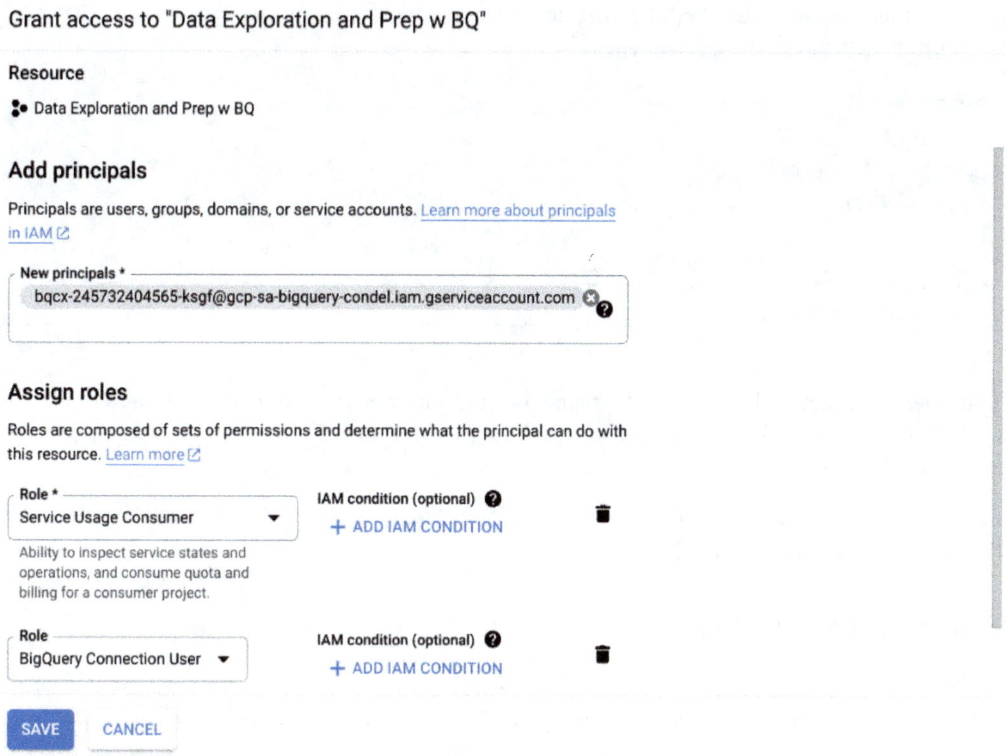

Grant access to "Data Exploration and Prep w BQ"

Resource

:• Data Exploration and Prep w BQ

Add principals

Principals are users, groups, domains, or service accounts. Learn more about principals in IAM ☑

New principals *

bqcx-245732404565-ksgf@gcp-sa-bigquery-condel.iam.gserviceaccount.com ⊗ ◕

Assign roles

Roles are composed of sets of permissions and determine what the principal can do with this resource. Learn more ☑

Role *

Service Usage Consumer ▼   IAM condition (optional) ❓
                                  + ADD IAM CONDITION   🗑

Ability to inspect service states and
operations, and consume quota and
billing for a consumer project.

Role

BigQuery Connection User ▼   IAM condition (optional) ❓
                                  + ADD IAM CONDITION   🗑

SAVE   CANCEL

Figure 13.19 – IAM permission setup for service account

3.   In **New principals**, enter the service account ID for your external connection. If necessary, open another tab with the BigQuery console to copy the ID.

4.   In the **Assign roles** section, select the **Service Usage Consumer** role.

5.   Click **+ Add another role**.

6.   In the **Role** field, choose **BigQuery Connection User** and click **SAVE**.

Creating a model

In the BigQuery console, run the following query to create a remote model with the CLOUD_AI_ NATURAL_LANGUAGE_V1 service type:

```
CREATE MODEL
ch13.sentiment
REMOTE WITH CONNECTION `us.1001`
OPTIONS (REMOTE_SERVICE_TYPE ='CLOUD_AI_NATURAL_LANGUAGE_V1');
```

https://tinyurl.com/mpmb2kpp

> **Note**
> BigQuery ML queries do not like table names or model names with hyphens (-) or underscores (_). Make sure not to include these if you give your model another name.

It may take some time for the model to be created. After the model is created, you will be able to use it to analyze the customer support datasets.

Querying the model

Run the following query to use the CLOUD_AI_NATURAL_LANGUAGE_V1 sentiment model that we previously created with the ML.UNDERSTAND_TEXT function on the STRING fields in our datasets:

```
#analyze sentiment on ticket_description STRING column
SELECT * FROM ML.UNDERSTAND_TEXT(
  MODEL ch13.sentiment,
  (SELECT instruction AS text_content from ch13.
bitextcustomersupport),
  STRUCT('analyze_sentiment' AS nlu_option)
);
```

https://tinyurl.com/26t948dn

It may take a while for this query to run. After the query completes, you will have results similar to the following screenshot.

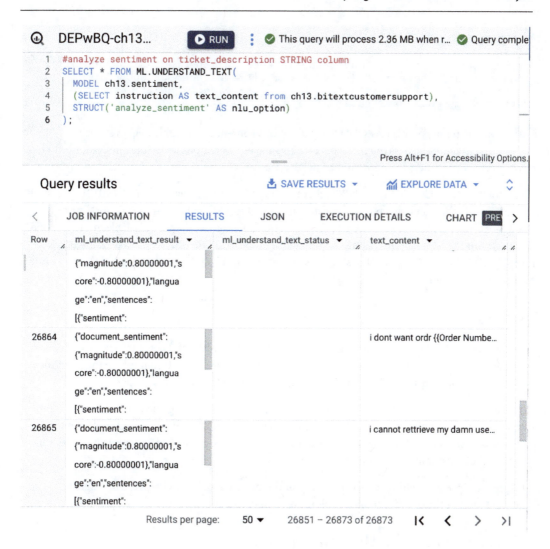

Figure 13.20 – Query results from the ML_UNDERSTAND_TEXT function and analyze_sentiment

The `ml_understand_text_result` needs to be interpreted to understand the results. As we know, `sentiment` represents the feeling associated with the text. `magnitude` indicates the overall strength of emotion within the text, with a range between `0.0` and `+infinity`. `score` indicates the emotional leaning of the text with a range between `-1.0` (negative) and `1.0` (positive). For more on natural language, visit the official docs: `https://cloud.google.com/natural-language/docs/basics`.

Let's examine row 26865:

```
{"document_sentiment":{"magnitude":0.80000001,"score":-0.80000001},"la
nguage":"en","sentences":[{"sentiment":{"magnitude":0.80000001,"s
core":-0.80000001},"text":{"begin_offset":-1,"content":"i cannot
rettrieve my damn user pass"}}]}
```

Interpreting the results of this row's data tells us that this content has a highly negative score (-0.80) with (0.80) magnitude. Sentiment scores can give us other data points to interpret emotions and attitudes across customer demographics or ticket types.

In addition to ML.UNDERSTAND.TEXT, there is a function for translation, ML.TRANSLATE, and a guide available that can help you translate data in a BigQuery table: https://cloud.google.com/bigquery/docs/translate-text. Additional remote services are available through Cloud AI to analyze BigQuery data such as ML_GENERATE_TEXT, ML_GENERATE_TEXT_EMBEDDINGS, and ML_ANNOTATE_IMAGE [5]. Using these functions and BQML models can help enrich your data and give you more valuable business insights.

Summary

Using BigQuery to analyze customer support data can provide highly useful insights to improve support and regular operations. Businesses can use customer support data insights to improve their products and services, resolve customer issues more quickly, and increase customer satisfaction.

In this hands-on exercise, we analyzed two customer support datasets and gained insights into common customer issues, customer demographics, and customer sentiment. This hands-on example is intended to be used as a starter guide and shows the value that BigQuery can provide to organizations looking to analyze their customer support data.

In the next chapter, we will review a summary of the prior chapters and provide foresight into the future direction of the practice of data exploration and preparation.

References and further reading

1. *Cloud Natural Language Sentiment*: https://cloud.google.com/natural-language/docs/reference/rest/v2/Sentiment

2. *BigQuery ML Understand Text*: https://cloud.google.com/bigquery/docs/reference/standard-sql/bigqueryml-syntax-understand-text

3. *Cloud Natural Language Basics*: https://cloud.google.com/natural-language/docs/basics

4. *BigQuery ML Create Model*: https://cloud.google.com/bigquery/docs/reference/standard-sql/bigqueryml-syntax-create-remote-model#remote_service_type

14
Summary and Future Directions

In this final chapter of *Data Exploration and Preparation with BigQuery*, we will recap the key points discussed throughout the book. We will provide a concise summary of the key points covered in our exploration, analysis, and data preparation using BigQuery. In addition to being a summary of concepts described earlier in this book, this chapter will look into the future and anticipate the emerging trends and transformative directions that will shape the landscape of data exploration, preparation, and analytics with BigQuery in the years to come. This chapter serves as a compass, guiding you through the insights and best practices we've discovered and pointing the way toward the exciting future of data-driven discovery and innovation.

This chapter will cover the following sections:

- Summary of key points
- Future directions

Summary of key points

Let's revise our chapter-wise journey in this book right from the beginning in the following sections, which contain a list of key points from each chapter.

Chapter 1, Introducing BigQuery and Its Components

- BigQuery is a fully managed, serverless data warehouse that enables users to analyze data with SQL.
- BigQuery uses a columnar format that is optimized for analytics queries on structured and semi-structured data.
- You can use common SQL queries to analyze data in BigQuery, as BigQuery supports a standard SQL dialect known as GoogleSQL.
- There are several access methods for administration tasks in BigQuery, including the Google Cloud console, the bq command-line tool, and the BigQuery API.

- **Role-based access control** (**RBAC**) is used to secure data and resources. You can control access to rows as well as views.
- There are two pricing models: on-demand analysis and capacity pricing (BigQuery Editions), offering predictable pricing for different analytic workloads.
- **BigQuery ML** (**BQML**) is a machine learning service that can be used to build and deploy machine learning models in BigQuery using SQL queries. *This makes data science work more accessible to data analysts.*
- You can add public and private datasets to projects to enrich proprietary data.
- BigQuery supports federated queries and external tables to support multi-cloud analytics.

Chapter 2, BigQuery Organization and Design

- Organizations, folders, and projects make it easier to manage users, billing, and access control. Folders help you organize projects, and projects help you isolate resources and make it easier to manage costs.
- Billing accounts, budgets, and resource quotas allow you to track and control costs.
- A dataset in BigQuery is a container for tables, views, and user-defined functions.
- Tables in BigQuery are like tables in a traditional database; they contain structured data and can be queried using SQL.
- BigQuery has automatic storage tiering for infrequently modified tables.
- Denormalization is not a requirement for tables but can speed up queries by reducing the need for joins.
- Take advantage of nested and repeated fields in denormalized tables when you have situations of related data.
- Design for performance – when designing your schema. you must consider how the data will be used. Keep it simple; the more complex your schema, the more difficult it will be to manage and maintain.
- Choose the right data types. The data types for each column should be appropriate for the data stored in the column.

Chapter 3, Exploring Data in BigQuery

- Data exploration is the process of examining, analyzing, and visualizing data in order to discover patterns, relationships, and insights.
- Data exploration is an iterative process that involves understanding the data, identifying outliers and missing values, identifying relationships between variables, discovering patterns in the data, and generating hypotheses about the data.

- BigQuery offers a variety of features that make it easy to explore data, including the BigQuery web UI and the bq command-line interface, and supports visualization tools such as Looker Studio, Tableau, Looker, and Power BI.

- Advanced approaches to data exploration in BigQuery include using BigQuery Studio, Jupyter Notebook, and Google Cloud's **artificial intelligence** (**AI**) and **machine learning** (**ML**) tools.

- Best practices for data exploration in BigQuery include understanding the data, using visualizations, and refining the analysis through an iterative process.

Chapter 4, Loading and Transforming Data

- Data loading and transformation are critical steps in the data analysis process.

- There are various ways to ingest data into BigQuery, including batch, streaming, and scheduled jobs.

- Data transformation is important to understand because, as a data analyst, you have options to transform data during data load, in a pipeline on its way into your cloud data warehouse, or after it has been loaded into BigQuery.

- The choice of whether to use **ETL** (which stands for **extract, transform, load**) or **ELT** (which stands for **extract, load, transform**) depends on a number of factors, including the size and complexity of the data, the performance requirements, and the budget.

- Explore the hands-on exercise, *Data loading and transformation in BigQuery* in *Chapter 4* for practice with a public data source.

Chapter 5, Querying BigQuery Data

- It is important to understand the structure of a BigQuery query, including the SELECT, FROM, WHERE, GROUP BY, HAVING, ORDER BY, and LIMIT clauses.

- Identify and use the appropriate data types for each column in a table to ensure accuracy and efficiency in querying.

- Utilize expressions and aggregations to perform calculations, manipulate data, and summarize results.

- Join tables using inner joins, outer joins, and self-joins to combine data from multiple sources.

- Leverage functions to perform complex calculations, transformations, and analytics on data.

- Use advanced querying techniques such as subqueries, common table expressions, window functions, and array functions to handle complex analysis scenarios.

- Saving and sharing query functionality can improve collaboration.

- Optimize queries to improve performance, reduce costs, and enhance productivity. Try to select columns instead of selecting `*`, and filter with the `WHERE` clause early to limit the amount of data processed.

- Troubleshoot and improve your queries by analyzing error messages, reviewing execution details and graphs, and monitoring query progress and durations.

Chapter 6, Exploring Data with Notebooks

- Notebooks are a powerful tool for exploring and preparing data. They allow you to run queries, visualize data, perform transformations, and execute all of your data analysis tasks in a single application.

- Notebooks make it easy to collaborate and iterate on your analysis and quickly see the results of your progress and changes.

Chapter 7, Further Exploring and Visualizing Data

- An important and often ignored topic in data analysis is understanding data distributions – the way in which the data is spread out or clustered around certain values or ranges.

- Descriptive statistics and SQL functions can help you understand data distributions in your tables.

- Equally as important as understanding data distributions is understanding the relationships in data. Uncovering patterns and using visualizations can help better understand correlations and help you get closer to insights.

- Exploring BigQuery data in Sheets and Looker Studio can help you quickly analyze and give you another view beyond query results.

- Visualizations can help you uncover data quality issues in tables and can help with extended functions beyond the query such as calculations.

Chapter 8, An Overview of Data Preparation Tools

- Start data preparation by defining your goals and understanding your objectives. Data preparation will follow in a way that aligns with your analysis goals.

- Evaluate your current data quality before moving on to data cleaning and transformation.

- There are several ways to approach data preparation: manual, automated, and hybrid data preparation.

- Focus areas with data preparation can include, data sampling, data integration, data cleaning, and data transformation.

- Data preparation tools integrate with BigQuery and can reduce the time and effort to prepare data.

- Cloud Dataprep and Cloud Data Fusion integrate well with BigQuery and provide a visual interface for data cleansing and transformations.

Chapter 9, Cleansing and Transforming Data

- Data cleansing and transformation are important steps in the data preparation process as data quality issues can negatively impact data analysis and reporting.

- ELT is the modern approach of ETL where transformation takes place *after* the data is loaded into the data warehouse.

- ELT has gained popularity due to the advancements in data processing and computing infrastructure and its ease of management.

- Dataset integrity includes the shape of the dataset, the skew, data profiling, data validation, and data visualization.

- SQL can be used for data cleansing tasks such as removing duplicates, handling missing values, standardizing and formatting data, and correcting inconsistent values.

- SQL can be used for transformation tasks such as aggregation and grouping, joining and combining tables, conditional transformations, and data type conversions.

- Cloud Dataprep can be used for visual cleansing and transformation.

Chapter 10, Best Practices for Data Preparation, Optimization, and Cost Control

- Data preparation best practices include denormalization data, optimizing schema design, considering nested and repeated fields, using correct data types, data cleaning and validation, partitioning and clustering, and optimizing data loading.

- Best practices for optimizing storage include table expirations, long-term storage (when a table has not been modified for 90 days), and compressed storage (with BigQuery Editions).

- Multi-cloud analytics across Cloud platforms is enabled by federated queries, external tables, and BigQuery Omni.

- BigQuery has several backup and recovery options including time travel, table clones, snapshots, and the ability to archive to Cloud Storage.

- Best practices for optimizing compute include determining whether On-Demand or BigQuery Editions fits best for your analytics workload.

- BigQuery commitments are allocations of dedicated resources and reserved capacity within BigQuery. Reservations are a reserved capacity that allows you to assign committed slots to critical workloads, enabling enhanced query processing and reliable insights.

- Query optimizations include using `select *` except, using `WHERE` to limit bytes processed, using `like` instead of `regex_contains`, using approximate functions over more generic functions, and using cached results on duplicate queries.

- BigQuery has tools to preview your table data before querying, check how expensive a query will be before executing it, and custom quotas, budgets, and alerts to keep you within a specific spend threshold.

Chapter 11, Hands-On Exercise – Analyzing Advertising Data

Chapters 11, 12, and *13* consist of hands-on exercises covering advertising, transportation, and customer support data. Each of these chapters used unique data sources to provide a solution and framework to analyze a use case for each industry:

- Google Ads, analytics, and e-commerce data can be added and queried together in BigQuery to provide insights into advertising, marketing, and sales efforts.

- Standardizing date formats across data sources makes querying and joining data easier.

- **Return on Ad Spend (ROAS)** is an important metric in digital advertising that measures the effectiveness of advertising campaigns by evaluating the revenue generated compared to the amount spent on advertising.

- Looker Studio makes it easy to visualize query results and display results to business users.

Chapter 12, Hands-On Exercise – Analyzing Transportation Data

- **Geographic Information System (GIS)** functions in BigQuery can be used to analyze transportation and GPS data.

- Data preparation such as changing the data type of date columns can make it easier to understand GPS data.

- Analyzing transportation data can provide insights into vehicle maintenance, activity, usage, high-value deliveries, and route optimization.

Chapter 13, Hands-On Exercise – Analyzing Customer Support Data

- Analyzing customer support data in BigQuery can provide insights into the most common support issues, average resolution time per ticket type, customer demographics, customer sentiment, and more.

- Renaming columns in BigQuery requires running a query and overwriting the table with query results. Descriptive column names make it easier to utilize data sources.

- BQML makes it easy to run sentiment analysis on customer feedback and ticket details. Sentiment analysis can give you an idea of overall positive or negative satisfaction among ticket types or customer segments.

Future directions

As we continue the final chapter of *Data Exploration and Preparation with BigQuery*, it is essential to turn our attention to the horizons of what lies ahead. The field of data exploration, preparation, and analytics is in a state of constant evolution, and BigQuery continues to be at the forefront of these innovations.

BigQuery is becoming more of a platform for all data services. For example, you can run SQL and Spark workloads from BigQuery using serverless DataProc. Data quality, profiling, and lineage on BigQuery tables can be done with Dateplex. Remote machine learning models that run on Vertex AI can be executed directly from BigQuery Studio with SQL. BigQuery as a platform will continue to evolve. In this section, we will explore the future directions and emerging trends that will shape the path of data analysis and decision-making with BigQuery.

More integration with AI and ML

AI and ML are increasingly becoming integral to data analytics. BigQuery, with its strong foundation in Google Cloud's AI and ML offerings, currently integrates seamlessly with AI and ML services such as Vertex AI. This integration will enable more data analysts access to the power of predictive modeling, recommendation systems, natural language processing, and anomaly detection within the familiar BigQuery environment.

AI-driven features will become more accessible, enabling users to derive deeper insights and predictions from their data. With the integration of AutoML capabilities within BigQuery, the process of serving models to make predictions on new data will enable a seamless integration of ML into decision-making processes.

Generative AI

Generative AI is a type of AI that can create new content such as text, images, music, and code. Generative AI models are trained on large datasets of existing content and they learn to identify patterns and relationships in the data. **Large language models** (**LLMs**) can generate new content that is similar to the data they were trained on. **Generative AI** (**GenAI**) has the potential to significantly impact data exploration and preparation in the future. LLM accessibility and integration will increase, and processes and regular data analysis practices will evolve.

Here are several areas in data analysis and engineering that will be impacted by GenAI:

- **Missing Data**: Generative models can be used to add missing values in datasets. When dealing with incomplete data, GenAI can generate values based on the existing data distribution, making data more complete.

- **Anomaly Detection**: A model of normal data can be established by GenAI, and anything that deviates significantly from this model can be considered an anomaly. This can be valuable in data quality assurance and data preparation.

- **Data Cleansing**: Generative models can be used to identify and rectify inconsistencies and errors in data.

- **Summarization and Report Generation**: LLMs can generate summaries of large datasets, making it easier for analysts and decision-makers to quickly understand the key insights from data. They can also automatically generate reports based on exploration results.

- **Enhanced Visualization**: Data visualizations and graphs can be generated by GenAI tools based on data analysis results.

- **Natural Language Interfaces**: Users will be able to interact with data in a conversational manner, making data exploration more accessible to non-technical users.

It is important to note that GenAI should be used carefully and results should be validated to ensure that they align with the specific requirements of the task. GenAI should be considered a valuable tool to assist in data exploration and preparation, but it should not replace human expertise and judgment entirely.

Natural language queries

Another use of GenAI is through **natural language processing** (**NLP**) for SQL queries. Natural language query tools are already making data analysis more accessible. Users can query data using natural language (for example, *Show me the top products sold in 2023*), reducing the need for technical expertise. Duet AI assistance is an early-stage technology that can help you generate an SQL query, complete an SQL query, and explain a SQL query. For more on Duet AI assistance, check the Google Cloud docs at `https://cloud.google.com/bigquery/docs/write-sql-duet-ai`.

DataOps

DataOps is an emerging concept that applies DevOps principles to data analytics. It emphasizes automation, collaboration, and agility in data pipelines, resulting in faster and more reliable data analysis. The Google Cloud service that supports this approach is called **Dataform** (`https://cloud.google.com/dataform`). Dataform allows users to build and operationalize data transformation pipelines in BigQuery using SQL. Dataform integrates with GitHub and GitLab and enables data analysts and engineers to collaborate on the same repository without managing infrastructure. Dataform is an open source, SQL-based language for managing data transformations.

Hybrid and multi-cloud data analysis

Organizations are increasingly using multiple cloud providers' infrastructure and services. Organizations may use one cloud provider as their data processing cloud and another as their data warehouse. Data marts may exist on other cloud providers due to their proximity to business-critical applications running on that provider's infrastructure. Technologies for seamless data analysis across hybrid and multi-cloud environments is an evolving area to watch and monitor to remain cost-effective and agile in your data analysis practice.

BigQuery Omni enables users to query data directly from Amazon S3 buckets and Azure Blob Storage, without the need to physically move the data into BigQuery. This capability allows organizations to analyze their data wherever it resides, without incurring the costs and complexities of data migration. BigQuery Omni enables organizations with unified data access, enhanced accessibility, and reduced transfer costs. Expect BigQuery Omni integrations to continue to support an open analytics cloud platform.

Zero-ETL and real-time analytics

Earlier in this book, in *Chapter 9, Cleansing and Transforming Data*, we covered the ETL and ELT data processing approaches. ELT is the modern approach and simplifies data pipelines and powerful data warehouses, performing transformations after the data has been loaded. Looking ahead, we must look beyond traditional ETL and modern ELT and embrace a future-forward approach known as "zero-ETL." This paradigm shift promises to streamline data pipelines, reduce latency, and enhance the agility of data exploration and preparation.

Historically, ETL and ELT processes involved extracting data from source systems, transforming it into a suitable format, and loading it into a data warehouse before it could be analyzed. The advent of cloud-based data warehouses such as BigQuery has changed the landscape. Platforms such as BigQuery can directly query source data, minimizing the need for traditional ETL. This leads us to the concept of zero-ETL.

Zero-ETL represents a significant departure from the traditional ETL approach. In a zero-ETL environment, data is not moved or transformed before analysis. Instead, it is queried and analyzed directly from its source location. BigQuery's federated query capabilities, external tables, and BigQuery Omni are key to enabling this approach. Zero-ETL is well-suited for a range of use cases:

- **Real-time Analytics**: In scenarios where real-time or near-real-time insights are crucial, zero-ETL ensures that data is analyzed as soon as it becomes available
- **Data Lakes and Data Warehouses**: Zero-ETL can be employed to directly query data stored in data lakes or data warehouses, making it easier to consolidate and analyze from diverse sources
- **External Data Sources**: Zero-ETL is ideal for federated queries that access data from external sources without the need for data replication
- **Dynamic Data Exploration**: Analysts can use zero-ETL to explore data without being constrained by predefined ETL processes

Zero-ETL represents a transformative shift in how we explore and prepare data for analysis. By directly querying and analyzing from source locations, organizations can improve latency, improve agility, and simplify data pipelines.

Data governance and privacy

With increased data regulations and concerns about privacy, data governance and privacy technologies are gaining prominence. This includes data masking, encryption, and tools for data lineage and auditability. The Google Cloud service for unified governance is called **Dataplex** (`https://cloud.google.com/dataplex`). Dataplex allows organizations to centrally manage, discover, and govern data across data lakes, marts, and warehouses with the goal of providing controlled access to trusted data and analytics at scale. Services such as Dataplex combine a data catalog with data lineage, security and governance, and life cycle management, enabling global control of assets.

Federated learning

Federated learning is an ML approach that allows a model to be trained across multiple decentralized edge devices holding local data samples, without exchanging them. Instead of sending all the data to a central server or cloud for model training, the model is sent to the edge devices, and the model updates occur locally. This privacy-preserving ML approach allows models to be trained on decentralized data without centralizing sensitive information.

Federated learning is used in various applications including personalized recommendations, predictive text input on mobile devices, healthcare, and more. It's an emerging area of ML that balances the benefits of data-driven insights with privacy and data security.

Data clean rooms

Clean rooms are a secure and privacy-preserving environment for organizations to share and analyze data without revealing the underlying data itself. In BigQuery clean rooms (`https://cloud.google.com/bigquery/docs/data-clean-rooms`), each organization retains control over its own data. Data is never copied or moved between organizations. Instead, organizations share queries and results with each other. This allows organizations to collaborate on data analysis without having to share their sensitive data. Clean rooms can be used for a variety of use cases, such as the following:

- Joint marketing analysis
- Fraud detection
- Risk assessment
- Product development

Data monetization

Data is often hailed as the new oil, and indeed its value is immeasurable. Data monetization is the ability to extract tangible value from data, and this concept will transform the way organizations perceive and utilize their data assets.

Data monetization is the process of converting raw data into revenue or other measurable benefits. It goes beyond the traditional use of data for internal-decision making and analysis. When effectively executed, data monetization can unlock new revenue streams, improve operational efficiency, and enhance customer experiences.

Data monetization takes various forms, and organizations can choose strategies that align with their goals and capabilities. Let's go over some common data monetization strategies:

- **Data Sales and Licensing**: Selling access to your data or licensing it to other organizations or individuals can be a direct and immediate way to monetize your data assets. This strategy is commonly seen in industries such as market research, finance, and healthcare.

- **Subscription Models**: Implementing subscription-based models for data access can generate recurring revenue. This is popular among providers of financial data, analytics, and industry-specific insights.

- **Data Exchanges and Marketplaces**: Data exchanges and marketplaces serve as intermediaries, connecting data providers with data consumers. These platforms facilitate data transactions, making it easier for organizations to buy, sell, or trade data. Analytics Hub (`https://cloud.google.com/analytics-hub`) is the Google Cloud data exchange that allows BigQuery users to securely exchange data assets across organizations. Data assets can be cataloged as internal and external assets and the platform takes care of publishing and subscribing to shared datasets in a secure manner.

- **Data-Driven Products and Services**: Building data-driven products or services can create entirely new revenue streams. For example, **Internet of Things (IoT)** devices that collect and transmit data can offer subscription-based services for data analysis and insights.

BigQuery plays a pivotal role in data monetization as a platform that enables external data sharing through Analytics Hub. Data monetization represents a transformative shift in the way organizations perceive their data assets. It's not just about storing and analyzing data, it's also about leveraging data to create value, drive, innovation, and foster revenue growth.

As technology and data analysis continue to advance, staying informed about these forward-looking technologies and concepts is essential for organizations to remain competitive and leverage the full potential of their data. Data professionals and analysts should continue to adapt and evolve their skills and practices in this dynamic environment. The future of data analysis is likely to be filled with new and exciting developments that will have an impact on the way that we collect, analyze, and use data.

Additional resources

Throughout the book, resources have been shared following each chapter. In the following list, you will find additional resources to support your journey in data exploration and preparation:

- *BigQuery documentation*: `https://cloud.google.com/bigquery/docs`. The official Google Cloud docs are the most up-to-date verified resource for BigQuery documentation.

- *Kaggle*: `https://www.kaggle.com`. Kaggle is a community of data, AI, and ML resources that can assist with your exploration and preparation.

- *Dataset Search*: `https://datasetsearch.research.google.com`. Google Dataset Search is a search engine for datasets that allows you to find datasets hosted across the world.

- *Coursera*: `https://www.coursera.org`. Coursera is a learning platform that offers several Google Cloud and BigQuery training courses.

Final words

The future of data exploration and preparation with BigQuery is bright. BigQuery is a powerful platform that can be leveraged to explore and prepare data for insightful analysis of large complex data across industries and sources. As BigQuery continues to evolve, it will provide data analysts with even more powerful tools and capabilities.

Data analysts who want to be successful in the future need to be aware of the trends and challenges that are shaping the field of data exploration and preparation. They need to be able to adapt to change and learn new skills. By doing so, they will be able to meet the demands of the future and make a valuable contribution to their teams and organizations.

As we conclude this book, I urge you to remain committed to continuous learning, exploration, and innovation in the practice of data analysis and preparation. The world of data is dynamic and ever-evolving, presenting a myriad of challenges and opportunities. It is through your dedication that you will continue to pave the way for transformative change and drive meaningful impact in the data-driven future that lies ahead.

Index

`Packtpub.com`

Subscribe to our online digital library for full access to over 7,000 books and videos, as well as industry leading tools to help you plan your personal development and advance your career. For more information, please visit our website.

Why subscribe?

- Spend less time learning and more time coding with practical eBooks and Videos from over 4,000 industry professionals

- Improve your learning with Skill Plans built especially for you

- Get a free eBook or video every month

- Fully searchable for easy access to vital information

- Copy and paste, print, and bookmark content

Did you know that Packt offers eBook versions of every book published, with PDF and ePub files available? You can upgrade to the eBook version at `packtpub.com` and as a print book customer, you are entitled to a discount on the eBook copy. Get in touch with us at `customercare@packtpub.com` for more details.

At `www.packtpub.com`, you can also read a collection of free technical articles, sign up for a range of free newsletters, and receive exclusive discounts and offers on Packt books and eBooks.

Other Books You May Enjoy

If you enjoyed this book, you may be interested in these other books by Packt:

Data Wrangling with SQL

Raghav Kandarpa, Shivangi Saxena

ISBN: 978-1-83763-002-8

- Build time series models using data wrangling
- Discover data wrangling best practices as well as tips and tricks
- Find out how to use subqueries, window functions, CTEs, and aggregate functions
- Handle missing data, data types, date formats, and redundant data
- Build clean and efficient data models using data wrangling techniques
- Remove outliers and calculate standard deviation to gauge the skewness of data

SQL Query Design Patterns and Best Practices

Steve Hughes, Dennis Neer, Dr. Ram Babu Singh, Shabbir H. Mala, Leslie Andrews, Chi Zhang

ISBN: 978-1-83763-328-9

- Build efficient queries by reducing the data being returned
- Manipulate your data and format it for easier consumption
- Form common table expressions and window functions to solve complex business issues
- Understand the impact of SQL security on your results
- Understand and use query plans to optimize your queries
- Understand the impact of indexes on your query performance and design
- Work with data lake data and JSON in SQL queries
- Organize your queries using Jupyter notebooks

Packt is searching for authors like you

If you're interested in becoming an author for Packt, please visit `authors.packtpub.com` and apply today. We have worked with thousands of developers and tech professionals, just like you, to help them share their insight with the global tech community. You can make a general application, apply for a specific hot topic that we are recruiting an author for, or submit your own idea.

Share Your Thoughts

Now you've finished *Data Exploration and Preparation with BigQuery*, we'd love to hear your thoughts! Scan the QR code below to go straight to the Amazon review page for this book and share your feedback or leave a review on the site that you purchased it from.

`https://packt.link/r/1-805-12526-5`

Your review is important to us and the tech community and will help us make sure we're delivering excellent quality content.

Download a free PDF copy of this book

Thanks for purchasing this book!

Do you like to read on the go but are unable to carry your print books everywhere? Is your eBook purchase not compatible with the device of your choice?

Don't worry, now with every Packt book you get a DRM-free PDF version of that book at no cost.

Read anywhere, any place, on any device. Search, copy, and paste code from your favorite technical books directly into your application.

The perks don't stop there, you can get exclusive access to discounts, newsletters, and great free content in your inbox daily

Follow these simple steps to get the benefits:

1. Scan the QR code or visit the link below

https://packt.link/free-ebook/9781805125266

2. Submit your proof of purchase
3. That's it! We'll send your free PDF and other benefits to your email directly